The Mistress of Paris

ABOUT THE AUTHOR

Catherine Hewitt studied French Literature and Art History at Royal Holloway, University of London and the Courtauld Institute of Art. Her proposal for *The Mistress of Paris* was awarded the runner-up's prize in the 2012 Biographers' Club Tony Lothian Competition for the best proposal by an uncommissioned, first-time biographer. She is currently at work on her next book, *Renoir's Dancer*, to be published by Icon in 2017. She lives in a village in Surrey.

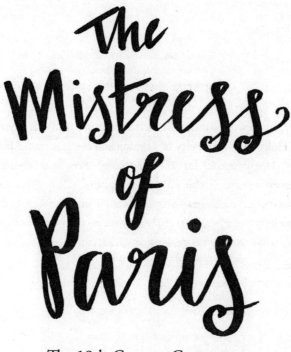

The Mistress of Paris

The 19th-Century Courtesan
Who Built an Empire on a Secret

CATHERINE HEWITT

ICON

First published in the UK in 2015
by Icon Books Ltd, Omnibus Business Centre,
39–41 North Road, London N7 9DP
email: info@iconbooks.com
www.iconbooks.com

This edition published in the UK in 2016 by Icon Books Ltd

Sold in the UK, Europe and Asia
by Faber & Faber Ltd, Bloomsbury House,
74–77 Great Russell Street,
London WC1B 3DA or their agents

Distributed in the UK, Europe and Asia
by TBS Ltd, TBS Distribution Centre, Colchester Road
Frating Green, Colchester CO7 7DW

Distributed in Australia and New Zealand
by Allen & Unwin Pty Ltd, PO Box 8500,
83 Alexander Street, Crows Nest, NSW 2065

Distributed in South Africa
by Jonathan Ball, Office B4, The District,
41 Sir Lowry Road,
Woodstock 7925

ISBN: 978-178578-044-8

Typeset in Van Dijck by Marie Doherty

Printed and bound in the UK by
Clays Ltd, St Ives plc

Contents

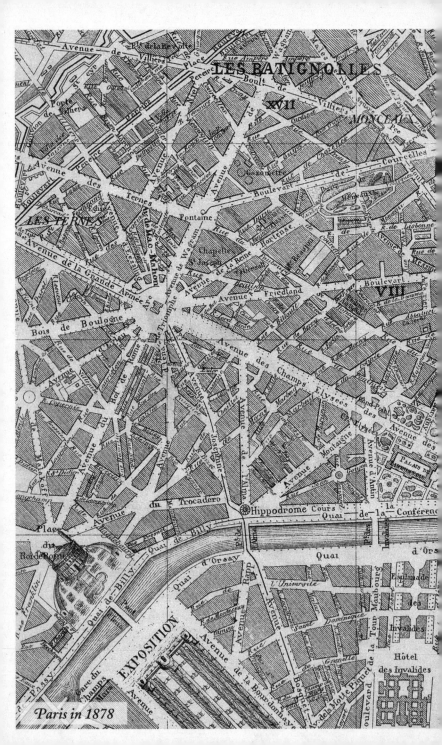

Paris in 1878

Prologue

One Sunday afternoon in May 1933, journalist Jean Robert found himself in the northern French town of Caen.[1] He had been invited to attend a lunch with some old school friends. Having spent several pleasant hours in their company, he hastened along to the town hall. The *Annual Exhibition of Lower Normandy Artists* was under way, and he was eager to see it before returning home. Once satisfied with his tour of the gallery, he stepped outside into the mid-afternoon sun. Checking his watch, Robert realised that he still had an hour before his bus left. As he pondered how best to use this time, his eyes alighted on a door just ahead of him. It was the entrance to the local museum. It had been left wide open, inviting. Delighted by the prospect of an absent-minded meander around the museum, the journalist hurried inside.

He climbed the stairs and entered the first room. But no sooner had his gaze begun its tour of the exhibition space than something peculiar caught his eye. It was a portrait of a well-to-do gentleman dressed in a blue, 18th-century costume. Robert recognised the name of the painter: Édouard Detaille. He was an artist Robert greatly admired. But Detaille was a painter of military scenes; this was not a soldier. As Robert stepped closer and read the inscription, he was taken aback: Etienne-Michel, Marquis de la Bigne. Then he noticed another painting by the same artist on display close by. This portrait showed an officer in Napoleonic uniform. The subject was identified as Sigismond-Tancrède, Comte de la Bigne. And both works, the journalist learned, had been bequeathed to the museum by a countess: Valtesse de la Bigne.

Robert was startled. He was friends with the current Marquis de la Bigne. Only a few years ago, he had assisted his friend in researching his family's history. He could not remember whether he had come across the names of these two men in the course of his research, but one thing was certain: he had never heard of this Valtesse.

How was this possible? De la Bigne was a local, noble name. Few people shared it. Those who did were almost certainly of the same family. How could he have missed the existence of a countess, and one who had died so recently? And how was it that these paintings had found their way into the museum in Caen?

As he left the museum, the strange name Valtesse ran through his mind. Who was this woman? He had to find out more.

Robert knew there to be some members of the de la Bigne family living in Paris, and he wasted no time in paying them a visit. Yes, they had heard about this woman. 'An adventuress', Robert was told. But the family could not provide him with anything more substantial. The journalist's curiosity mounted.

Then, on his return home, something rather wonderful happened, quite by chance. Robert received a letter from a reader of the journal he wrote for. It told him about some research that was being done on Valtesse de la Bigne. Feeling it might be of interest, the author of the letter had included an article with his correspondence. Robert could hardly contain his excitement. He began to read. And as he did, an incredible story started to unfold.

This was no ordinary countess or art connoisseur. She had usurped the noble name, invented the men in the paintings, and then bequeathed them to the museum to cement a false association with local nobility. And more: this woman, though born into poverty and destitution, had risen to become one of the most powerful courtesans of 19th-century Paris.

Her tale begins with another young woman and a flight from Normandy to Paris in the tumultuous years of the 1840s.

CHAPTER 1

A Child of the Revolution

It would still have been dark when the young peasant girl, Emilie Delabigne, boarded the *diligence* or stagecoach which was to carry her from Normandy to Paris early one morning in 1844. Having loaded a small bundle of possessions on to the roof, *diligence* passengers took their seats among the strangers who would become their travelling companions over the next three days. The coach must set off before sunrise if they were to maximise the daytime travelling hours – *diligences* were not as costly as the faster mail coaches, but they would not drive through the night. Passengers were obliged to stop at one of the post stations dotted along the route to Paris where they would rest and eat. Eight people, sometimes more, could be packed into a *diligence*; at 24, Emilie might well have been the youngest woman of the party setting out that morning.[1]

Country folk travelled to the capital for all sorts of reasons: perhaps some pressing business matter to attend to, or an illness in the family that would demand an extended stay with relatives. But it was too far for a humble peasant to travel simply for leisure. Emilie had a more serious reason for taking the coach to Paris.

Diligences were a notoriously uncomfortable mode of transport, particularly when the roads were rough, as they were in Normandy. Slowly, steadily, the vehicle would pick up pace, creaking as it went, swaying precariously from side to side. Passengers frequently complained of being thrown this way and that.[2] Emilie had to steady herself to watch her childhood home gradually disappearing from view through the carriage's tiny windows. It was a sight charged with poignancy, anticipation and trepidation. For at this moment, only one thing was certain: she was unlikely ever to see her home again.

Emilie was not the only young peasant moving to Paris at this time. Migration from country to city had always occurred, but the momentum increased from the mid-century as industrial and commercial development heightened the demand for labour.[3] With improved communication, news of Paris's wonders and delights began to reach the ears of the countryside's impressionable young. 'All over France the peasant displays the same foolish awe for the city of Paris. Everything which comes from Paris seems magnificent to him,' lamented one female commentator.[4] Paris dazzled and entranced, enticing the young with the promise of well-paid jobs, better standards of living, opportunities and adventure. By the middle of the 19th century, the mass departure of the young for the capital had become the bête noire of the regional press.

For many, communication with townsfolk was to be viewed with suspicion. The disappearance of the countryside's female population caused particular alarm. 'Just count the losses to our agriculture brought about by our young village girls' excessive appetite for luxury,' spat a vicar from Emilie's region.[5] 'Boarding schools and fashion have turned them into precious little madams, begloved, corseted and crinolined, unable to bend down and reach the ground, incapable of hoeing wheat, of binding sheaves, of feeding the animals.' Village girls were forgetting their primary responsibility to become virtuous wives and mothers. Worse, they were developing a taste for independence.

The most dangerous influence of all was felt to be the idealised figure of *la Parisienne*. Elegant, fashionably dressed, turning heads wherever she went, *la Parisienne* cast a spell over impressionable young peasant girls. Home, family and friends would be forgotten as girls set out eagerly to transform themselves into this revered – and reviled – model of femininity.

But not all youngsters migrated with such fanciful notions. The capital boasted very real practical advantages, too. Jobs were not only more numerous; they were more secure. Agriculture was a notoriously unpredictable business. Many peasant children leaving for Paris had watched incredulously as their parents struggled in vain to maintain paltry little farms. The young were realising that such suffering was futile.

Marriage remained a peasant's principal means of securing his or her property and future, but in ever-shrinking village populations, opportunities for prosperous partnerships were few and far between. A country girl who could only ever hope to become a farmer's wife might realistically aspire to marry an artisan or even a bourgeois if she moved to Paris. And many girls whose families were unable to supply the all-important trousseau, so vital to securing a good marriage, found that a temporary job in Paris increased their value on the marriage market when they returned to the countryside as well.[6]

But Emilie did not set off to Paris that morning with the idea of one day returning. There was no previously arranged marriage to fund. Her departure was to be permanent.

Emilie's parents were approvingly described as an 'honest' family, a term generally understood in 19th-century France to mean 'of modest income' but 'hard-working'.[7] Unlike the children of many of the poorest labourers, Emilie had learned to read and write (though she would always struggle with her spelling).[8] Her literacy casts her father not as a labourer, but rather a member of the 'middle' peasantry, involved in commerce and thus part of a social community.[9] Still, Emilie's departure suggests that M. Delabigne was not affluent enough to support a daughter of working or marrying age, or to secure her an advantageous betrothal to the son of a local farmer. In the absence of secure, well-paid jobs, many parents encouraged their children's departure for the city.

But even with her parents' support, once she left Calvados, Emilie would be utterly alone, probably for the first time in her life. She would need to be resourceful and resilient. Fortunately, these were qualities that the young Normandy girl had in abundance.

A female *diligence* passenger like Emilie would have arrived in Paris exhausted, her skirts crumpled and her limbs aching from three long days on an unforgiving road, broken only by snatched hours of sleep in strange beds. But as the vast city of Paris came into view, even the weariest of travellers would be inclined to forget their fatigue. After the quiet backwaters of the provinces, Paris's splendour could not fail to dazzle and amaze.

When Emilie arrived in the 1840s, the capital was slowly waking up to industrialisation. New buildings were being constructed to accommodate the growing industries, and Paris had seen its first railway open seven years earlier, turning the capital into a hub of activity and cultural interchange. On the surface, Paris was transforming itself into a lavish metropolis which impressed foreign visitors with France's prowess. As industry swelled, the promise of jobs saw the city's population double in size in the first half of the 19th century. Hopeful migrants flocked to the city from all corners of France. In the year Emilie arrived, Paris's population was nudging 1 million.[10]

Career opportunities for women were limited for most of the 19th century. There was no state secondary education for girls until the 1880s, meaning that the options were restricted to shop work, dressmaking, laundering or repairing clothes, cleaning, and waitressing or bar tending. There was industrial work, but this was often less well paid than these domestic tasks. A more fortunate young girl might secure a live-in post as a domestic servant. She might be employed as a maid or, if she were educated, a governess. In all cases, the hours were long and the work demanding. A marriage, even if it were loveless, was often a more attractive alternative.

For an unmarried country girl like Emilie, determined or obliged to find work, a move to the city was her best chance of finding employment. Even then, women's wages were meagre compared to men's. But this did not deter Emilie. Calvados was a department that relied heavily on the fickle industry of agriculture; any regular paid employment was to be celebrated.[11]

Emilie was lucky. No sooner had she arrived in Paris than she began work as a *lingère* or linen maid in a boarding school on the outskirts of the city. To secure such a position so quickly, a young girl would need to have some familiarity with the textile industry and the work of a domestic servant. If she were skilled and had contacts, a country girl like Emilie could even be offered a post before leaving and have her travel expenses paid by her employer.[12]

A *lingère* was a position with heavy responsibilities. Emilie was in charge of checking in and distributing the soiled and clean laundry for the whole school. She had to ensure that all the linen was in good repair and stored appropriately. She would make minor repairs and occasionally be expected to make curtains or other soft furnishings for the school. Above all, she had to be cleanly, meticulous and physically strong. The work was laborious and the hours long. She would rise early, work relentlessly and retire late, exhausted, her body aching and her mind numbed. And at the end of each day, she would have barely 1 franc to show for her labours.

It was a punishing existence that left little time for pleasure, and in any case, conduct manuals advised employers to limit the number of social excursions enjoyed by their staff. Still, Emilie's board and lodgings were paid for, and a school was a social community in itself. As a newcomer to the city where she was yet to make friends, Emilie no doubt welcomed the company of her colleagues. These were people with whom she could share her new experiences and exchange gossip as the day passed.

However, for a girl of Emilie's age, much of the colour and interest of her job came from the men she was now working closely alongside. And as a new face with a fresh, country complexion and an earthy, natural beauty uncommon in Paris, she soon attracted the attention of one of the male teachers, a Monsieur T.[13] By chance, Emilie's new admirer was also of Normandy extraction. Separated from family and friends, in a city where everything was strange and unfamiliar, Emilie was easily seduced.[14] A romance quickly blossomed.

The period that followed marked a parenthesis in Emilie's life, during which the monotonous routine of the working week was punctuated by romantic interludes and stolen moments of intimacy. But then one day towards the end of 1847, Emilie made a terrifying discovery: she was pregnant.

Some accounts claim that Monsieur T. was already married; others paint him as a bachelor fond of his freedom and his drink. Either way, he never married Emilie. Still in her twenties, Emilie had become the figure that 19th-century society most reviled: the unmarried mother. She knew that both she and her illegitimate child would be social outcasts and she would need to seek alternative lodgings. Her story was only too familiar.

In 19th-century Paris, single mothers were almost always poor and without family, and frequently drawn from the textile and domestic industries. Emilie knew her options to be severely limited. She could hardly return to Calvados, where she would face unemployment as well as contempt. Her wisest move was to see out her pregnancy in Paris. There, she could at least work for most of the term and then make childcare arrangements afterwards. Perhaps the baby's father would even assist her financially. It was not so much a chance worth taking – it was her only choice.

But by the time Emilie was nearing the end of her pregnancy in the summer of 1848, France had been thrown into uproar. If Paris's face appeared to glitter and sparkle, beneath the surface the country's economy had been faltering since the middle of the 1840s. The Orléanist regime watched in horror as its popularity began to crumble. In February 1848, a banquet in Paris escalated into a full-scale political demonstration, leading protesters to take to the streets and form barricades. A dismayed Louis-Philippe I abdicated, a provisional government was hastily put in place and a republic declared. But when discontent with the new administration's political approach reached a head in June, radicals once more took to the streets. The Parisian landscape was transformed into a maze of barricades and the streets reverberated with the sound of gunfire and shouting. Tens of thousands of Parisians participated; at least 12,000 were arrested and some 1,500 were killed.[15]

Barely three weeks after the conflict's bloody climax, with gunfire still echoing through the streets and the smell of smoke lingering in the air, Emilie went into labour. She was far away from her home town with no female family members to support her. Paris had its attention elsewhere. On 13 July 1848, alone and in the sweltering heat, Emilie gave birth to a baby girl.

Emilie adhered to common practice and gave her new baby her own name. But for convenience as much as caprice, the little girl soon came to be known as Louise.

Louise's birth certificate does not identify her father. The blank space where his name should appear betrays a complicated relationship. Though Louise's father joined her mother when she moved nearer the centre of Paris, he never officially recognised his lover or her child. He was often absent, and when he did return, his fondness for drink placed a constant strain on the household. Emilie Delabigne had to manage alone with her baby.

She could have given the child up. In 1844, 66 per cent of

single mothers abandoning their infants at the children's home, the Hospice des Enfants Trouvés, were *lingères*.[16] But Normandy women were renowned for their sense of family and duty; Emilie refused to give up her daughter.

As baby Louise grew, she began to develop a curious, striking appearance. She had a flush of golden red hair and pale skin, against which the piercing blue of her large eyes was accentuated. She was not exactly pretty by conventional standards; but there was something disarming, ethereal, even bewitching, about her appearance.

By the time Louise had learned to walk, her mother had moved to a tiny top-floor apartment in the Rue Paradis-Poissonière in Paris's poverty-stricken 10th arrondissement.[17] It was a lively area of the city, populated with shopkeepers, artisans and factory workers, and animated by a scattering of little theatres and café concerts. Workers' apartments like the one Louise and her mother inhabited were cramped and stuffy with low ceilings.[18] The rooms were poorly lit and dingy, and the few possessions the mother and daughter owned would instantly have made it look cluttered. And Louise and her mother were not alone in the apartment; the little girl's father was unreliable, but his presence was consistent enough for him to father six more children. Mme Delabigne, as she was now known, being over 25 and a mother, showed no resistance. Living as a concubine was common, particularly for girls who had migrated and could not easily acquire the necessary written consent of their parents to wed. Besides, the formalities of marriage presented a great expense.[19]

Living conditions became more and more uncomfortable as the family grew. Money was hard-won and quickly spent. Finally, Louise's mother realised that the cost of her lover's presence outweighed the gain. She severed relations with him for good.

Louise would never truly get to know her father. Her childhood was spent on the Rue Paradis-Poissonière, and she could not have begun her life at a more difficult time, both for her mother and for France. The revolution of 1848 had done little to improve the daily life of the poor. In Paris, the consequences of the wave of migration that brought Emilie to the capital were taking their toll. The golden opportunities so eulogised had proved a limited fund, reserved for the quick and the lucky. For the poor, living conditions were squalid. The putrid air made the stomach turn, while disease and sickness spread uncontrollably through the filthy, overcrowded streets.

The Rue Paradis-Poissonière was a microcosm of the city's ills. On either side of the dirty, narrow street, tightly packed buildings housed a growing number of workers, shopkeepers and dressmakers. The majority of the street's working-class inhabitants harboured bitter resentment at their lot. The theatres, café concerts and dance halls may have enlivened the area, but they also led to widespread alcoholism. It was an unsavoury place to grow up. A child had to be permanently on his or her guard. But Louise had little choice. Her mother had to continue working, and when she was away Louise found that the street became both her playground and her school.

Children of all ages would mix in the streets, the older ones teaching the younger what they knew, the young listening wide-eyed as the world was revealed to them. A child had to be perceptive and make quick judgements about characters and their surroundings. By the age of ten, Louise was becoming sure-footed. She was rapidly learning the skills needed to survive on the street, her bright eyes watching, looking, absorbing everything around her. She grew skilled at adapting to her changing surroundings. This facility would serve her well throughout her life.

For Louise, the street was often the preferable place to be. Even when her mother was at home, she was seldom alone. Conscious of her marketable assets, the resourceful Mme Delabigne would frequently return to the tiny apartment with a lover. More often than not, she was paid for her troubles. Prostitution was a common way for poor girls to make ends meet. In 1836, Alexandre Parent-Duchâtelet, the vice-president of the Conseil de Salubrité, declared there to be over 3,500 prostitutes in Paris, and a further 35–40,000 working on a clandestine basis.[20] Peasants new to the city were, he felt, particularly at risk of falling into this profession owing to their vulnerability and naivety. The garment trade was notorious for supplying a wealth of young girls eager to earn some extra sous through prostitution.[21] As a *lingère*, Mme Delabigne would often have found herself the butt of caricaturists' jokes. For such girls, a common trait was a lack of family support to fall back on.[22]

For Louise, her mother's sideline business established unconventional reference points from which to judge the world. From an early age, she learned by example that success was measured by a woman's ability to seduce a man. Years later, the little girl would speak proudly of her mother's sexual charisma:

'Mama was so beautiful, my dear, that every time she went out she would seduce at least three men.'[23]

Still, as a child, Louise learned that her mother's profession meant there were times when it was wise to be absent.

In this period of political upheaval, social rituals became vitally important. They offered stability and reassurance. Normandy was a region renowned for its piety and superstition, and Mme Delabigne clung to these familiar rituals when she moved to Paris. She made sure that her daughter took part in all the religious and social rites appropriate for her age. So in her tenth year, Louise joined the other girls and boys of the area at the Église Saint-Laurent to prepare for her First Communion. For children like Louise, the preparation and the ceremony were above all a marvellous social occasion. It was also a rare chance to wear a pretty dress and be admired. Everything about the event was a glittering contrast to the monotony of everyday life.

The Église Saint-Laurent was a modest yet elegant building. Louise could see it standing proud at the end of her road, a beacon of tranquillity, every time she stepped outside the family's apartment. It took barely five minutes to walk there, but when she left home on the day of the ceremony, each one of Louise's light, bouncing steps was another precious moment to savour the pomp and grandeur of the occasion.

Mme Delabigne washed and arranged her daughter's long red hair specially. Then, when Louise shed her dreary everyday dress and pinafore, the frothy white Communion dress – even if it were borrowed – seemed to transform her into a princess. A delicate crown of white roses was carefully placed on her head to complete the outfit. The purity of the white lace against her red hair and blue eyes made her unconventional, Pre-Raphaelite appearance even more striking than usual. Curious onlookers turned their heads in admiration as the children filed out of the church after the ceremony.

Louise instantly caught the attention of one of her neighbours. This was the young Jules Claretie, who would go on to become a prolific journalist. The little girl was eight years his junior, but the young man was spellbound by the child as she walked past him, the light catching 'her beautiful red hair'.[24] Already, Louise's social skills were flourishing. Well aware of the impact she was making, she bounded up to greet the young man clutching her prayer book. Louise had learned that survival depended on how you interacted with others.

Claretie became a firm friend. With his insatiable appetite for culture, he would often amuse himself by staging a makeshift puppet show for his younger neighbours. He was both director and puppeteer of these amateur performances, but the shows never failed to attract a keen audience, of which Louise was the most dedicated member. Seated on the little chair that Claretie had arranged for the purpose, she watched mesmerised as he performed crude interpretations of Victor Hugo's tragic drama *Ruy Blas* and the same author's courtly romance, *Hernani*. Claretie was always struck by the intensity with which Louise's big blue eyes fixed on the wooden puppets as she attentively absorbed the dialogue. At the end of each performance, her delicate hands would applaud enthusiastically. Perhaps, Claretie fancied, she was dreaming of conquering the world of theatre as she watched those shows.

However, the friendships Louise was cultivating were not restricted to her peer group. The renowned landscape painter Camille Corot lived close by, and along with the other local children, Louise would go and visit 'père Corot'. His studio represented a haven of peace in the bustling 10th arrondissement. When Louise stepped inside, closing the door behind her to the sounds of the street, she entered a whole new world. The artist's studio was not claustrophobic and cluttered with objects as her home was, but spacious and simply furnished.[25] The only decorations to be seen were the paintings and sketches that adorned the walls. The studio was cool, and the comforting smell of wood and oil paint filled the air. As Louise gazed upwards towards the high ceilings, she could see a large window that allowed the daylight to pour in.

Corot was a grandfather-like figure. He could often be found sitting at his easel, dressed in a comfortable, flowing blue smock and a soft hat. Once she arrived, Louise would sit and watch the master paint, singing while he worked; for Corot 'would begin his day singing and end it singing'.[26] Louise spent long summer afternoons lost in the painted world of the beautiful town of Ville-d'Avray, which Corot would bring to life through stories. Louise watched as a magical landscape built up in thick, glossy layers before her eyes. She had never travelled beyond Paris; and yet, in that quiet, peaceful space, with the sound of the artist's voice echoing through the studio, Louise could almost believe she was there, sitting by the lake or strolling in the shade along a meandering pathway.

Louise's life education had begun, but her childhood was to end abruptly. She had reached the age of thirteen. And it was then that she truly came to encounter the sordid underbelly of Parisian society.

CHAPTER 2

The Child Becomes a Woman

The young girl was beginning to blossom into an attractive teenager, her childlike figure growing curvaceous and womanly. Below the dramatic arch of her eyebrows, her huge blue eyes sparkled as she gazed back at all those she met. Her features were perfectly even, her nose fine and straight, and when she smiled, her dainty mouth recalled the quiet self-assurance of the Mona Lisa. But it was her hair that would turn people's heads. The thick mane of lustrous red tumbled down her back, glinting like spun gold when the light caught it. It was unusual and people would remark on it.

To Mme Delabigne, her daughter was now a young adult. She would have to get a job.

It was common for daughters of working-class families to be sent out to earn as soon as they became employable. Few parents saw any value in sending children to school. Attendance figures in Paris were erratic even among the youngsters who were enrolled.[1] Young adults were considered an asset designed to improve the family economy. This was felt most keenly in single-parent families. The memoirs of Jeanne Bouvier, the daughter of working-class parents living in Paris in the second half of the 19th century, paint a vivid picture of parents' reliance on their children's income:

'I was a good worker at the factory, but I almost never got a raise. My mother, who was always short of money, would get angry to the point of beating me. She thought that I was not working hard enough and she would call me lazy.'[2]

The consequences of unemployment could be terrible. It was vital that a youngster be found a position at the earliest possible opportunity. Each time she stepped outside her home, Louise's mother would see wretched women clothed in rags and men huddled in doorways, robbed of both soul and ambition. Unemployment was an ever-present threat and the Delabignes' neighbourhood provided a daily reminder.

Having been raised in the countryside, Mme Delabigne was used to children starting work as young as seven or eight.[3] It would not have struck her as unreasonable for Louise to begin work at the age of thirteen. So it was that in the early 1860s, Louise found herself arriving to begin her first day of paid employment in a dress shop.

It was a fortuitous time for the teenager to be starting her first job in the clothing industry. The market for luxury items was flourishing. After the financial crisis of the late 1840s, France was now enjoying an economic boom as the new Emperor, Napoleon III, set about nurturing the country's prosperity. Under the Second Empire, industry was thriving, communications and transport were improving, and money was being poured into housing. On the surface, Paris sparkled with affluence and possibility. There reigned a spirit of joie de vivre, and youth and beauty were particularly sought-after commodities.

The tone was firmly set by the Emperor and his entourage. The Imperial Court was renowned for its extravagance, its spectacular balls and parties, its elaborate costumes and gastronomic excess. Its example filtered down the social scale and was imitated by the rest of society. Everyone wanted to copy Napoleon and Eugénie.

'In general, people believe that luxury is the state most favourable to health,' complained critic Philarète Chasles in 1863.[4] This was the Paris of dances, parties and theatre excursions. Gaiety and frivolity had become the city's guiding principles.

The bourgeoisie found that they now had money to spare, and the leisure industry was quick to respond. Cafés, balls, operas, ballets and the theatre drew pleasure-seekers from across the capital. Ostentatious department stores began to appear from the middle of the century, and mechanised manufacture made fashion available to the masses. Paris firmly established itself as the world capital of luxury, good taste and pleasure.

At the centre of this lavish fashion show was *la Parisienne*. 'The Parisienne is not in fashion,' declared man of letters Arsène Houssaye, 'she is fashion.'[5] More than ever, a lady's appearance was of the utmost importance. 'By simply inspecting the external appearance of a woman,' explained the Comtesse Dash, the author of etiquette manuals, 'another woman, if she has intelligence and skill, will know to which class she belongs, what her education has been, the kind of society she has frequented. She will even be able to guess her tastes, her character, if she gives herself the trouble to observe; often the way she wraps her shawl about her, the placement of her hat, the way she puts on her gloves, tells of her life.'[6]

The burgeoning fashion industry depended on a steady supply of laundresses, seamstresses, milliners and shop assistants. Louise was one of many young girls whose first experience of luxury was preparing it for other women's consumption. As an impressionable teenager, Louise was swept up in the reigning spirit of extravagance and consumerism. But as a dress shop employee, her life was a stark contrast to that of the customers she was now serving.

A dress shop assistant's working day was long, lasting up to twelve hours. An 1841 law limiting the hours a youngster could work was rarely adhered to by employers.[7] Louise would leave home early, while the great city of Paris was only just stirring. The streets were being swept in preparation for another busy day and as Louise made her way along the pavements and passages, she would pass market sellers, factory workers and shop assistants, all hurrying to take up posts which would bring the city's bustling industries to life. Louise had to walk briskly. It was important that she arrive punctually. Few employers tolerated lateness, and time would have to be made up at the end of the day. A girl could not risk her parents discovering that her performance had been found wanting.

A young girl's wages could be pitiful by comparison with those of an adult. Under the Second Empire, the average adult worker earned a daily wage of 2 francs 50, though the more fortunate employee could be paid as much as 5 francs. The 40 sous (approximately 2 francs) Louise took home at the end of the day was a respectable wage for her age and profession.[8] Those precious coins brought personal pride and parental affection. But Louise soon discovered that they were hard-won.

Her day was filled with preparing garments for clients, adjusting ribbons and trimmings, adding adornments, and handling all manner of luxurious fabrics. A wealth of new skills had to be acquired and perfected. But Louise had always been an observant child. She responded as she always had to a new environment: she studied the people around her. By closely watching her co-workers and mimicking the work of their delicate fingers, she quickly mastered all the techniques of the trade. Soon, Louise became known in the local area for her intricate lace ribbons and pretty taffeta dresses.

Once the anxiety of the first day had passed, a new girl like Louise would fall into a routine. After an early start, a simple lunch was taken at about midday, usually in the workshop. Louise's contemporary Jeanne Bouvier also worked in a dressmaking shop and was struck by her colleagues' frugal eating habits: 'how they would scrimp and save so they could buy gloves, perfume, and a thousand other accessories. The midday meal was often reduced to its simplest expression.[9] Work then continued into the evening. It was draining, but conversations with fellow workers could make the time pass more quickly.

Dress shop owners typically employed several girls who would work alongside each other. Jeanne Bouvier recalled how the women she worked with were 'pleasant comrades' who would sing as they sewed; 'I had fun with them.'[10] In *L'Assommoir* (1877), Émile Zola's fictional tale of a working-class Parisian family, the florist's workshop where the teenager Nana is employed is abuzz with the sound of girls' voices chatting and gossiping as they work, giggling at each other's jokes, quietening only when the *patronne* enters.

For a young girl, the work environment provided a very particular form of education. Older girls could be doubtful teachers. In *L'Assommoir*, the jokes shared among the girls are frequently crude, and Nana soon becomes well versed in sexual double-entendre. Like Nana, Louise was exposed to the life experience of the girls around her. Zola's acerbic view of such establishments was shared by many: they provided 'a fine education', with girls gathered together 'one on top of the other', so that, just like a basket of apples containing a single overripe fruit, 'they rotted together'.[11]

Years later, Louise wrote a novel, *Isola* (1876), based on her childhood experiences, in which she denounced the corrupting influence of the workplace on a young girl. But it was not her colleagues' tales that shook her confidence. The place was:

> one of those workshops where young girls learn, among other things, to defend their honour. Uneasy about what I sensed, not daring to confide in anyone, unaware of good as of evil, I spent three years in this way. When, without respect for my childhood, a man spoke words to me which I suspected to be indecent, I left the workshop, occasionally regretting the company of the

woman whose husband had insulted me; and when I was alone,
I asked myself what it could possibly be about me that made
men harass me in this way.[12]

But for contemporary social observers, it was the employee's walk
home that gave most cause for concern. The journey to and from
work was riddled with danger, not least because it provided an
opportunity for men and women to meet. Louise's contemporary,
Suzanne Voilquin, also began work at a young age to help her family. She described her anxiety about walking home late after work:
'I had a horrible fear of meeting on my return one of those con-
temptible men who make a game of accosting young women and
frightening them with disgraceful remarks.'[13]

As she walked to and from work, Louise would come face-to-face
with the city's less glamorous side and its full cast of disreputable
characters. For all that the capital glittered and dazzled, poverty
and corruption simmered below its surface. It was a city tainted
by alcohol and prostitution. While the bourgeoisie and the upper
classes revelled in their new-found luxury, the poor were growing
poorer – and increasingly resentful. The areas inhabited by the
lower classes remained squalid. Living where she did, Louise could
not escape the capital's more sinister face.

Looks could be deceiving, too. As the century progressed, it
was becoming harder to make judgements based on appearances.
'Vice is seldom clad in rags in Paris,' wrote an English visitor to
the capital.[14] 'These days, one can no longer tell if one is dealing
with honest women dressed as good time girls, or good time girls
dressed as honest women,' warned Maxime du Camp.[15] Even age
and experience offered no shields against deception. But then Mme
Delabigne never queried the company Louise was keeping. When a
girl arrived at the Delabigne residence one day introducing herself
as Camille and asking if Louise was free to go out, she assured Mme

Delabigne that she was a friend from the shop.[16] Camille seemed harmless enough. It did not occur to Mme Delabigne that two girls together might get up to more mischief, encourage each other and attract more male attention than one. She allowed Louise to accompany the stranger out into the street.

Years later, in her semi-autobiographical novel, Louise drew on her encounters as a teenager:

> The people around me whispered strange words in my ears which made me blush without knowing why. I did not understand, and look at the terrible consequence of my ignorance. I was embarrassed not to understand.
>
> I wanted to see, so I drew nearer to this world which was spinning around me and to which I did not seem to belong.
>
> I was swept up in the terrible chain.
>
> Carried away, dazed, not seeing clearly, I let myself go, mad, stupid, laughing so as to show my teeth and hide my tears.
> I continued in this way until the day when, coming to my senses again, I realised that I was lost.[17]

Like Zola's Nana, Louise caught the eye of an older man. Any man could pass himself off as a gentleman if he knew how to present himself. Louise's mature admirer gave her her first sexual experience. It was brutal.

> Why is he protected by the world, the man who led me to that place, and who knew where he was leading me? Why does society have indulgent treasures to offer the wicked person whose good fortune and gallant adventures people talk about behind their fans?
>
> Yes, in that first journey, I saw what I did not suspect, the illusions, the naive aspirations, the dreams and hopes of

my childhood, it was all gone in an instant because a brutal
passerby had taken advantage of my gullibility, and society,
which owed me assistance and protection, became my cruel-
lest enemy.[18]

The experience lifted a veil for Louise, revealing the harsh reality
of life for a working-class Parisian girl. She had known poverty and
hunger. She had also seen luxury, felt the rich textures of expensive
fabrics, watched women of fortune as they left the shop with their
colourful dresses and chic bonnets tied with ribbons. As a child on
the streets and as a teenager in the workplace, she had overheard
whispered tales of sordid affairs, and she had passed shady figures
coming and going on visits to her mother. But a glimpsed silhouette
and a second-hand tale lack the bitter edge of first-hand experience.
Now, her innocence had been irreparably shattered.

All at once she could see clearly: happiness came at a price.
Tenderness and emotional warmth were conditional, unreliable,
untrustworthy. And material pleasure required money. Louise was
poor. To taste the luxury those elegant ladies enjoyed, she must
have something else to offer, something the keyholders to all that
splendour desired. All around her, in her neighbourhood, on her
route to work, there were girls just like her whose innocence had
been destroyed. Often, as their naivety vanished, girls began to
realise that they had the means to escape poverty. To satisfy their
material needs, they had only to respond to men's physical urges.
They would give men exactly what they wanted: their bodies.

'How many young girls I have seen fall,' lamented Jeanne
Bouvier, 'because they earned such miserable wages. I have seen
them go down into the streets. Poverty is an insufferable situation,
and those who do not escape into suicide escape into prostitution.'[19]

In Louise's case, the shock of losing her virginity coincided
with the natural curiosity of an adolescent impatient to grow up

and the hunger to taste the pleasures she had watched the rich girls enjoying. Once her purity had been sullied, there was nothing left to lose. Added to which, Louise lived dangerously near Notre-Dame de Lorette, an area known for its flourishing sex trade. Her fall into prostitution was perhaps inevitable. 'A fact worth noting,' observed A. Coffignon in his study of corruption in Paris, 'is that the worker who later submits to prostitution has almost always been deflowered by a man of her class and her immediate entourage.'[20] Louise's example was typical.

Her new career was a well-established profession, and there were always opportunities for new recruits. In 19th-century Paris, the industry was thriving as never before, largely due to the extreme contrast between rich and poor. The capital boasted one of the most highly regulated systems of prostitution in the world. While other countries sought to eradicate it, the French system worked from a simple premise: prostitution was unfortunate but inevitable. Fighting it was futile. It was better to control it.

To this end, Alexandre Parent-Duchâtelet's *Prostitution in the City of Paris* (1836) sought to record the state of the industry and assess the scale of the problem. His findings gave rise to countless stereotypes and revealed the rigorous methods of control that officials attempted to put in place.[21]

As far as the authorities were concerned, girls working in the industry could be grouped into two categories: *filles soumises* or *filles insoumises*.[22] A *fille soumise* was a prostitute who had been officially registered. A girl could register herself, or she would be registered by an official. Either way, she would have to adhere to strict rules and regulations. Besides being forbidden to appear in public outside specific hours or to live within a certain distance of a school, she would have to undergo regular health checks. These were universally dreaded. An unsatisfactory report (usually a diagnosis of a venereal disease) could lead to forced admission to the fearful prison-hospital, Saint-Lazare. Girls whispered that you could be locked up and even have your hair cut off if you were detained.

Being registered as a *fille soumise* brought frustrating restrictions. But the alternative was far worse. An unregistered prostitute or *fille insoumise* led an even more precarious existence. She was constantly on her guard for fear of being caught by the police. And yet to the irritation of rigorous information-gatherers like Parent-Duchâtelet, clandestine prostitution continued to thrive uncontrollably.

When Louise first turned her hand to the profession, unregistered to begin with, she joined thousands of girls in a complex social hierarchy.[23]

The lowest status was that of the common prostitute. Such a girl would walk the streets soliciting potential clients, or work in a brothel, and usually lived in a state of abject poverty. If a woman had not sunk to this lowest of stations, she automatically joined a superior category: the *demi-monde*.

Demi-monde provided a convenient umbrella term for an indefinable, shady 'half world' and all those who occupied it. It was a place hovering between destitution and respectability, and within it were further categories and gradations of sex worker.

At the bottom of the hierarchy was the *grisette*. Young, lighthearted and coquettish, the *grisette* often worked in the clothing industry or sometimes as a florist, and used prostitution to supplement her meagre income. The synonymy between the garment trade and prostitution became a cliché that aroused knowing smirks, but the stereotype was based on statistical fact. So frequently was it proved accurate that it gave this class of prostitute her name: *grisette* derived from the inexpensive grey material from which working-class women's dresses were made. A *grisette* was still achingly poor and had to live a frustratingly modest existence. But she could hold her head higher than the common prostitute. According to popular perception, when the working week was done, the *grisette* loved nothing more than to have fun, to go to dances, cafés and student balls, and she adored the theatre. But more than anything – more than parties, pretty trinkets or a hunger-relieving supper – the ambitious *grisette* dreamed of becoming a *lorette*.

Taking her name from the area of Notre-Dame de Lorette where her kind were found in abundance, the *lorette* was still a relatively new class of prostitute when Louise started working in the industry. Initially identified by Nestor Roqueplan in the 1840s, the *lorette* was proud to be able to distinguish herself from the *grisette*. Crucially, she would have secured the protection of a man of considerable income, who would often set her up in her own apartment, turning her into a *femme galante* or kept woman. And this source of income enabled her to enjoy a more comfortable lifestyle than the *grisette* could ever hope for. A *grisette* would make do with a handful of practical shirts, skirts and bonnets; a *lorette* spent every last sou on the latest dresses made of fine silk and rich velvet, trimmed with delicate lace, and she would purchase sumptuous hats and accessories. A *grisette* would gratefully accept what she was offered; a *lorette* would expect the best and always want more. However, the *lorette* mixed in relatively lowly bohemian circles. She knew she had not yet reached the summit of her profession.

The highest echelon to which a girl working in the sex industry could aspire was the title of courtesan. Known variously as *les grandes horizontales*, *les grandes abandonnées*, *les grandes cocottes* or *les lionnes*, with the top ten or so leading courtesans referred to as *la garde*, these were the women who commanded Paris. The courtesan was worlds apart from the common prostitute. The difference came down to two simple factors: the degree of choice a girl had, and her level of earnings. A courtesan had the luxury of cherry-picking her lovers, and the material benefits could be outstanding. Courtesans lived in palatial *hôtels particuliers*, and would be seen riding like royalty in gilt carriages through Paris's most fashionable parks and gardens, dressed in furs and velvets, glittering with jewels. But a courtesan had to know how to promote and present herself. She must dress exquisitely, be well-mannered and cultured, have read widely and possess an innate understanding of the appropriate protocol for every occasion, for she would be mixing in elegant society. A courtesan commanded prestige. She was a celebrity.

Thousands of girls dreamed of becoming courtesans, but only a few would ever scale such heights.

When Louise began her career, she could not even consider herself a fully fledged *lorette*. She still lived with her mother and had no wealthy protector. She entered at the bottom of the *demi-monde*'s hierarchy. But circumstances had set her firmly on a path that could lead her to the top.

The teenager was soon living the lifestyle of a typical *grisette*. She considered her appearance carefully – *grisettes* were experts at dressing to please on a limited budget – and experimented with a little make-up. The goal of every *grisette* was to attract the attention of a suitor who would, in exchange for the pleasure he derived from her body, treat her to a good dinner, a trip to the theatre, a pretty trinket or some other present. To do this, the *grisette* had to go where men with spare sous would be likely to see her. Louise would follow her friends to cafés, brasseries and dances around the Latin Quarter and the area of Notre-Dame de Lorette.

Notre-Dame de Lorette was notorious: 'Whenever people talk of pleasures, of clandestine love, of ephemeral liaisons, ruined elder sons […] one's imagination turns, irresistibly, towards Notre-Dame de Lorette […] As soon as you mention the name in the provinces, young girls avert their eyes, mothers cross themselves, and eligible young ladies look at you with displeasure.'[24]

With its thronging student population and exhilarating nightlife, the Latin Quarter was a magnet for *grisettes* seeking male attention and fun.[25] Many of the students were new to the capital and had come in search of pleasure as much as an education. They often came from good families, and were bursting with newly acquired knowledge and youthful enthusiasm. And they arrived with an allowance. It was small and intended to last the month; but Paris's wonders and attractions beckoned. The allowance rarely lasted long.

Between lectures, these young men spilled out onto the terraces of budget-friendly cafés, filling the air with laughter, cigarette smoke and the sound of cheerful banter and chinking glasses. In the evenings, they would swarm towards the Latin Quarter's brasseries to take a modestly priced meal. The quality of the food could be doubtful, the drinks mediocre; but since most students lived in tiny attic rooms starved of both pleasure and company, the jovial atmosphere and the pretty women more than compensated.

A *grisette* was pleased to win the heart of a student. Besides the usual treats she greedily received, a student could also teach her something of the world. These lessons might prove useful if she were ever to progress to the status of a *lorette*, when she would need to mix in more cultivated society.

Louise threw herself into the bohemian lifestyle of the Latin Quarter's cafés and brasseries. She drank, smoked, laughed loudly and began using coarse language.

But a wise *grisette* like Louise knew that the café and the brasserie were not the only settings in which she could catch a man's wandering eye. In the evenings, students and other men flocked to Paris's numerous *bals publiques*. This was where a *grisette* stood the best chance of ensnaring that wealthy suitor who would finally make her a *lorette*.

'The true Parisian does not sleep,' boasted one observer, 'or at least, very little.'[26] It was on this premise that the *bal publique* or public ball was founded. When the Revolution ended the government's strict regulation regarding the frequency and location of *bals publiques*, a veritable dancing frenzy rippled out across Paris.[27] The public ball swept away the cobwebs of tradition and became a defiant symbol of uninhibited pleasure. Students, foreigners, *grisettes* and *lorettes*, society girls and wealthy gentlemen all congregated at Paris's *bals publiques* in the evenings. Men would go to admire the prettiest members of the opposite sex – and perhaps find a partner for the night; *grisettes* and *lorettes* set out with the explicit intention of attracting a rich benefactor. And both sexes arrived determined to have a good time. It was an explosive combination.

But the choice of ball would depend on social status and this would determine the kind of person one might meet. Louise had to consider this carefully. The Bal Mabille, with its enchanting garden twinkling with soft gas lights, had become one of the most fashionable balls in Paris by the mid-19th century. It was here that many great courtesans launched their careers. But when she was starting out, Louise would have found the ball at the Closerie des Lilas more to her taste. The entrance fee was cheap and the venue was brimming with students. As one English visitor remarked, this was where *grisettes* could be seen 'in full feather'.[28]

The Closerie des Lilas was run by a M. Bullier, an enterprising tycoon in the entertainment industry, who had modelled his establishment on the Alhambra, the Moorish palace in Granada.[29] A superb garden, generously planted with the lilac bushes that gave the venue its name, provided young lovers with leafy corners and shaded groves behind which to conduct their affairs. A swing aroused squeals of delight from giggling girls, while sly members of the opposite sex could sneak a look at the ankle of whichever girl was enjoying the ride. At the end of the garden was a billiard room, and just beyond it, a covered dance space; not even bad weather could stop the frenzied dancing at the Closerie des Lilas. Between the dances, patrons could take a moment to catch their breath and enjoy a refreshment at one of the round green tables, just big enough for two. It was one of the most lively, raucous evening haunts in the area. Every corner of the garden was overflowing with young people chatting, drinking and laughing.

The venue had seen some great stars in its time, including the sensational dancer Clara Fontaine. Dances were held every night of the week, and when Louise started frequenting the Closerie des Lilas the venue was beginning to attract the more ambitious *grisette*, with aspirations of grandeur and a hat to match; a cheap bonnet would be met with disdainful looks.[30] Any self-respecting girl at the Closerie des Lilas would proudly appear in a *bibi*, the feathered hat favoured by *lorettes*.

The ability to dance well was essential. Dancing was how a girl attracted attention. This served two purposes. Firstly, it enabled her to secure a client, and for a *grisette* maybe even to progress to the status of *lorette*. But for a *lorette* it was also a potential audition. It was a chance to be spotted by a theatrical producer and offered a part on stage. In the *lorette*'s eyes, nothing could rival the thrill and glamour of being an actress.

By attending such dances, Louise was now rubbing shoulders with actresses, *lorettes* and men of all ages and classes. Students were all very well, but she found she had a particular weakness for military men. She sought out the prime spots they frequented, such as the Champ de Mars and the popular ball at the Salon de Mars. She loved the smart uniforms, the carefully waxed moustaches, the gleaming buckles and medals. There was something about the discipline, the rigour and the air of tradition that impressed her.

Poverty fuelled both Louise's need for basic necessities and her yearning for luxuries. And then there was alcohol, that potion that made a person forget their worries. Louise began to rely on it more and more. But all these things had to be paid for; an unmarried girl simply could not survive in Paris, let alone console herself with a little luxury from time to time, without some spare sous. A sexual favour here and there seemed a small price to pay for a hot meal, a swig of gin or a pretty hat.

Sometimes, if Louise had offered her services to a student, a cramped attic room might be available. But occasionally she would be obliged to take a lover home. Mme Delabigne was accommodating. She knew the flavour of poverty and the ache of hunger. She had found her own body to be a renewable source of income. And Louise was disarmingly attractive. It was a simple calculation.

Louise later confided to an acquaintance how her mother complied willingly when she brought a man home, and had helped manage her career by ensuring that she always looked her best. Referring to Mme Delabigne, the confidant explained:

> In the morning, when the lover had gone, she would come into her daughter's bedroom. Finding the young girl, without stopping to worry whether or not she was tired, she covered the shivering pink body with a damp sheet. It was heroic of her, because she could have killed the youngster. That was too bad. Under the icy sensation, her breasts filled out, her skin grew firm again. The mother could feel that she had done her duty and she would say to herself: 'You will see. The little one will be marvellous. She will be fabulous.'[31]

But men could be cruel. The profession forced Louise to develop a tough exterior. She had to feign pleasure when a fat and sweaty man pressed his naked body close to hers. Then she might be ordered to carry out peculiar sexual acts. And the richer the man, the more exotic his requests could be. Some men were violent; on a bad night, she might be spat at, slapped and kicked. But Louise persevered, using her charms and her body to survive. She took the blows, drawing strength from her naturally ambitious streak. Working in a dress shop had left her with a taste for finery and the power and security it brought. She would never have been satisfied as a simple *grisette*. From the very first, she had a loftier target in her sights.

A *grisette* ideally sought to build herself a small register of regular clients. It was easier than constantly hunting for men, and far less precarious. Having an established client base was also an indication that a girl was moving up in the *demi-monde*. A practical way to do this was to find a job as a waitress or a barmaid. Girls who did so enjoyed the reassurance of a reliable weekly income (albeit small), and had the advantage of being able to supplement it through a steady stream of potential clients who might become regulars.

When a job came up working in a *brasserie de femmes*, Louise seized the opportunity. She desperately craved security.

The *brasserie de femmes* was a new concept that was growing fashionable in the 1860s.[32] The particularity of the bars was that they were staffed exclusively by women. As one contented patron remarked, the idea was 'founded on a simple principle: it is pleasant to smoke a cigar while you watch a creature whose job it is to please strutting up and down in front of you'.[33] The waitresses would often be dressed provocatively in provincial costume, and were more than happy to supplement their income. Men were delighted by the gimmick and the craze soon took off.

Countless *brasseries de femmes* sprung up in the 10th arrondissement near the Delabignes' home. Louise fitted in well: the girls were typically pretty and known to be fierce with clients who took liberties. Many people deplored the corruption they believed these venues encouraged. 'Of all the young girls, the brasserie girl is the one who most easily turns into a monster void of all sense of morality,' fumed A. Coffignon. 'Beware he who falls into her clutches.'[34]

The girls earned tips from the beverages they sold, and were instructed to throw out customers who had stopped buying drinks. The waitress's job was to use her feminine wiles to persuade men to spend more. To encourage them, she would often drink as well.

Despite her aspirations, Louise's life was spiralling into a vortex of alcohol and promiscuity.

Then one day, an unexpected glimmer of hope appeared. It caught Louise off guard, but it would change her life forever. In 1864, the sixteen-year-old fell in love.

CHAPTER 3

First Love, First Appearances

ichard Fossey was different from other men. Four years older than Louise, he was kind and gentle. He knew how to listen. He came from a good family, his father was well-connected, and his parents had high hopes for his future. And while the young man's career was being decided, he was making his transition from boyhood to manhood in the heart of the capital.

Louise and Fossey shared a mutual acquaintance, their friend Camille.

When the girls met as teenagers, Louise quickly warmed to Camille. Louise was sharp-witted, passionate and physically alluring, and though her interior was growing embittered and hardened to pain, the teenager masked her core with a captivating veneer of girlish coquettishness which was designed expressly to please. By contrast, Camille was straightforward, sturdy and placid. She was fun, but she was also dependable. Louise's world was coloured by uncertainty; she valued the loyalty and discretion she found in her new friend. The pair formed a close and lifelong bond.

After a while, Louise's comrade began to make Mme Delabigne uneasy. One way or another, she needed her daughter to earn. An acquaintance who diverted the youngster's attention was a threat to the whole family. Mme Delabigne felt certain that it was Camille who had orchestrated her teenage daughter's meeting with Richard Fossey during one of the girls' pleasure-hunting forays in the capital. But Louise preferred to circulate a different story.[1]

In her version of events, fictionalised later in her novel *Isola* (1876), the couple's encounter was more serendipitous and romantic. One dismal evening, Louise had slumped in despair beneath a coach entrance in a side street. As she sat crying, unsure whether to return home and face the latest violent lover her mother had procured, or to brave the cold night air and sleep huddled at the side of the street, a man approached. It was Fossey. Noticing the shivering young woman, he stopped to ask the cause of her upset. Tentatively, Louise began to tell him of her traumatic upbringing. 'He possessed that extraordinary kindness that comes with youth,' Louise remembered.[2] Fossey listened in earnest. He was moved by her tears, sympathised with her misfortune, and tried to console her. As she spoke, Louise could see that her youth and fragility had touched Fossey's heart. He seemed compelled to protect her.

Fossey did not fit the mould Louise had come to know. She had never been treated with such care. Like many *femmes de brasseries*, she had grown accustomed to male contempt and she concealed her resentment beneath a thick skin. The encounter was the first of many meetings.

Mme Delabigne told people how, as the relationship blossomed, Camille would come to the house to collect Louise.[3] Then, having coaxed Mme Delabigne into giving her permission, the two girls would hurry out to the corner of the street where Camille's lover and Fossey would be waiting for them. Camille became a convenient messenger, surreptitiously sliding Fossey's passionate love letters into Louise's hand when Mme Delabigne's back was turned.

Before long, Fossey announced that he intended to make Louise his wife – when the time was right. The prospect had everything to appeal. Aside from his connections, Fossey seemed to genuinely care about her and could offer her a respectable life. She could have a husband and a home. She could be somebody's wife. Louise had never known security. She gave herself to him completely.

Acquaintances held that it was the idea of love and the future Fossey offered that most captured Louise's heart. But Louise insisted: 'What people say may not always be true.'[4] 'Nothing was too much for him,' she explained, 'I had everything a woman could wish for, and I was perfectly happy.'[5]

Looking back, Louise would see this as the great – and only true – love affair of her life. As they spent more and more time together, Louise anticipated the formalising of their union. She waited. The proposal did not come.

Still, she had plenty to keep her occupied. She had to earn a living, and in 1864 she got a lucky break: one of the minor actors she had met in the Latin Quarter said he thought he could get her work as an extra. She might lack experience, but her looks were a considerable advantage. After a series of meetings and discussions, Louise began playing walk-on parts at the Théâtre Saint-Germain (later to become the Théâtre de Cluny).[6] It was an enviable opportunity for a girl of Louise's age. It was her first step up the social scale.

Under the Second Empire, Paris's theatre scene was prospering. In 1806, Napoleon I had abruptly quashed the liberty of theatres that had been established following the Revolution. Only eight closely monitored venues were authorised to continue staging performances in Paris.[7] When liberty was finally restored in 1864, Parisians, starved of entertainment, poured into the auditoriums. In response, a host of new theatres sprang up across the capital, and by 1875 Paris boasted 58 in total.[8]

The pleasure-hungry middle and upper classes had money to spend, while the working class craved light relief to colour their dreary routine. Behind the scenes, playwrights were brimming with new ideas, producers and designers bursting with originality. It was a winning combination.

Each theatre held a distinct position in a hierarchy and specialised in a particular genre.[9] An audience member's class would guide their choice of establishment; for in 19th-century Paris the theatre was more than just an entertainment venue – it was where you went to be seen.

The upper classes were proud to be spotted at the opening night of a tragedy or a work by Molière at the prestigious Comédie Française. Meanwhile, a working-class spectator would more likely be found laughing heartily at one of the Théâtre des Variétés' popular farces. Ticket prices were pitched to cater to this social diversity. In 1862, spectators could enjoy a performance at the Bouffes-Parisiens for as little as 1 franc; at the Théâtre des Italiens, they could expect to pay as much as 12 francs for a top-price box.[10] The average weekly wage for a worker under the Second Empire was 12 francs 50.[11]

When Louise first appeared on stage, these class boundaries that had so clearly distinguished theatregoers and establishments were beginning to blur. As more and more people came to see plays, the theatre was undergoing an *embourgeoisement*.[12] If a person wanted to be noticed by the masses, the stage was the place to be.

Certainly, many regarded the stage as a breeding ground for immorality, and the actress was a problematic figure in the eyes of 19th-century society. Outwardly, she could appear impeccably groomed, as polished as the next fine lady. But then in private she might be given to wild passions and sexual libertinism. Yet despite popular preconceptions, the actress remained distinct from the common prostitute: she wielded power.

'The visitor to Paris cannot fail to have been struck by the important part that actresses play in that gay city,' observed an English journalist. 'They set fashions; they are received in the salons of the haute finance, they are to be seen everywhere, at the races, the theatres, always at the best places; many of them live in very elegant style, and are apparently never in want of money.'[13]

Louise knew that, as she stepped on to the stage, she would be walking away from her past and her perilous life of prostitution. It was glamorous, it was exhilarating; she had begun to climb.

Situated on the busy Boulevard Saint-Germain, the Théâtre Saint-Germain was a small venue in an area where theatres were few. Although many considered it a welcome addition to the left bank, the theatre struggled from the very beginning. When it first opened, the theatre turned to young, inexperienced writers for its popular repertoire of dramas and comedies – to its detriment. When a theatre's nearest neighbour was the acclaimed Théâtre de l'Odéon, 'a work which lacks wit, like all those it has presented so far, can never succeed', warned theatre critic Adrien Desprez.[14] Throughout the 1860s, the venue was perpetually closing and reopening, changing name several times. For its performers, it made an uncertain profession even more precarious.

Still, the theatre's position in the heart of the Latin Quarter made it a lively place in which to perform. There was hardly an hour of the day when the Boulevard Saint-Germain fell quiet. The chatter of voices and the rumble of carriage wheels were an intrinsic part of the boulevard's character. The swarms of fashionable young Parisians it attracted were loyal patrons of its many bars and cafés.[15]

Louise's time in Paris's brasseries had left its mark. With temptation all around, she could not resist a drink, and often arrived for a performance the worse for wear. Her acting did little to redeem her in directors' eyes. She was offered no stretching roles and was relegated to the chorus. No critics mentioned her in their reviews, and there seemed little chance of her acting career progressing.

Thankfully, she possessed one attribute that outweighed all these flaws. Her unconventional yet beguiling appearance more than compensated for her lack of talent. Her looks were an asset to any production. Eventually, a man with influence and vision spotted her and came to the same conclusion. His name was M. Soëge.

M. Soëge was a familiar face on the theatre scene, and he boasted contacts with many important directors. Catching sight of the striking redhead one evening at the Théâtre Saint-Germain, M. Soëge calculated that she could tempt other directors. It was in his power to propel this girl's career, and he decided to use his influence. Naturally, he would need to be thanked in some way. But rewarding male benefactors was an area in which Louise excelled.

With M. Soëge's expert salesmanship, Louise was offered a golden opportunity. In 1866, she was invited to join the cast at one of the most popular theatres in Paris: Jacques Offenbach's Bouffes-Parisiens.

If Paris was a musical hotspot in 19th-century Europe, then Offenbach was undoubtedly its figurehead. The triumphant airs of his frivolous operettas captured the spirit of the time, and Parisians rhapsodised about the upbeat, catchy melodies the composer brought to the stage. Offenbach's music was in direct harmony with the Parisian obsession with farce and light-hearted entertainment.[16]

Though a German Jew, Offenbach considered himself every bit the Frenchman. Born in 1819, his musical dexterity was spotted early by his father, who sent him to study in Paris as a teenager. After a year at the prestigious Conservatoire, Offenbach performed as a cellist in a series of theatre orchestras, but he remained unfulfilled. He yearned to write music for the stage. When he began to do so, his musical gift truly started to shine.

Like a magician, he captivated his audience. 'There was something demonic about him,' one listener mused.[17] He had a glitter in his eye and boundless energy that magnetised people towards him.

By 1855, Offenbach had been conducting the orchestra at the Théâtre Français for five years and he was restless. He longed to start his very own musical theatre. It would be a place for 'gay, witty music', he enthused.[18] It must exude life.

Fortune was smiling on Offenbach. He got word of a small theatre that had become vacant near the Palais de l'Industrie, where the much-hyped Exposition Universelle was about to open. It was a tiny wooden building with steep seating that could hold barely 50 people. But it had a quaint charm. It seemed worth the risk. And there was no time to lose; in a matter of days, crowds would be flocking to Paris from all corners of the globe to see the exposition. Offenbach hurriedly made enquiries and soon took up residence at the theatre that would become known as the Bouffes-Parisiens.

He had to work quickly; the influx of visitors to the capital could fill his auditorium for weeks. Under pressure, he took a chance on an unknown librettist, Ludovic Halévy. It was another fortuitous decision; the chemistry between the pair was immediate, and the first performance in July 1855 was a wild success.

The Bouffes-Parisiens soon became one of the most popular theatres in Paris, and night after night the actors would perform to full houses of delighted spectators. By the end of the summer season, Offenbach had proved that he could fill the auditorium. The Bouffes moved from its original home in the Salle Lacaze on the Champs-Elysées to the Salle du Théâtre Comte on the Passage Choiseul for the winter, installing itself there permanently in 1858. The new venue was larger, warmer and more luxurious. But its primary selling feature was that it adjoined the Passage Choiseul; audience members could enjoy some fresh air or a cigar outside before the performance and remain dry, even in bad weather.[19]

Parisians raved about the theatre. 'The chocolate box' – as people affectionately termed it – was exactly what was wanted.[20] The music was 'not just French, but Parisian'.[21] Visitors' guides recommended it as an unmissable venue 'where you always have fun and where the crowd is invariably gracious and full of pretty women'.[22]

Crowd-pleasing operettas appeared in quick succession. Then, in 1858, after a hesitant beginning, a new operetta surpassed all those that had gone before it, taking the music scene by storm. *Orpheus in the Underworld* got the whole of Paris dancing to Offenbach's infectious melodies and chuckling at his gentle satire of the current regime.

By the time Louise was beginning her career as a theatre extra in the 1860s, the charismatic composer's reputation was firmly established. Offenbach's fine features, spectacles and side whiskers were recognised all over Europe. And recognition gave rise to sociability. This suited Offenbach; he hated solitude. His Friday evenings were invariably given to entertaining. These informal gatherings saw friends and acquaintances packed into the rooms of the Offenbachs' elegant home, banter and laughter filling the air. 'He had an extraordinary number of friends who were always dropping in promiscuously. His Friday evenings at home were wildly amusing,' his grandson remembered.[23] 'If he noticed that voices were being purposely subdued, he would look up and ask if anyone was dead.'

Offenbach was famed for his 'soupers de Jacques', parties he would throw ritually after the first night of any performance. These events nourished his creative appetite. Guests recalled that it was not unusual for him to seize a pencil in the middle of a party and plunge into a state of deep concentration, then begin frantically composing while the conversation continued around him.[24]

Offenbach was fastidious about the tautness of his theatrical productions. Like many creative geniuses, he lived at high pressure and was the victim of nervous tension. He possessed a fortuitous instinct for sensing when he was in the presence of an undiscovered star. And he never missed an attractive woman. 'You know,' he explained to a friend by way of justification, 'that in my little theatre the public sits very close to the stage, and consequently the women have to be even more beautiful than elsewhere.'[25] They always were. Women wanted to be noticed by Offenbach.

Unfortunately, his magnetism and musical talent were not matched by his business sense. In the early 1860s, Offenbach was obliged to hand over the management of the Bouffes to Alphonse Varney.[26] But his popularity never wavered. When his *La Vie Parisienne* came to the stage in 1866 to a thunder of wild applause, it merely reinforced the composer's position as society's most popular, empathetic musical impresario; he was the toast of Paris.

It was at this point, just as Offenbach reached the height of his fame, that Louise was offered the chance to work for him. She would appear in a rerun of one of his most successful operettas: *Orpheus* was to return to the Bouffes-Parisiens.

Louise knew that this would be markedly different from her experience in the Théâtre Saint-Germain. For one thing, her name would now be printed in the daily announcement of productions that appeared in the papers. It was the custom for actors to be identified by a single name when the cast lists were published, so this name was critical. It was how they would be remembered. Louise decided that hers must change.

She wanted to make an impression, to stand out. A new life had begun. She was now climbing in society and she wanted a name that reflected the heights she was aiming for, the person she was determined to become. After years of humiliation, she wanted to be worshipped. She deliberated. Finally, she believed she had found the perfect stage name.

Louise renamed herself 'Valtesse'. The name was a witty contraction of the French 'Votre Altesse', or 'Your Highness'. It delighted her. From now on, everyone who addressed her would be her subject and she their queen.

On 2 February 1866, Valtesse's name appeared for the first time in the Parisian newspapers.[27] Readers learned that this new face was to appear in the minor role of Hébé. This was her chance to shine.

'Offenbach is still an idol this winter,' confirmed *Le Monde Illustré* in its announcement of the rerun of *Orpheus*.[28] The composer's *Barbe-Bleue* was due to premiere in the same week at the Variétés, where *La Belle Hélène* had packed the auditorium for months in 1864. Parisians could not get enough of Offenbach's music. *Orpheus* was bound to be a success.

But it was not. *Orpheus* met with a cool reception. Was it due to the renovations that had recently been carried out to increase the size of the theatre, wondered critic Albert de Lasalle? The Bouffes used to be so intimate: 'You were sitting so close to the actors that you could see the slightest grimaces with which they accentuated their lines; it was as though you were performing in the show with them,' recalled de Lasalle.[29] The decor and costumes were still spectacular, but the voices had lost something of their exquisite clarity. It was not that the show was poor; it just failed to retain its audience's interest as it had in 1858. Had people seen one performance too many of *Orpheus*?

Historically, shows usually ran only for a few weeks. Until the second half of the 19th century, city populations were considered too small to justify runs of several months.[30] But this situation was starting to change. Even so, by early April, one newspaper journalist reported having spotted a notice displayed in the theatre: 'Due to popular demand, we announce the final performance of *Orpheus in the Underworld*.' 'People must have really disliked it to have called so vehemently for the last performance,' joked the journalist.[31] The production closed.

As a minor part, Valtesse did not receive attention in the reviews of the show. But it hardly mattered; through *Orpheus*, she had firmly established herself as part of the troupe at the Bouffes-Parisiens. This was her first production of many.

When *Orpheus* finished, Valtesse was awarded her next role. She was to play Mme Annibal in the theatre's production of *Didon, Reine de Carthage*. The show received still less critical attention than

Orpheus. But the cast was smaller; Valtesse stood a greater chance of being noticed. That was what she wanted; she had not pursued a career in the theatre to remain unremarked.

Valtesse had yet to be awarded a main part. Nevertheless, by the end of the year, she could feel confident; she had marked her territory at the Bouffes-Parisiens. If she could fine-tune her skills as a performer, this could be the start of a glittering career. It was the opportunity she had been waiting for to mix with influential figures who could help her continue her social ascent.

In the 19th century, the theatre was an institution apart from any other. It was structured around a social code unique to itself. Gas lights now lit the stage more brightly than the candles of the 18th century had been able to do.[32] Their warm glow made costumes sparkle, brought sets to life and transported enchanted audiences to another world for an hour or two. In the auditorium, everything centred around appearance and status. Even the seating was socially codified. High above the crowd, beautiful women adorned in luxurious silks and furs edged their way to the front of expensive boxes, glittering with diamonds, self-aware and determined to be seen. Men stood back chivalrously, offering their status-affirming partners the best possible view – and affording themselves a discreet vantage point from which to peer down at other women through their opera glasses. Young dandies celebrated their bachelorhood by taking a seat in the male-only orchestra pit, the closest point to the action. And between the boxes and the orchestra pit, a whole cross-section of Parisian society could be seen looking, whispering, assimilating, judging.

Valtesse soon came to understand the complex code that governed the auditorium. She explained to a later readership:

A first night, oh Parisians, is not what frivolous, foolish people might think. It is an occasion of utmost importance […] For gallant ladies, it is a chance to display their charms […] *Tout-Paris*, that chicest fraction of Parisian society, is there: the one which writes, which thinks, which pays.[33]

But to meet the individuals who could truly propel her forward in society, Valtesse needed to familiarise herself with another domain: backstage. This was a world apart from the activity in the auditorium and on stage. It demanded a very different kind of protocol. In his novel *Nana* (1880), Émile Zola describes:

> the heavy, overheated, backstage atmosphere, with its strong underlying stench of gas, stage-set glue, squalid dark corners, and the smell of the female extras' unwashed underwear. The passageway was even more suffocating; from time to time the sharp scent of toilet-water and soap drifting down from the dressing-rooms blended with the pestilential odour of human breath [...] Upstairs there was a sound of wash-basins, laughter, shouts and banging doors releasing female smells in which the musky odour of make-up mingled with the harsh animal scent of hair.*[34]

This shady warren of passages and side rooms was inhabited by two kinds of people: performers and wealthy men. Men who subscribed to the main – most expensive – boxes were granted virtually unlimited access to the backstage area. Theatre managers were keen to stay in favour with wealthy and prestigious patrons, so these men could be found in the green room, or roaming the corridors, the theatre wings and even the dressing rooms.

The stereotype of the rich older man and the young female performer had long been the stock in trade of caricaturists by the time Valtesse negotiated the stuffy corridors backstage at the

---

* © By permission of Oxford University Press.

Bouffes-Parisiens. The theme received renewed attention in the 1870s and '80s. Few men were better placed than Offenbach's own librettist, Ludovic Halévy, to take an ironic view of the social interaction that went on backstage. His satirical novel, *La Famille Cardinal* (1883), playfully sketched the exchanges between young female dancers, their male admirers and their domineering mothers, to the delight of tickled readers. 'Ah,' exclaims Mme Cardinal after a series of calamities between her cosseted daughters and a succession of male suitors, 'two daughters dancing at the Opéra, what a trial for a mother!'[35] The world backstage made an impression on artists as well, notably Edgar Degas, in whose pastels the viewer peers voyeuristically through the cropped doorway of ballerinas' dressing rooms to see pretty young dancers changing before their elderly male admirers.

Sexual commerce was an accepted part of the social fabric backstage. It was what earned actresses and dancers their dubious reputation. However, for a girl wishing to secure the financial support of a prestigious benefactor, this was their means of doing so. It was the very crux of what made acting an attractive profession. The Duc de Morny (the illegitimate son of Napoleon Bonaparte's stepdaughter, Hortense), the military professional the Comte de Castellane, and the composer Giacomo Meyerbeer were regular visitors to the Bouffes-Parisiens when it first opened, Meyerbeer invariably requesting an orchestra seat on the second night of every new production.[36]

But for all the important, well-placed men she was now encountering backstage at the theatre, Valtesse remained attached to Fossey. Other men could admire her body, but they could never have her heart. Her dream of marriage still flickered tantalisingly. She was not prepared to give it up.

When writers like Zola taunted the middle and upper classes over their social hypocrisy, their criticisms were not unfounded.

If they relished their secret forays backstage, in public, men of Fossey's background often found acting a problematic profession to accept. But Valtesse showed her heart to be loyal, however much she longed to climb the social ladder. In turn, Fossey continued to protect her and ensured that she was never led too far astray. Finally, Valtesse could begin to look to the future with hope in her heart. Everything seemed possible.

But then a surprise befell her. It threatened to destroy all she had worked for over the last two years. She discovered she was pregnant.

CHAPTER 4

Creation

Valtesse appeared in her last performance at the Bouffes-Parisiens in the spring of 1866, and she did not return for the summer season. She disappeared entirely from the public scene. Her pregnancy was veiled in secrecy, concealed from all but those directly affected.

On 3 March 1867, Valtesse gave birth to a baby girl. She was still a teenager, and entirely unprepared for motherhood. For the last three years, all her thinking, energy and focus had been channelled into establishing her stage career. She had tenaciously pursued auspicious contacts, taken care to appear in the smartest places, and made sure that she was seen by the most influential people. And Valtesse was punctilious: wherever and whenever she appeared, she always looked her very best.

Motherhood had not featured in her plans. Still, her predicament offered one consolation: it might prompt Richard Fossey, the baby's father, into marrying her at last.

But there were further complications. Fossey had yet to establish himself in a career. When Valtesse gave birth, he had no salary to support a family, and he was frivolous with the little money he did have. A young man in Richard Fossey's position often received an allowance from his parents until he embarked on a career.

But Fossey knew his father's stance. Any financial assistance would cease if he married Valtesse. His father would never allow a prostitute-turned-actress to sully the family name. He would forbid a marriage.

Valtesse understood the implications of her past. A woman who had resorted to prostitution was thereafter branded with an indelible stigma. The courtesan Céleste Mogador explained in her memoirs: 'Love cruelly retaliates against women who have profaned its image! [...] For the woman who has fallen so low, there is no family. [...] Marriage is out of the question.'[1] For Fossey to marry Valtesse, he would need the courage to cut his ties with his family – and their money.

Maternal sentiment did not come naturally to Valtesse. Her own mother had never provided an inspiring maternal role model, so motherhood carried no positive associations for her. She could survive on the street and defend herself against the drunken advances of lecherous men. She knew how to negotiate the complex internal politics of the theatre. But maternity was a strange and unfamiliar domain. Valtesse had no notion of what was required or where she should begin.

Adhering to common practice, Valtesse sent her newborn baby away to be cared for by a wet nurse. While etiquette manuals and social discourse encouraged maternal breastfeeding, it was primarily among the upper classes that this trend was taking hold. Working-class mothers relied heavily on wet nurses, and even in the upper classes many women still employed a *nourrice sur lieu* or live-in nurse.[2] For a young woman in Valtesse's position, this was considered the natural thing to do with your child.

But sending the infant away did not absolve her of responsibility. A nurse would only care for the child until it was weaned, and she must be paid for. Valtesse had to accept her new role. And she had scarcely begun to acclimatise to it when she discovered that she had fallen pregnant to Fossey again. Within a year, a second daughter was born.

Neither infant was strong and healthy. If the firstborn, Julia-Pâquerette, was a delicate child, her sister Valérie-Albertine was even weaker and more sickly. There was at least something interesting about Pâquerette's fine little features. But Valérie was more concerning. It soon became clear that her weakness extended to her mental faculties. Valtesse had never wanted to be a mother. Now, she had two frail children to support and no reliable source of income. Her situation was becoming desperate.

Aside from Fossey, Valtesse's sole financial resource depended on her achieving success in the theatre. She had seen the dedication, commitment and energy that demanded; and for a young woman, looks counted for everything. While she was pregnant and convalescing, such a career was impossible. Valtesse urgently needed to marry. Fossey was her only hope. The young man's father, however, had very different ideas.

Knowing his father, Richard Fossey can hardly have been surprised. When the news reached M. Fossey senior that his son had a mistress, he was outraged and immediately forbade a marriage. A girl of such humble origins who was caught up with the suspect world of the theatre? It was unthinkable. M. Fossey wasted no time. Using his connections, he speedily negotiated a respectable position as a civil servant which his son could take up immediately. The job was in Algeria. Unable, or unwilling, to challenge his family's wishes, Richard Fossey boarded a ship and left France.

Valtesse was devastated. Fossey wrote to her, assuring her that he would return, that all would be well. He made her swear that she would wait for him. She waited.

Eventually, another letter arrived. Fossey was not going to return. He had met a girl in Algeria. The Parisian press reported, approvingly, that they were to be married, 'respectably'.[3]

The blow validated Valtesse's deepest fears about society and the opposite sex. Fossey's kind treatment had restored her faith in men. It had encouraged her to hope. She had started to view the future optimistically. Now, this dream too had been snatched away.

Hurt, angry, she vowed that she would never allow herself to be deceived again. Henceforward, Valtesse trusted no man. The best were weak and spineless. Even a good-natured man like Fossey buckled under family pressure and became powerless in the face of financial need. With Fossey's departure, Valtesse's whole outlook changed. So did her identity.

While 'Valtesse' had been making her way in the theatre, off-stage, 'Louise' had continued to love and to hope. Valtesse now resolved that Louise must disappear for good, and her stage persona should rise triumphant. The final traces of the delicate, curious little girl were buried once and for all and a resilient woman with an unshakeable self-preservation instinct took her place.

Valtesse stopped communicating with her remaining siblings and repudiated her role as a mother. Life had taught her to trust nobody. Her faith in society had been shattered. She needed to think of herself now. She developed a fierce attachment to her independence, convinced that her survival depended on her ability to fight for what she needed.

Valtesse's pain and sense of injustice drew out the ruthless streak she had had to learn to survive on the streets. Some years later, she put her emotions into the words of her fictional heroine, Isola:

I do not love nor do I wish people to love me.[4]

And:

I will take your husbands, your brothers, your sons and your lovers just as it pleases me [...] With your fortunes, I will buy

myself family, parents, friends, children, the world if it takes my
fancy.[…] I must acquire riches if I am to restore my honour.[5]

Valtesse was under no illusions; she was living in a man's world. 'It
is always the way,' she grieved, 'they kill the fatted calf to celebrate
the return of the prodigal son […] For a daughter, it is different;
she is rejected, damned.'[6]

Valtesse was justified in her grievance. A deep-rooted gender
bias underpinned 19th-century French society. Only a few years
earlier, Flaubert had horrified his readers with the critique of the
bourgeois marriage and the woman's lot he presented in *Mme Bovary*
(1857). Behind the public outcry lay unease; the novel had tres-
passed uncomfortably close to the truth. Flaubert's anti-heroine
laments:

A man at least, is free; he can explore each passion and every
kingdom, conquer obstacles, feast upon the most exotic pleasures. But a woman is continually thwarted. Both inert and
yielding, against her are ranged the weakness of the flesh and
the inequity of the law. Her will, like the veil strung to her bonnet, flutters in every breeze; always there is the desire urging,
always the convention restraining.[7]

People knew that Emma Bovary's situation was more than a fantastical creation. Valtesse was feeling the legacy of years of female
subservience.

The Revolution of 1789 had the long-term effect of emphasising family values and differentiating more clearly between the
roles of the sexes.[8] Order in society, it was felt, started with order
in the home. Marriage was therefore vitally important. Under the
ancien régime, the family had been characterised by its patriar-
chal character; marital unions were guided by family ambition and

financial concerns rather than love, and primarily designed to produce an heir.[9] Women were placed under the legal authority of their husbands once married, and divorce was prohibited. For all the challenges it had faced following the Revolution, the authoritarian, paternalistic family model was far from obsolete as the 19th century dawned. And throughout the century, it was women who most felt the effects.

By the time Fossey abandoned Valtesse, social discourse was calling for a more affectionate family model and greater equality between the sexes. But change occurred only slowly. Throughout the 19th century, a single female courted social disapproval. She was viewed with suspicion – she might be a prostitute, or, worse, a lesbian. If she wished to be thought respectable, a woman could not attend all the entertainment venues men frequented and she was advised against going out in the street unaccompanied. A working woman's wages were a fraction of what a man earned. Her principal vocation was to become a good wife and mother. As such, a woman was answerable to her husband. It was not until 1881 that a married woman was allowed to open a bank account without her husband's permission, and it would be a further 25 years before she could spend her salary as she chose. Traditionalists of both sexes agreed: any lot other than marriage was simply 'abnormal'.[10]

A woman had two ways of conducting herself in this male-orientated society: either she conformed to its rules and conventions or she refused to submit to them and instead turned them to her advantage. Only one path guaranteed social approval. But the other was often a woman's sole chance of attaining independence.

Valtesse knew that marriage was now out of the question. But she had to survive. She refused to continue life as a victim. The pain and anger of abandonment made her hungry for independence. This drive gave her the strength to renounce marriage and commit herself wholeheartedly to her social ascent. She wanted to be somebody. Her determination spurring her, Valtesse began her quest where she had already laid the foundations for her rise: the theatre.

Valtesse entrusted the supervision of Julia-Pâquerette and Valérie-Albertine's care to her mother. It was a practical decision. The theatre was a world and a lifestyle that left no space for children. Mother and starlet? The one, unremarkable and emotionally generous; the other, glamorous and guarded – the two roles were simply not compatible. She knew she could not risk the existence of children tarnishing her theatrical persona. Their basic needs would be met but maternal affection was a luxury they would have to do without.

The arrangement suited both Valtesse and her mother. After leaving her post as a linen maid, Emilie Delabigne had been working in Paris as a domestic help for the eminent Doctor Jobert de Lamballe.[11] However, the elderly surgeon passed away in 1867. Mme Delabigne received 5,000 francs by way of compensation, but her employment was abruptly terminated. The monthly supplement of Valtesse's childcare allowance was welcome.

Henceforward, Valtesse rarely saw her daughters. She was determined: she was going to rise and Paris would be hers.

∽

At the end of September, 1868, Parisians opened their newspapers to find an announcement publicising the reopening of the Bouffes-Parisiens. The theatre had temporarily closed in June for redecoration. 'The refurbishments are now complete,' declared *Le Figaro*. 'Notable improvements have been made to the stage and the auditorium, which has been decorated with the utmost care, very luxuriously. Nothing has been neglected so that it calls to mind the elegant public who used to frequent this stylish theatre.'[12] Other critics agreed: 'The auditorium at the Bouffes-Parisiens is now one of the most charming and luxurious in Paris,' eulogised another journalist.[13]

Theatregoers were burning with curiosity to see the revamped theatre. There was to be a new director and a revised cast. Excitement rippled through Paris as the night of the opening performance approached. And there, among the names on the list of the Bouffes's regular cast members, was that of Valtesse. The theatre's reopening was just the comeback she had been hoping for.

Still, she had to wait a little longer to be awarded a named part. She was not selected to appear in the four opening productions. But by October, she was back on stage. However, as her first performance approached, Valtesse noticed that an error had been made in the publicity for the autumn line-up. *Le Figaro* announced that one of the minor parts in the October production of *Le Fifre enchanté* and the role of Saturnin in *La Chanson de Fortunio* in November would be played by a young actress named Waltesse.[14] The mistake threatened to delay even further the public recognition Valtesse craved.

It did not pass uncorrected for long. By the time she won the role of Berthe in *La Diva* the following spring, the paper had rectified the error.[15] It was just as well, since the next production Valtesse was to appear in would get all of Paris talking. It was her first significant role. At last, she would be named in press reviews. But by far the most attractive boon was that it steered her directly into the path of Offenbach.

On Thursday 9 December 1869, *La Princesse de Trébizonde* premiered at the Bouffes-Parisiens. The show had been publicised for weeks before. The previous summer, it had met with enthusiastic applause when it was performed for the first time in Baden-Baden:

The orchestra was conducted by Offenbach himself, and it was marvellous to see this little man, standing behind the rostrum, conducting with that devil in his body which, in the words of Voltaire, is what makes genius [...] After every act, the

composer had to appear before the adoring crowd and be sub-
jected to a thunder of applause.[16]

The show was a resounding success, and champagne flowed late into
the night at the after-show party.

The Parisian public arrived at the Bouffes-Parisiens for the
opening night primed with expectation. The crowd was 'already
intoxicated' before the show, remarked one journalist.[17] The production was bound to be spectacular.

The opéra bouffe told the tale of a travelling showman named
Cabriolo who wins a castle, land and the title of Baron in a lottery,
and arrives at the property to take up residence with his troupe
of performers. He brings with him a wax figure of the Princess of
Trebizond, but since the figure's nose is broken, the showman's
daughter dresses up as the wax figure and takes its place. The son of
a prince falls in love with her and the tale ends with them marrying.
The story was entirely fantastical, and the critics showed no mercy
for the plot or the score. With its bouncy rhythm, 'the music',
wrote the authors of the *Dictionnaire des opéras*, 'is as unpleasant as
possible'.[18] Parisians loved it.

'The performers make for a rather risqué troupe, I would not take
my fiancée along,' observed one audience member. But, he conceded,
'the formula was foolproof: arrival of the father, dancing, singing,
marriage. Pour onto it Offenbach's music, serve up to an audience of
cocodès and *cocodettes*; and you have a successful premiere.'[19]

The opening night was a sensation. The cream of Parisian society was there: counts and countesses, dukes and duchesses, colonels
and their wives. There was the actress Augustine Brohan and the
Romanian Prince Ghika. Nobody wanted to miss the first night.
'People had fun, enormous fun,' raved one journalist.[20] 'The corridors were full of people. You could barely move. The conversation
was noisy and animated.'[21]

Valtesse played one of the twelve pages. When she stepped out in front of the audience for her first scene, she was dressed in a smart jacket, breeches and satin culottes. Her figure-hugging costume followed the shapely curves of her body, while the outline of her calves was suggestively traced by tight white stockings. Her hair was scraped back beneath a blonde wig for most of the performance; the production demanded it. But Valtesse made sure that the critics at least noticed her proudest asset.

'Redheaded like one of Titian's Virgins,' one critic reported. 'But that is as far as the resemblance goes. Very shy – on stage. Hides behind her colleagues. People sat in the orchestra pit complained about it. Distinguishing feature: wears a blonde wig.'[22]

Valtesse was forging herself a reputation. If her acting failed to impress, her charms were winning her admirers nonetheless. And she took full advantage of the attention; after all, her survival depended on it. When she left the stage, she shed her coy persona and became bolder and more flirtatious. She had good reason to grow in confidence: on the opening night, she had the personal encouragement of an experienced theatrical impresario – Offenbach himself.

Throughout the show, Offenbach could be seen gesticulating vigorously, agitating his arms with incredible energy. Valtesse and her fellow performers were spurred on by his passionately delivered stage directions. 'My dears,' he could be heard shouting, 'remember the break! One, two, three! That is it, very good!'[23]

As the final curtain fell, thunderous applause erupted from the auditorium, and theatregoers filtered out of the Bouffes-Parisiens drunk on good feeling and frivolity.

'Offenbach is ecstatic,' one paper subsequently reported. 'The day before yesterday, *La Princesse de Trébizonde* took 4,750 francs at the box office, more than any performance so far at the Bouffes.'[24]

That performance did more than boost the audience's spirits

and box office takings. It afforded the performers the privilege of an acquaintance with Offenbach and the opportunity of working closely with him. This intimate relationship between maestro and cast proved a turning point for Valtesse, professionally at first – and then rather more personally.

Offenbach studied the newcomer in the chorus closely. He could see that she was eye-catching. Critics might disparage her talent, but the public found her delightful. Their opinion mattered. It was decided: Valtesse should be given the chance to shine. *La Romance de la Rose* was scheduled to open shortly after the premiere of *La Princesse de Trébizonde*, and the two productions would run alongside each other. Finally, Valtesse was awarded her first major role.

Taking musical inspiration from Friedrich von Flottow's *Martha*, *La Romance de la Rose* told the tale of an American widow, Mistress Johnson, who is seduced by a beautiful voice that she hears singing one day. She mistakenly attributes the voice to a musician, when it actually belongs to his friend, a painter. The musician cannot repeat the performance, and the painter has a jealous partner, so he dreams up all sorts of schemes to sabotage the quality of the song and divert the widow's interest.

Valtesse took the starring role of Mistress Johnson. She was required to sing a series of verses in a baffling Franco-English tongue with a heavy American accent. Quite apart from public stardom, the role gave Valtesse the enviable opportunity of bringing a smile to the composer's lips; one of her verses opened with an English expression that had always tickled him:[25]

> Oh very good!
> Oh very well!
> Joli, charmant, spirituel.
> Oh, sire, c'était très bien très chic!
> Oh! What is sweet love in miousic [*sic*].

Later in the performance, Valtesse's soprano voice could be heard singing:

> Monsieur, je suis veuve très riche!
> Will you épouser moi, my dear?[26]

Reviews were mediocre at best. Critics complained that the music scarcely differed from Offenbach's other operettas. As for its originality, the production was scorned as being 'the most redundant in ideas' of any show that had ever preoccupied the public.[27] One critic was more generous:

> This charming little vaudeville is performed with much talent by M. Hamburger, Victor, Mlle Périer, who has a rather small role, and Mlle Valtesse, who, for the start of her career, has shown proof of talent, grace and charm in the very successful role of an English [*sic*] lady.[28]

But such flattery was an exception. Reviews praising Valtesse for her acting ability were rare.

By the end of the 1860s, it was becoming increasingly clear: Valtesse lacked the talent required to become a star of the calibre of Offenbach's renowned protégé, Hortense Schneider. But she had her looks and she now had Offenbach's attention. She recognised that these were her most valuable assets. The time had come to capitalise on them.

CHAPTER 5

A Courtesan Must Never Cry

altesse did not continue in the role of Mistress Johnson in the new year; the actress Léa-Lini took over in 1870. Valtesse still had her minor part in *La Princesse de Trébizonde*, in which she appeared for the remainder of the spring. But winning a starring role was no longer her chief objective. Her focus had shifted to a more absorbing project: Valtesse had begun an affair with Offenbach.

Novelist and man of letters Arsène Houssaye recalled how Offenbach's cheerful disposition tended to cloud over whenever he was troubled by one of his professed extramarital affairs.[1] Even close acquaintances remained uncertain as to the number and importance of these liaisons, but their occurrence should have been no surprise; Offenbach was at the centre of a profession whose ground was notoriously fertile for passionate affairs. Despite that, his marriage to his wife of 25 years, Herminie, remained strong, the pair being bonded by mutual respect. Besides, his dalliances were mostly harmless flings. Their flame burned bright on ignition, but guttered quickly.

However, in 1863, a singer caught Offenbach's eye in a way no other had before. Zulma Bouffar was young, blonde-haired, blue-eyed, and vivacious.[2] Offenbach made routine visits to the spa town of Bad Ems in the hope that the waters might remedy his rheumatism. It was during one of these visits that he first heard the haunting soprano tones of Zulma's voice; she was singing at a theatre in Bad Homburg. Zulma had spent her childhood among travelling players. Encouraged by her father, she had titillated diners by singing risqué songs in restaurants from a young age, where she became affectionately known as 'the Little Parisian'. Zulma's childhood experiences resonated with Offenbach's own: he too had been supported in his musical pursuits by his father from a young age, and he and Zulma had even performed in the same brasserie in Cologne as youngsters. Contemporaries found Zulma's looks a little odd: her nose was awkwardly shaped, her face rather flat and her chin turned up.[3] But with her bright blue eyes and charisma, her draw was magnetic. The fluctuating moods of her passionate gypsy temperament only made her more appealing. Offenbach fell in love, and his creative zeal flourished.

Zulma was the most significant and long-lasting extramarital affair the composer ever had. She even bore him two illegitimate children.[4] But however much Zulma captivated him, Offenbach's heart remained devoted to Herminie. In August 1869, they hosted a memorable party at Etretat to celebrate their silver wedding anniversary. The superb dinner, masked ball and general good spirits of the occasion gave guests the impression of nothing but marital harmony.[5]

But just a few months later, *La Princesse de Trébizonde* and *La Romance de la Rose* began rehearsals. In the composer's new love interest, both Herminie and Zulma encountered a serious rival. Valtesse was the fiercest competition either woman had ever faced.

When Valtesse and Offenbach first met, the celebrated maestro was 50. She was just 21 – barely a year older than Zulma when the composer had begun his affair with her. Valtesse could not boast Zulma's fine soprano tones. But with her red hair and porcelain-white complexion, she too had a unique, arresting form of beauty, and she shared Zulma's dynamism of character. Furthermore, Valtesse was younger, fresher; her energy was inspiring and her bright disposition infectious.

It was true that as a child, she had been denied the educational opportunities she had craved. It had been a constant frustration to Valtesse that her mother's financial situation had made it impossible to indulge her love of books. The thinnest volume had required saving for weeks. Tuition had been unthinkable.[6] But she had a naturally sharp mind and she listened attentively to the conversations she was now hearing around her, absorbing linguistic flourishes and turns of phrase that made her own conversation sparkle and conveyed her dry sense of humour. Such quick wit in one so young was as rare as it was attractive. Valtesse could smooth an ageing man's furrowed brow. She could make him forget his worries. Offenbach fell deeply, hopelessly, under her spell.

The affair was a magnificent coup for Valtesse. Offenbach was a celebrity. He was powerful, charismatic, wildly sociable and notoriously generous with his money. She had set out to rise in society; connecting herself to Offenbach, her goal had been achieved. She continued to harbour great venom towards her rival, though, and based a fictional character on Zulma some years later:

In the neighbouring box, a most ugly creature was prancing around: Zuléma Tonneau, who gained more from her ugliness than her colleagues did their beauty. Zuléma's nose is quite a burlesque poem. She powders it like a Louis XV wig, paints it, highlights its shadows, admires its reflection in a little hand mirror, anticipates all its needs, pats it, strokes it, delights in it, and lets it make her way in the world. Oh yes, Zuléma has a good nose. She may only have one, but people say that it does the job of four![7]

The new couple made a striking pair. Though visibly ageing, Offenbach's dark, beady eyes still exuded energy, animating his fine, birdlike features. His wiry frame never weighed more than 50kg, and the nervous energy which positively crackled through it gave him a remarkable intensity.[8] With his trademark moustache, sideburns and spectacles, he had a permanent aura of refinement and dignity – even if his eyes had grown sunken with age, his hair was thinning and he was plagued by gout (and not rheumatism as he had first believed). Valtesse, meanwhile, was fresh and bright, with clear skin and enormous blue eyes that sparkled teasingly. Impressively for her age, she could converse informedly on a range of topics; and once Offenbach began leading her into more elevated circles, she quickly realised that she must educate herself, and started to read widely. When she spoke, whether about the latest morsel of Parisian gossip, or one of the classic works of literature she was now discovering, her dainty smile radiated quiet self-assurance. Valtesse was confident in her beauty and triumphant in her conquest.

Offenbach was careful never to publicise his affairs; he knew how fond his friends were of Herminie. But the liaison did not stay secret for long. And to those in the know, the people Offenbach trusted, he could present Valtesse with his head held high. She was the perfect trophy mistress.

Throughout the early months of 1870, Valtesse's new lover was insatiably busy. While *La Princesse de Trébizonde* and *La Romance de la Rose* were still drawing eager theatregoers, *Les Brigands* was delighting audiences at the Théâtre des Variétés, with Zulma in the lead role. Offenbach had been planning to go to Vienna in the first months of the year. However, he changed his mind at the last minute when a charity performance of *The Grand Duchess of Gerolstein* starring his protégé, the singer Hortense Schneider, was scheduled to take place in Nice. When he received a telegram from the star, Offenbach immediately arranged to travel to Nice to conduct the performance in person. It was impossible to ignore how pale and gaunt he looked, and people were alarmed when he had to stand down after the first two acts feeling unwell. Undeterred, Offenbach was soon back in Paris hosting a gala supper at the Grand Hôtel to celebrate the success of *La Princesse de Trébizonde* and *Les Brigands*.

The gala supper was a star-studded event, to which Valtesse was naturally invited. If the presence of Zulma gave the evening a sour edge, there was consolation in the opportunity it provided to rub shoulders with the uppermost of Paris's influential elite. *Tout Paris*, that superior stratum of fashionable society, was there in all its glory. As Valtesse scanned the room, she could see journalists, the music publisher Brandus, Robert Mitchell, editor of the political paper *Le Constitutionnel*, the great actress and courtesan Blanche d'Antigny, and Hortense Schneider herself.[9] Between the courses of a sumptuous dinner, Offenbach, dressed in a black suit and white tie, delighted his guests when he stood to deliver a witty speech entirely in German. Champagne flowed late into the night and the evening was declared a resounding success. A military captain named O'Donnell enjoyed himself so much that he announced he too would throw a ball at the Grand Hôtel so that the same guests – particularly the ladies – might repeat the experience.[10]

With the gala supper complete, Offenbach was immediately back to work, toiling over another comic opera, *Fantasio*. Then there were the usual dinners and restaurant visits: Offenbach was a loyal patron of the fashionable eating establishments Bignon, Noel et Peters, La Maison Dorée and the Café Riche, and commandeered a regular table in each.[11] There were also soirées and invitations, on top of his regular Friday night gatherings and time spent with the family. Though it was in his nature to be sociable, Offenbach was exhausted. His health was suffering.

Though there was little leisure time to spend with a mistress, for Valtesse Offenbach made the time. In March 1870, he decided to treat her to a trip away. He would take her to Italy.

It was almost certainly the first time Valtesse had travelled abroad. Although political and military tension had coloured the relationship between France and Italy in the past, Italy remained one of the most highly regarded destinations for those with means to travel. 'Italy is the classic land of travels,' exclaimed one guide-book author in 1864.[12] 'It is the garden of Europe and the home of the arts [...] Everything there attracts attention and excites curiosity.'[13] From the beautiful landscapes, the mild climate, the churches, museums and art collections to the lifestyle, fashions and people, travel writers flooded the French mindset with the wonders of Italy. And there was no more popular time to visit than in the spring at the time of the Carnival and Holy Week, 'the two moments which are the richest in entertainments designed to please the eye'.[14]

Valtesse had good cause to be excited. Quite apart from the new sights, sounds and smells to be discovered in a foreign country, she would be travelling as the lover of one of the most celebrated composers in Europe. If, as one journalist declared, Offenbach was the Empire, then Valtesse was now its mistress.[15]

To the fashion-conscious Parisienne, Italy was the ultimate travel destination. A lady's appearance during her stay was of the utmost importance. As the arrival of railways made it possible to travel more frequently and further afield, fashion responded to women's changing habits. A woman embarking on a trip abroad could consult fashion journals and guidebooks to familiarise herself with what to take, and more importantly what to purchase and bring back. Tourists travelling to Italy in the early months of the year were advised to take warm winter clothing: 'After sunset, the temperature gets considerably colder, and it is a sorry traveller indeed who walks around in a summer jacket.'[16]

With a trip from Paris to the connecting city of Turin taking only 22 hours in the 1870s, rail was the most practical means of travelling to Italy. But even once the couple arrived, excessive walking was unlikely to feature in the itinerary; Offenbach's gout led him to seek out carriages whenever possible.[17]

Still, Valtesse had spent enough time among coquettish actresses to know that a person did not travel to Italy to remain cooped up. Italian cities were rich in enticements to tempt the discerning Parisienne consumer. French travellers complained bitterly that Italian merchandise was overpriced, but Valtesse had a weakness for beautiful things, and she especially loved Venetian glass and delicate Italian lace.[18] She knew first-hand the time and labour a simple lace ribbon demanded. In her mind, those luxury items represented the ultimate in refinement and good taste, everything she sought to possess and project. Jewellery, clothing, hats, gloves and, particularly, exquisite tableware and objets d'art made her blue eyes sparkle. Offenbach was happy to oblige her whims.

When word of her husband's illicit romantic break reached Mme Offenbach, she was unsettled. Usually so resigned to – or at least discreet about – her husband's extramarital dalliances, Herminie felt strangely uneasy about this new young girl. She hastily made the necessary travel arrangements and set off for Italy in pursuit of the couple.

By the time Mme Offenbach arrived in the hotel foyer where her husband and his latest love interest had checked in, Offenbach had already spent a fortune on his 21-year-old mistress. The papers back in Paris did not report what took place when the maestro and his lover were confronted by Mme Offenbach. But an account of the explosive scene Herminie created at the hotel soon reached the Parisian police, who reported the incident in their records. The confrontation was, the report declared, nothing short of a scandal.[19]

Valtesse withdrew gracefully. It was common knowledge that Offenbach and Herminie enjoyed a solid relationship. Offenbach had converted to Catholicism in order to marry Herminie, and she had stood loyally by him throughout the many trials he had faced in his career.[20] He respected her immensely and he valued her opinion, always rewriting anything that did not meet with her approval.[21] The couple had five children, and had worked tirelessly to build a comfortable existence. Even Zulma had been unable to tempt the composer away from his wife for long. Furthermore, age and ill-health were beginning to take their toll. Both the man and his financial resources were already spread desperately thin.

Valtesse was not prepared to fight for a man in such conditions. It would be futile. There was her pride to think of, too. But more than that: the affair had brought her to a pivotal moment of self-realisation. It was not the life of an actress, or even a composer's lover, that she yearned for. She wanted more.

On Offenbach's arm, she had tasted riches and all the luxury, power and material security it could bring. She had begun to live the life not of the shop girl she had been, but of the elegant ladies she used to serve. The composer had introduced her into the circles in which those incredible creatures, the courtesans, moved. Her eyes had been opened to the world they inhabited. Blanche d'Antigny, Cora Pearl, Hortense Schneider: Valtesse had watched the best of them command an audience with just a look. She had heard the swish of their rich skirts as they passed, been dazzled by the glitter of their diamonds. Courtesans were the focus of all eyes as they drew up in resplendent carriages. Then they made their exit gracefully, leaving only the lingering souvenir of their perfume and a longing for their return. Princes, noblemen, bankers and men of letters competed for their attentions. They dined in grand restaurants and enjoyed an endless flow of costly gifts.

Cora Pearl was said to have inspired a present of a box of

marrons glacés, in which each sweet delicacy was individually wrapped in a 100 franc note.[22] Another lover presented her with an enormous silver horse that turned out to be brimful of jewels. Blanche d'Antigny's smile could light up a room, and she was rewarded with showers of diamonds, a gem with which she became firmly associated.[23] The spirited Hortense Schneider boasted a chain of aristocratic lovers, and her carriages were the envy of all those who promenaded the leafy avenues of the Bois de Boulogne. So plucky was Schneider that she even gained access to the Exposition Universelle through the entrance reserved exclusively for royalty.[24] These women had everything. The courtesan possessed grace, charm and, above all, utter confidence in her own sexual magnetism.

Valtesse saw that all this was now within her grasp. She had learned how to please a man sexually, mastered the techniques needed to arouse him, the irresistible feminine touches that would keep him coming back time and time again. Why should she not enjoy the benefits that skill could bring? As a *grande horizontale*, she could possess it all. So Valtesse made a life-changing decision: she would become a courtesan.

Becoming Offenbach's mistress had gained her the recognition needed to launch herself in this new career. The experience had required her to smooth her rough edges, and quickly, in order to fit in. Valtesse now saw her separation from the composer in strategical terms: it was both prudent and essential. Besides, she had promised herself that she would never again become dependent on any one man. That was too dangerous.

Valtesse returned to Paris and a new life began.

∽

As 1870 unfolded, Paris looked set to continue in the affluent, fashionable and glamorous manner of the previous decade. Sounds of discontent could still be heard among the working classes, and the Emperor's foreign policy left many people uneasy. It was true that nothing had yet matched the spectacular climax of the 1867 Exposition Universelle. Nonetheless, for the bourgeoisie and the upper classes, daily life was still firmly structured around balls, parties and entertainment. Extravagant living remained the norm.

Valtesse knew that the arts played a starring role in this social comedy. Offenbach had served a valuable purpose; he had catapulted her to the realm of minor celebrity and gained her access to the arts scene. She would now use her improved status to pursue powerful contacts within this sphere. All were potential benefactors.

Valtesse returned to the Bouffes-Parisiens to complete the season in *La Princesse de Trébizonde*, and she read for a part in the forecasted production of *Mam'zelle Moucheron* (which, in the event, would not premiere in 1870 after all). However, for her the attraction of the theatre was no longer the glamour of being an actress. Her interest was motivated by the advantageous connections she could forge.

Before long, Valtesse's strategy bore fruit. By the middle of the 1870s, she had found a new lover and benefactor. Albert Millaud was a well-regarded playwright and journalist for *Le Figaro*, as well as being the son of the banker, Moïse Millaud, who founded *Le Petit Journal*.[25] The young Millaud had everything Valtesse could wish for: money, power and a strong connection to the arts.

Millaud showered Valtesse with gifts and money. Her lifestyle went from comfortable to semi-luxurious. The days of struggling appeared to be over, the anxiety of how she would pay for things gone. No more was she having to make tired dresses presentable for yet another wearing. The pangs of hunger that had gnawed her stomach as a girl were a distant memory. Dining in fine restaurants, elegantly dressed in the latest fashions, became her new reality.

Valtesse was beginning to grow accustomed to her upgraded lifestyle when suddenly, in the summer of 1870, daily life in Paris was turned on its head.[26] The rumblings of political unease that the capital's pleasure-seekers had so gaily dismissed erupted into a full-scale war. In July 1870, a Prussian prince came forward as a candidate for the vacant Spanish throne. The threat this posed to the southern frontier horrified France. The country's reaction was so fierce that the Prussian candidacy was withdrawn. With no assurance that a similar move would not be repeated, France declared war on Prussia on 19 July 1870. It was a fatal decision. On 1 September 1870, Napoleon III was defeated at Sedan and taken prisoner. The end of the Empire was officially proclaimed.

Pinning the problems on the Emperor, people relaxed once more, confident that France could return to normal. But it was not to be. The Prussians stormed Paris, determined to bring the city to its knees. Reluctantly, the provisional government, now based in Tours, continued to fight. A full-scale siege set in, and for four months the country's political upheaval penetrated every aspect of daily life in Paris. Communications were cut off; food shortages spiralled into starvation and citizens were reduced to eating cats and dogs. Once a glamorous centre of luxurious living, Paris was now a war zone ravaged by hunger.

'We are moving fast towards starvation or, for the moment at least, towards an epidemic of gastritis,' wrote Edmond de Goncourt on 7 January 1871. 'Half a pound of horsemeat, including the bones, which is two people's ration for three days, is lunch for an ordinary appetite.'[27] The price of poultry and meat pies rose so much that few could afford them. Butter was a long-forgotten luxury.[28] 'Soon the animals observed that man was regarding them in a strange manner,' observed Théophile Gautier, 'and that, under the pretext of caressing them, his hand was feeling like the fingers of a butcher, to ascertain the state of their embonpoint.'[29]

For the upper classes and the social elite, the besieged city was no place to enjoy their accustomed comfortable lifestyle. They had thrived on Paris's rich array of entertainments; once war was declared, leisure was all but forgotten.[30] Theatre audiences dwindled, and on 9 September, the *préfet de police* officially closed all theatres and entertainment venues. The Bouffes-Parisiens did not reopen for the rest of the war. Even when the concession was made in October that some theatres could occasionally show a performance, if only to boost morale, auditoriums remained eerily empty. The gas lights that had illuminated Paris's stages only a few months before were replaced by candlelight once more. At 10.30pm, a curfew bell rang out and put a stop to any performance that overran.[31] The carefree gaiety of Paris's social scene had evaporated. In its place was a mood of resolute seriousness.

Pleasure-seekers with foresight fled before the city was completely cut off at the end of September.[32] Valtesse was one of them. Abandoning her life in Paris, her friends, her mother and therefore her link to Pâquerette and Valérie (whose ill-health had made it necessary to place her in special care), Valtesse got herself safely out of the capital. By the end of the year, she was staying in Nice.

The choice of Nice as a temporary refuge was fitting. The town had established itself as a fashionable winter holiday destination for the Parisian elite, and its popularity would soar as the century progressed.

'Life in Nice is exactly like that in the capital,' explained one contemporary journalist.

Intelligent pleasures, charming walks, fashionable parties, balls, receptions, dinners, everything there has the character of the Parisian highlife, with the additional attraction of prodigious nature and an endlessly clear sky. [...] Nowhere do you dine better than in Nice. Sovereigns, princes, great lords of every country have their dining habits copied.[33]

With winters typically eight to ten degrees warmer than in Paris, multiple entertainments (not least its carnival) and a lively social scene, Nice became the favoured winter retreat of the Russian Imperial family, and regularly welcomed German, Swedish and Norwegian princes.[34]

In Nice, Valtesse could continue to enjoy the lifestyle to which Offenbach and Millaud had enabled her to grow accustomed in Paris. Of course, theatre trips, fine dinners and such pleasures required money. Luckily, Millaud, who had stayed in Paris, was in a position to provide it.

But alerting Millaud to her financial needs was not straight-forward. Communications between the capital and the rest of the country became hampered once the siege set in. Resourceful Parisians began using balloons to pass messages to and from the capital.[35] When trial runs proved effective, the Minister of Posts in Paris set up a balloon post, and two or three balloons would take off each week to transport messages around the country. But the balloons required vast quantities of gas, and they offered only a one-way method of communication. This problem was eventually overcome by a more lowly method of transportation: the carrier pigeon.

The government established a microphotography unit in Tours and later in Bordeaux, and messages were shrunk down into minute form so that several could be sent with just one pigeon. So success-ful did the concept prove that the service was opened to the public at the beginning of November.[36]

People were soon eagerly dispatching messages to Paris. The situation was critical, and before long the service was inundated. Conversation in the provinces centred on the developments in the capital, and every day provincials scoured the regional papers to bring themselves up to date with the current state of affairs. Food and morale were running low, the press reported. Citizens were starving. Violence could erupt at any moment. There seemed to be no end in sight. Those with loved ones in Paris faced the very real possibility that they would never see them again.

On 9 December, Valtesse dispatched a message to Millaud by pigeon. 'Received money,' she wrote, 'am in good health.'[37] Her location in Nice gave her another advantage, too: she could report to Millaud as to the well-being of his parents. On 31 December, she assured him: 'Your parents are well, love you, am well, need nothing.'[38]

When she posted her messages to Millaud, Valtesse also wrote to another man. It was Richard Fossey. 'I send you all my heart, am in good health, in a good situation.'[39]

Fossey had returned to France, and Valtesse knew to address his message to a residence in Montmartre. She had another correspondent at this address: her mother. 'All my heart for Dick, you, Pâquerette, Emilie,' Valtesse wrote to Mme Delabigne as the year drew to a close.[40]

Messages dispatched by pigeon were sent in desperation. Senders were restricted to twenty words per dispatch.[41] At 50 centimes a word, it was an expensive procedure. Words had to be chosen carefully. People only sent communications they considered absolutely necessary. Valtesse made no reference to the reasons for Fossey's return to Paris or the arrangement that had led to him sharing a postal address with her mother. In a time of national crisis, she had two priorities: maintaining communication with Millaud (and his money), and sending what she believed could be her last ever message to her family (even her younger sister Emilie, with whom her relationship was fractious at best) and to her first true love.

In Paris, the war ground on. While Valtesse celebrated the New Year in Nice, diners in Paris feasted on cuts of elephant from the local zoo.[42] On New Year's Day, the local paper in the city Valtesse had made her temporary home told its readers:

We had intended to summarise the events that have marked the gloomy year of 1870 in this article; but when we began this painful resumé, we lost courage. Why think back on this sombre past when it is only the future that should concern us? The year 1871 begins more promisingly.[43]

It was an optimistic New Year's greeting. In reality, the Prussians still held Paris in a vice-like grip. 'Never since there was a Paris has Paris had such a New Year's Day,' lamented Edmond de Goncourt.[44] 'Cold, bombardment, famine: these are the New Year's gifts of 1871.'[45] It would be ill-advised for Valtesse to return to the capital yet. The city was in chaos and deprivation, and Valtesse was building a career based on pleasure – other people's and, ultimately, her own.

And yet while Nice could offer luxurious living, it was in Paris that reputations were forged and the best contacts made. Now that she had decided herself on her profession, she could not afford to grow complacent. Competition was fierce. She must always be thinking ahead. As she was entertaining one man, she should be calculating where her next source of income would be coming from. Besides her own comfort, there was the upkeep of her daughters to think of. Valtesse knew that to reach the glittering heights of notoriety, a woman had to be tough. Her friends were struck by her stoical, single-minded approach to her career: 'A courtesan must never cry, never suffer [...] She must stifle all sentimentality [...] I have a soul of iron [...] I will tolerate no obstacle in my path.'[46]

As soon as it was practical, Valtesse knew she must return to Paris.

CHAPTER 6

The Lioness, Her Prey and the Cost

As the new year began, Paris and its glittering high life remained out of reach. Further problems were brewing.

It was not until the end of January 1871, after the Prussians had begun bombarding the city, that France's president, General Trochu, finally accepted that he must ask Bismarck for an armistice.[1] The defeat saw France's loss of Alsace and Lorraine, and was crowned with a humiliating 50 billion franc war indemnity.

Parisians were furious. The new Republican assembly (led by Trochu's successor, Adolphe Thiers, from February) was greeted with hostility. Before long, revolutionaries set up a rival regime in Paris which became known as the Commune de Paris. The Commune brought together a colourful medley of parties, from veterans of the revolution of 1848 to radical feminists. Their interests were diverse, but their grievance the same: all were profoundly dissatisfied with the government of Paris. With the Commune having set up its headquarters in the Hôtel de Ville and Thiers's party based in Versailles, the tension broke into civil war.

With no time to recover from the Prussian siege, citizens watched in despair as the streets of Paris were reduced to a scene of devastation and destruction once more. Buildings including Thiers's private house and monuments – most poignantly the

Vendôme column, erected by Napoleon Bonaparte to celebrate his victories of 1805 – were brutally demolished. Violence swept across the city and, in one of the most barbaric acts in Parisian memory, the Archbishop of Paris was taken hostage and executed. Barricades were erected and buildings mercilessly burned to the ground. One of the most devastating sights people recalled was the burning edifice of the Tuileries Palace as it lit up the sky with a sinister glow. Paris was in chaos.

Finally, Thiers's army succeeded in entering the capital and, after a bloody confrontation that would become known as *la semaine sanglante*, emerged victorious against the Communards. By the end of May, the conflict was over, but the cost had been horrific: an estimated 20,000 Parisians had lost their lives and the city's landscape was altered beyond recognition.

The Paris Valtesse beheld in 1871 was a mere skeleton of the vibrant city she had left. Buildings were in ruins, the remains of barricades littered the streets, and every now and then the unnerving creak of a house beginning to collapse could be heard. But despite the devastation, the capital's migrants were impatient to return home. As soon as peace was declared, Parisians flooded back to the capital they had abandoned. 'This evening you begin to hear the movement of Parisian life which is being reborn, and its murmur is like that of a distant high tide,' wrote Edmond de Goncourt on 29 May 1871.[2] 'The clocks no longer strike in the silence of the desert. [...] On the paving stones which have been replaced a swarm of Parisians in travelling clothes taking possession of their city once again.'[3] The capital began to buzz with energy.

By June, Paris's regeneration was under way and the citizens who had fled were returning in their masses. Their city was battle-scarred, but it was still standing, resilient and proud. Soon, Parisian life was resuming its old shape. 'Crowds reappear on the boulevard des Italiens, on the pavement which was deserted a few days ago,' remarked Edmond de Goncourt. 'This evening for the first time it begins to be difficult to make your way through the lounging of the men and the solicitation of the women.'[4] Paris was reborn, and after months of deprivation it was ravenous for pleasure. Valtesse was ready to take advantage of the situation.

A courtesan, Valtesse once explained to a friend, was outside society and its pettiness. 'What independence, what intoxicating liberty!' she enthused. 'No more principles, no more morals, no more religion … A courtesan can do anything openly.'[5] Valtesse declared that as a courtesan, she had no more duties, not a single responsibility, except towards herself and her desire. This was what attracted Valtesse to the profession.

But female independence came at a price. Valtesse knew in her heart that society could not be dismissed; it was the courtesan's lifeblood. A fledgling courtesan must be seen out in fashionable circles. Only then would she be recognised as belonging to that social group. This was essential if she were to procure herself wealthy suitors within that sphere. Millaud's assets and attentions could not be counted on indefinitely. Having laid the foundations of a respectable fortune, Valtesse was anxious that it should grow. *La vie parisienne* was re-establishing itself, and she had to secure her position within it. Being a courtesan meant playing a complex game of wit and strategy. Valtesse wanted to win. She made Paris's revitalised social scene her chessboard.

As the sparkle and animation was breathed back into Parisian high life, Valtesse returned to the theatre. But a transformation had taken place since her last appearance. No longer was the pretty redhead waiting nervously in the wings; now, confident and self-assured, she could be seen in the VIP section of the audience. She glittered with jewels, wore elegant dresses, and attracted attention wherever she went.

By making regular public appearances, always impeccably turned out and entrancing onlookers with a sweet but knowing smile, Valtesse soon gained recognition as a prominent society beauty. All the society pages were interested in her. 'That beautiful sunset, the radiant Mlle Valtesse' turned heads when she appeared at a premiere at the beginning of March 1872.[6] The following month, she was spotted alongside the celebrated courtesan Cora Pearl and the eminent banker Gustave de Rothschild at the opening night of *La Timbale d'Argent* at her old home, the Bouffes-Parisiens.[7] In November, she attended a performance at the Vaudeville, and raised eyebrows by being seated 'in what was formerly the Imperial box, if you please, with five ladies and a gentleman.'[8] Valtesse had elevated herself and become part of Paris's most glamorous social elite.

Her physical appeal was indisputable. She dressed and moved with an understated grace, favouring dresses with intricate bodice work and high collars which gave her a proud appearance. She kept her makeup simple in an effort to look as natural as possible; a heavily powdered face and garish lipstick were hallmarks of the common prostitute. Once men were introduced to her and discovered that the cool beauty they had been admiring from a distance also possessed intelligence, charm and a lively sense of humour, they were smitten. With 'small breasts, a flat stomach, sensual lips, her breath had a wonderful scent of sugared almonds, and something indefinable, a kind of fiery spice which drove a man wild.'[9] Valtesse made herself intoxicating.

Her efforts were soon reaping enviable rewards. Valtesse was not yet 25 when she caught the eye of a man who made Offenbach and Millaud seem paltry conquests. Her new admirer was far superior to a journalist or a composer: he was a prince.

Prince Lubomirski belonged to one of the most ancient, noble families in Poland.[10] The family wielded substantial political, economic and military power, and over the course of several centuries had established a sizeable empire. It boasted vast estates in Poland, Austria and France, and was associated with numerous profitable investments and charitable works. The Lubomirskis' foreign residences ensured that the family maintained an esteemed profile across Europe, notably in the French capital. It was there that, having spent time travelling, Valtesse's prince eventually chose to settle.

The prince was an enthusiastic patron of the capital's entertainment scene, and a familiar figure on the Parisian social circuit. He wrote and was passionate about the arts, attending theatre opening nights, concerts and balls, and he was often spotted dining at the fashionable restaurant Offenbach patronised, Bignon.[11] His financial acumen was perhaps not his strongest quality; he had lost large sums, and his fondness for women was said to be the cause of his undoing. However, his family connections and inherited wealth provided something of a cushion. The prince was one of the most eligible suitors Valtesse could have won.

Valtesse had become a society darling; her affair with a prince could not stay secret for long. The couple became the talk of Paris. The paper *L'Événement* delighted in publishing an extract from an album that the author claimed belonged to 'Mlle. V':

> Prince Lubomirski
> having gobbled up his riches
> takes a pretty mistress.
>
> Prince Lubomirski
> dismissing public thought
> to brunettes and blondes pays court.[12]

Valtesse coolly dismissed the jibes. Her dignified mien and enigmatic smile fostered her public's admiration and respect. But privately, the conquest was a source of deep satisfaction and pride. Valtesse was not in the least bit displeased to learn that, behind the closed doors of private salons, her name was being whispered in connection with nobility. Press attention was invaluable. Being seen out in fashionable society on the arm of the prince, exhibiting the lustrous jewels and diamonds he had bestowed on her, she could almost have been a princess.

As the affair flourished, Valtesse watched her fortune swell. The prince considered no sacrifice too great for his beautiful mistress. Valtesse was treated to fine dinners, as many trips to the theatre or the opera as she desired, and the most costly jewels and dresses money could buy. From the delicate lace collars she so favoured to diamond and pearl chokers, brooches and bracelets, through Prince Lubomirski Valtesse could have them all.[13] She moved into an apartment in the Rue Saint-Georges and Paris's gossip-mongers insisted that it came courtesy of the prince.

Not even a prince can boast an inexhaustible income, though. Having denied Valtesse nothing, he eventually found he was left with nothing in return. Prince Lubomirski had ruined himself. He had compromised his entire noble fortune on a girl from the back-streets of Paris.

The fairy tale was over, but there was no space for sentimentality. Valtesse had accepted the demands of her profession. Her livelihood depended on moving swiftly on to the next suitor. She saw men as stepping stones on a path that guaranteed her survival and success; once the support beneath her began to give way, she would spring lightly to the next foothold.

Prince Lubomirski's successor was also rich. He too was well regarded in Parisian society. But Valtesse's new admirer possessed an additional quality to tempt her. In the American general, M. Commandos, Valtesse found an answer to both her desire for riches and her weakness for the military.[14]

The general lived in the smart Hôtel du Helder off the Boulevard des Italiens. The hotel's elegant decor and distinguished ambience had earned it an excellent reputation and an elite clientele.[15] Its à la carte menu was considered among the finest on the boulevard, and contemporary travel guides declared its wine cellar one of the best in Paris. Few decisions betrayed class as explicitly as a person's choice of restaurant in the 19th century. Patronising an à la carte dining establishment like the Hôtel de Helder won social respect. It guaranteed diners the impeccable standard of service usually reserved for royalty, and the assurance of being served the finest culinary delicacies available in the capital. 'Listen to true gourmets,' advised the writer of the *Guide Conty*, 'they will tell you that à la carte restaurants are the only eating establishments to be recommended [...] the prices in these restaurants are higher; but the service is better, the cooking more succulent, the wine cellar finer, the menu more varied and the portions larger.'[16]

Valtesse set great store by chic, luxurious living and social prestige. As for General Commandos, money was no obstacle when it came to pleasing his beautiful French mistress. In the space of six months, he spent over 60,000 francs on Valtesse (just short of £580,000 in today's money).[17] In addition to fine meals out, he lavished gifts on her. There were exquisite pieces of jewellery packaged in dainty boxes, and dresses hand-stitched from rich fabrics, carefully wrapped in crisp tissue. And in addition to the usual entertainments, presents and treats, Commandos had something special to offer Valtesse. It came with a 3,700-franc price tag. In October 1872, Valtesse became the proud leaseholder of a superb apartment at number 10, Rue Blanche.[18]

Situated on the second floor, Valtesse's spectacular new home comprised an antechamber, kitchen, sitting room, dining room, three bedrooms, an additional reception room with a fireplace, and – the height of modern advancement and luxury – two bathrooms and lavatories.[19] The apartment was magnificent, and it was all hers. At last, Valtesse held the keys to her very own home, which she could decorate just as she desired.

Valtesse was happily growing accustomed to the luxuries she had seen other courtesans enjoying. She had embarked on a complex game and she was winning – for the moment. If a young girl succeeded in this profession, the gains could be spectacular. But Valtesse knew there was a price to pay: 'the day I became a courtesan, I erased every memory from my life, every attachment [...] I renounced the so-called sensitivity of the soul.'[20] She had to be tough. Expending her time on one primary lover was all very well while he was rich and besotted, but it was an approach fraught with risk. A man's affections could turn at any moment. Worse: he could find himself bankrupt. Valtesse had learned that men were not to be relied on. Her strategy for dealing with this inconvenient truth was simple: she had relationships with several men at once.

Valtesse was strategic in her choice of partners. Entertaining a regular chain of high-profile lovers enabled her to maintain her lavish lifestyle. The names of countless prominent figures were associated with her in the 1870s. Besides Prince Lubomirski and General Commandos, statesmen such as Pierre Waldeck-Rousseau, writers including the novelist Octave Mirbeau, the painter of military scenes Édouard Detaille and the younger painter Henri Gervex were all seen coming and going at Valtesse's address.[21]

Yet discretion was her calling card. Valtesse never publicly identified her lovers. People whispered that she had even received visits from Emperor Napoleon III before the war when she was still new to the profession, and that she had been a regular guest at the Tuileries; questions about the supposed affair merely aroused an enigmatic smile. Valtesse became adept at teasing the public's hunger for gossip. She realised that, used wisely, the Parisian imagination could be a formidable marketing tool.

Men returned to see her time and time again. Lovers often arrived to find Valtesse pacing the length of her boudoir, deep in thought, a cigarette between her lips and her hands thrust into the pockets of her sumptuous black silk dressing gown, which only a costly jet pin kept from slipping to reveal her breasts.[22] But cool and reserved though she appeared, Valtesse had learned much during her time in Paris's *demi-monde*. She knew exactly how to ensnare a man – and his money. Her glacial exterior was sharply contrasted by a well-versed sexual repertoire. The duality made her irresistible. No accessory or request fazed her; she knew the value of assuming sexual authority. At times, her work could be disgusting, but Valtesse had grown skilled at affecting ecstatic pleasure whenever a fat, panting, sweaty client's wealth gave reason to suppress her repulsion. And she became known for one feature in particular, something people spoke about in hushed voices and which brought curious men hurrying to see her: she was always 'ready to make love', and could do so without foreplay.[23]

Valtesse's approach to her suitors was businesslike and rigorous. Her men were divided into three categories.

In the first group were those who were permitted to take her to the theatre, the opera and concerts and, of course, to buy her gifts. But to such men, she acted merely as an escort; she refused to sleep with them.

This additional privilege was only granted to a second, select group of men. The price they paid was accordingly higher. And Valtesse attached a proviso: men who enjoyed this advantage were forbidden to speak of their experiences.

Valtesse distinguished a third category of client, too. These men formed a very particular group. They could be seen with her in public. They were permitted to sleep with her. And they paid little, or sometimes nothing at all, for the privilege.

It was a puzzling concession, since Valtesse had reached a point in her career where she could command a high fee for her services. She explained her methodology to an acquaintance: 'I could not deny my poor friends such a pleasure.'[24] Though proud and stoical about her liaisons, Valtesse harboured an innate sympathy with essentially good souls to whom life had dealt an unfair hand. She understood their suffering; she had shared it.

However, poverty alone did not grant a man access to this group. Valtesse allowed into it any man she felt attracted to. If he wore a uniform and a moustache, he was likely to find favour with her.

One of Valtesse's *amants de coeur* was Edmond Comte de Lagrené, a diplomat. His father had been an ambassador, and in 1862 Edmond too joined the Ministry of Foreign Affairs. Although he had worked abroad in such far-flung locations as Peking and Moscow, Edmond could not boast a sizeable fortune. He was permanently frustrated that his modest financial means led the great courtesans to pity rather than respect him. The authorities took a dim view of his conduct. He was, the police recorded, 'notorious in the demi-monde for living off women'.[25] But Valtesse was empathetic. Besides, men with exotic Eastern connections always fascinated her.

Valtesse had a particularly soft spot for her old gentleman. Every Sunday at two o'clock sharp, he would arrive and be granted half an hour of pleasure for a token of a coin or two.[26] Provided she did not make an unreasonable amount of these concessions, Valtesse knew she could afford herself such whims of the heart. The financial rewards she reaped from men like Commandos and Prince Lubomirski were ample compensation.

But for all the luxury and independence she was enjoying, Valtesse had to accept that as a courtesan, her life must be 'a continual performance'.[27] She could not afford to make enemies. Her success depended on being seen, and on altering her behaviour to suit the company she kept. She must appear bright and lively when her body ached with tiredness, sound interested in conversations she found dull, and feign pleasure at crude male caresses and sexual encounters which left her cold.

Furthermore, as a courtesan, the law was an indomitable enemy. Before long, the police were alerted to the suspicious activity of the pretty former actress from the Bouffes-Parisiens. In 1872, Valtesse was listed as a courtesan with the *police des moeurs*.[28] From then on, the file they held on her grew. And the year Valtesse's name first appeared on the register, she also learned that a formal complaint had been lodged against her.

In January, the police received a visit from an agitated lady who gave her name as Mme Crémieux.[29] She wished to make a complaint. She had taken a lover – a confession that would hardly have raised an eyebrow with the police. But, she continued, the man in question had previously been the lover of a renowned red-headed courtesan: Valtesse. Mme Crémieux insisted that Valtesse had become so enraged when her lover left her for another woman that she immediately set to work seducing Mme Crémieux's husband by way of revenge. Valtesse being a professional, M. Crémieux was soon her willing servant. Having won his trust, she encouraged his jealousy of his wife's affair, so much so that his rage culminated in a violent outburst towards his spouse. A separation became the only possible solution. However, still not content, Valtesse was accused of having bombarded Mme Crémieux with threatening letters, and as an extra precaution, enlisted the help of a friend to follow the estranged wife.

The police made little of the complaint. Paris was teeming with disgruntled wives. In practical terms, the accusation was a trifling matter for Valtesse – a nuisance, but no more. The police were already aware of her activity. With growing confidence, Valtesse learned that a prying officer could always be pacified when a woman knew how to work her charms. It would take more than a trivial complaint to sabotage her prospering career. However, even close friends described Valtesse as 'haughty and proud'.[30] Mme Crémieux's argument was not incredible.

Still, Valtesse was soon enjoying the attentions of a new primary lover, the elderly – but fantastically rich – M. Gunsbourg. Previously a banker in the Russian court, Gunsbourg furnished her with 15,000 francs a month (close to £150,000 by today's values).[31]

By the mid-1870s, Valtesse could feel satisfied with her burgeoning empire. She became an expert at managing her career, which ran like a well-organised military operation. Valtesse adhered to a meticulous timetable. Courtesans tended to rise late, but the remainder of the morning was ideal for dealing with accounts. It was a task about which Valtesse was punctilious. Then there might be couturiers, decorators, or furniture makers to see. Visits were made and visitors received in the afternoon. It was also essential that she be seen promenading in her carriage in the Bois de Boulogne on fine days, for as one contemporary guidebook author observed, 'Where else can one see such a crowd, such society and so finely turned out?'[32] Theatre visits, dinners and receptions were a necessity for which time must be made in the evening. And when she received her gentlemen – an appointment tended to last an hour – she rigorously timed the rendezvous to the minute. Once a suitor's time had elapsed, she swiftly hastened his exit. Time, after all, was money.

Valtesse had not long been resident at Rue Blanche when she managed to secure yet another, particularly powerful, benefactor. The Prince de Sagan came with a noble title, a vast fortune and connections to the most esteemed sectors of Europe's social elite. Although issuing from Polish aristocracy, the prince had been born and resided in Paris, where he was a noted member of high society. A true bon viveur – 'notorious', according to English papers – the prince adored the opera, particularly Italian, and was one of the most enthusiastic supporters of Paris's musical scene.[33] With his dignified moustache and his measured gestures, the prince exuded an air of gentlemanly elegance and studied refinement. His bright eyes seemed to smile, and women frequently fell victim to his charms. An ardent admirer of all things chic, the prince dined in the finest restaurants and hotels, favouring Claridge's whenever he was in London, and he was intimate with members of royal and aristocratic families across Europe.[34] He had joined the Prince of Wales and the Duke of Edinburgh for a splendid breakfast in the Pavillion Gousset during their visit to Paris for the 1867 Exposition Universelle.[35] Before the war, he had regularly attended balls and soirées with the Emperor and Empress. And the prince's fortune was prodigious: he had thought nothing of purchasing the hunting ground at Chantilly in 1860 when the estate was about to be broken up, acquiring the dogs, horses and attendants and paying compensation to the proprietors of the land, which amounted to a staggering 50,000 francs (over half a million in today's money); such sums did not faze him.[36]

The prince was a covetable suitor. His marriage to the Baron de Seillières's daughter was no obstacle for Valtesse. The prince loved women, and Valtesse had mastered the power of her own charms. The Prince de Sagan joined the list of Valtesse's most enviable conquests, and her fortune was soon reflecting the happy results of her success.

But Valtesse did not realise the full magnitude of her victory straightaway. That only became apparent later into the relationship. The prince was preparing a very special present. It would be the most incredible gift she had ever received – and it testified indisputably that she had joined the ranks of the greatest courtesans of her time.

CHAPTER 7

Names and Places

Valtesse's star had risen and was shining brighter than ever. In 1873, the police estimated her fortune to be in the region of 300,000 francs (nearly £3 million in today's money).[1] The following years saw it increase still further. Valtesse was a committed saver.

She had reached the zenith of her career at a fortuitous time. Reeling from the shock of the siege and the Commune, post-war Paris had made itself drunk on pleasure. Aristocrats no longer ruled the city – the nouveau riche now reigned supreme. Money was there to be made and the entertainment industry ensured that it was spent. Status ceased to be determined by class. Wealth and social respect were available to anyone shrewd in their conduct and discerning in their alliances. Identity was a matter of personal choice. Culture could be acquired, connections forged, and a person's past was whatever they claimed it to be.

Perched high on the throne of the new social landscape was its queen: *la Parisienne*. This figure was a model for fashion-conscious women, the heroine of male fantasies, and an unofficial ambassador for France. 'She is the glory, the renown and the raison d'être of Paris,' proclaimed journalist and social observer Adrien Marx.[2] 'Paris would not exist without la Parisienne!' She could be a member of high society or an actress, a countess or a kept woman. Her class was irrelevant; her appearance was everything. *La Parisienne* was the ultimate fashion icon. She lived in a chic apartment, surrounded by exquisite objets d'art and exotic plants. She was elegant and cultured, cool yet well-mannered. Women across the world strove to emulate her, artists from Manet to Renoir paid homage to her – and for a courtesan like Valtesse, *la Parisienne* was at once her role model and a standard against which she knew she would be measured.[3]

The ingredients for success lay before Valtesse. But using them effectively and maintaining her position required hard work and dedication. She made it her daily occupation.

Valtesse decided to modify her banal family name to the more aristocratic 'de la Bigne'. She was now socialising with princes and dukes; ennobling herself reduced the unspoken gap between them. All around her, Valtesse saw her peers inventing patronymics. Courtesans were particularly known for doing so. In changing her name, Valtesse was following in the path of some of the greats, not least Marie du Plessis and Blanche d'Antigny. But the nominal alteration served another purpose, too: 'de la Bigne' was not just an empty poetic construction. The de la Bignes were one of the most ancient, noble families in Normandy, where Valtesse's ancestral roots lay. The link to the esteemed family was pure invention on Valtesse's part, but the implied alliance was both credible and priceless. By changing her surname, Valtesse instantly acquired a venerable ancestral heritage and a respectable past.

Valtesse was delighted to see correspondence arriving bearing her new mode of address. She decided to complete the effect with a fitting title. No longer satisfied with 'Mme', Valtesse became 'Comtesse'.

Such was the climate in Paris at this time that it had become impossible to distinguish true nobility from noble-sounding self-creations. Titles, like surnames, were being fabricated on a daily basis. Society welcomed Comtesse Valtesse de la Bigne into its fold. Few questions were asked.

So when Valtesse had a bouquet of flowers sent to the Emperor and Empress in Chislehurst on the anniversary of Napoleon Bonaparte's birthday – for she had always admired the leader of the First Empire – the Empress Eugénie, no longer enlightened on the configuration of Parisian society, exclaimed in delight: 'We have not been forgotten, even the Faubourg Saint-Germain has extended its regards. The Comtesse de la Bigne has sent us flowers!'[4]

Valtesse's new title was in perfect keeping with the image she sought to project. She presented herself as a woman of refinement and good breeding, cultured and surrounded by grandeur, yet who remained unknowable, untouchable – thus more desirable.

Her appearance was intrinsic to her image. 'The *cocotte* knows that her toilette is her most powerful tool of seduction,' explained Adrien Marx.[5] Valtesse attended to it scrupulously. Being naturally creative and sensitive to aesthetics, she carefully picked out dresses that slimmed her waistline and showed off the natural curve of her hips. But while her lower half hinted suggestively at her feminine curves, there was a decidedly masculine quality to her look from the waist up. This served two purposes. Fitted bodices and high necks gave her a haughty, dignified air, which commanded respect; they also diverted the male gaze from her chest, for it had been said that 'she has no breasts to speak of'.[6] Valtesse abhorred criticism.

She would often appear at a costumed ball dressed in male clothing. The opening night of *Les Merveilleuses* in 1873 was a star-studded occasion, and Valtesse's outfit was the first of the 'exquisite toilettes' to which the reporter from *Le Gaulois* was drawn.[7] She wore a sexy ensemble with a masculine twist, comprising a long black velvet skirt, a white satin waistcoat and a fitted black velvet jacket. She looked the perfect dandy, and people declared her to be 'glowing'. Gender-blurring entertained Valtesse. It disconcerted and raised questions – and creating mystery was what she liked best. It made her feel empowered.

But black was not Valtesse's favourite colour. For a courtesan to secure her position among the greats of her profession, she had to make a lasting impression. Her audience must hold an image of her long after she had left. Many courtesans assumed a trademark, a personal quirk. Diamonds immediately called to mind the lovely Blanche d'Antigny; Cora Pearl ensured that her hair and the upholstery of her carriage were a perfect, matching shade of golden yellow. Valtesse followed suit.[8] She adopted blue, one of the traditional colours of Paris, as her personal theme. She ordered clothing, accessories and furnishings for her home in assorted shades of blue.

Then, just as the camellia had grown indissociable from Marie du Plessis, the violet was selected by Valtesse as her trademark flower. Its symbolism was no coincidence; apparently delicate, unassuming and reputedly shy, it was nevertheless the flower associated with Napoleon Bonaparte, the powerful emperor Valtesse held in such high regard.[9] Whenever an appearance demanded a bouquet or a posy, Valtesse's florist received an order for violets.

Valtesse made no secret of her Bonapartist leanings and surrounded herself with friends of the same persuasion. The world of politics was a rich fabric interwoven with power – and money. Beside the Emperor's political convictions, his personal attributes – courage, determination and a boundless capacity to seize and maintain power – were qualities Valtesse held in high regard. Her correspondence was always written on the finest quality blue writing paper bearing the Bonapartist symbol of a golden eagle.

Blue was regal and patriotic, and it enhanced the natural beauty of Valtesse's eyes, but few colours conveyed sovereignty and grandeur as powerfully as gold. Bonaparte had understood that. Rare was the portrait that did not depict him adorned in the colour. Valtesse wanted to harness its connotations, so in 1874, she coyly assigned herself a nickname: 'Rayon d'or' or 'Ray of Gold'. Royalty, power, the Sun King, Versailles, Bonaparte: Valtesse chose the name carefully for its multiple associations. It conveyed a certain romanticism. And it drew attention to her proudest attribute: her hair, whose red tones shone gold whenever the light caught it.

Valtesse was turning herself into a commercial product. She was determined to secure her social position – and mindful of what could happen if she did not.

'Ray of Gold' was an admirable nickname, but Valtesse felt she needed a more concise soubriquet, too. It should convey strength, intelligence – in short, her very essence. Valtesse's love of the classics led her to a name which doubled as a motto. Valtesse became the simple and superb 'Ego' (which she spelt Εγω, using Greek characters). She congratulated herself, considering the notion inspired. She had her stationery, and even the ceilings in her home, embossed with the name.

Valtesse had fashioned a self-image and it was promoting her across Paris with remarkable efficiency. 'Is she really "de la Bigne"?', ventured one journalist. 'It does not matter. She is Valtesse and "Ray of Gold" – and that is enough.'[10] Now, she was worthy of any prince.

But however concerted her efforts, the past could not be erased. She still had two daughters whose care continued to be overseen by her mother. And both children were sickly. Valérie-Albertine seemed permanently unwell, and even Julia-Pâquerette had lately fallen ill – alarmingly so. It was decided that she should be sent to a clinic for treatment.

Friends said that it was Fossey who, discovering the girls to be in poor health on his return from Algeria, suggested that the grandmother take them to live with her in the country. Country air was said to hold no end of health benefits, and Valtesse approved the project.

The arrangement suited Mme Delabigne as well. After her post as a domestic help for Doctor Jobert de Lamballe was terminated in 1867, Mme Delabigne had found a position as a supervisor in a girls' boarding school in Paris, run by a Mme de Barral.[11] The job brought some security, but Mme Delabigne was now in her fifties and had no spousal support. The prospect of leaving Paris with an increased monthly allowance for taking full responsibility for the girls was appealing.

Mme Delabigne left the capital with her granddaughters and moved west of the city, closer to her native Normandy, settling in the village of Limay near Mantes. The extolled benefits of country living had a pleasing effect on Julia-Pâquerette, whose health was soon restored. But Valérie-Albertine's condition was less responsive. She died soon afterwards.

Valtesse never spoke of her feelings when she learned of her daughter's death. Her friends and general acquaintance were still unaware that she was a mother. That was how she liked it. She had become an expert in concealing her emotions. The life Valtesse had created in Paris demanded her undivided attention; her security depended on it. That world was all-consuming and it could crumble if she did not nurture it. It was her cocoon and she immersed herself in it, refusing to leave.

Valtesse had the Prince de Sagan, her other lovers and Paris's insatiable social scene to occupy her. Few capital cities were as rich in diversions and, with the prince, Valtesse's attention was absorbed as she hungrily tasted them all.

The Prince de Sagan was especially fond of horseracing. He was a member of the infamous Jockey Club, an exclusively male club that was one of the most prestigious in Paris. Capitalising on the wave of Anglomania that was sweeping through Paris in the 1830s, the Jockey Club was founded with the official purpose of encouraging and improving horse breeding in France.[12] In practice, the club and its smart headquarters on the corner of the Boulevard des Capucines and the Rue de Scribe provided a social distraction for some of the richest, most fashionable sporting gentlemen in Paris. Admission had to be granted and membership was exorbitant. However, the financiers and industrialists who joined calculated that the benefits and prestige justified the expense.

Cards, horses, duels and most of all gambling were common interests. When entertainments were wanting, members could be found smoking and sipping brandy as they placed titillating bets on the speed of their horses, the chastity of their wives or even the probable death dates of their fellow members.[13] But by far the most enticing advantage of club membership was the access it granted to the society's private box at the Opéra. The seats boasted one of the most privileged views of the stage – and gave men easy access to the stage door and the dancers' dressing rooms beyond.

The Jockey Club were notorious for their love of women. Rumour had it that every member had spent a night with the fiery Italian courtesan La Barucci.[14] La Barucci was no fool: with their wealth and distinction, Jockey Club members made enviable catches. Some courtesans refused to even look at a man if he were not a member. Valtesse was well aware how auspicious her relationship with the prince was.

As a woman, Valtesse was denied access to the club headquarters. But she could attend the races.

In 19th-century Paris, the horse races were a great social occasion. The race itself was merely a convenient pretext; like the theatre and England's Royal Ascot, the racecourse was the place to see and be seen. 'The races, which for a long time have been the meeting place of elegant society and magnificent teams, can be divided into spring races, summer races and autumn races,' explained one guidebook in the 1870s.[15] The Prince de Sagan was a devoted spectator of all the big Parisian races. There was the

Grand Prix de Paris with its 100,000-franc prize at Longchamp (the racecourse made famous by the paintings of Édouard Manet and Edgar Degas, and later by Émile Zola's novel *Nana*).[16] The Grand National took place at Auteuil in the week of Pentecost, and no fashion-conscious Parisian would miss the Concours Hippique – 'the great event of the moment' – in the spring.[17] And perhaps most importantly, there was the Jockey Club prize, which was held every May at Chantilly, the racecourse the Prince de Sagan had purchased.[18]

The races opened Valtesse's eyes to a colourful new world. From the thrill of being seen and admired to the reassurance that she was forging contacts in the best circles; from the anticipation as the bell rang to announce the horses' arrival and the flutter of the starter's red flag to the surge of adrenaline as the horses thundered away from the starting line and the explosion of applause when a favourite horse won; the races had everything to appeal to Valtesse. They were exhilarating. She attended as many as possible.

At each race, Valtesse studied the elegant crowd mingling around her. She listened attentively to their conversations, taking note of their views, their political opinions, the current literary and artistic debates. Then she mimicked the behaviour she observed, so that she blended in seamlessly.

In such circles, it was becoming increasingly fashionable to own a country property. 'Paris smothers, it searches the wider horizon,' wrote P. Juillerat in 1861.[19] In the second half of the 19th century Parisians' insatiable appetite for leisure and diversion combined with the expanding rail network and an economically favourable climate to propel Paris's rural suburbs to the height of popularity. What could be more pleasant, manuals and guidebooks enquired, than to travel just a short distance on the train and discover the countryside, nature in all its glory, and an array of pleasant diversions?

Parisians were charmed by the carefree existence the countryside offered. For many, a day trip satisfied the whim for country air. But for others – notably the moneyed upper classes – a second home in one of the quaint little villages around Paris was deemed the only civilised way to appreciate the beauty of the countryside. Formerly the prerogative of just a small elite, country homes were being purchased by a growing number of middle-class Parisians.[20] City dwellers spent the summer enjoying the charms of the countryside, with all the benefits of an entertainment schedule that, aside from the surroundings, scarcely varied from that of Paris.[21]

The idea of a rural retreat captured Valtesse's imagination. Her apartment in Paris was handsome, but if she owned a country property, she could travel there whenever she had the urge. She could escape Paris and reassert her independence. Its decoration would provide an outlet for her creative flair. She could invite just who she pleased, and she would appear terribly grand. Besides, her fortune would now easily cover the expense. Valtesse's mind was made up, and in 1873 a property became available which exceeded her wildest hopes.

The large house was situated on the outskirts of Paris.[22] It boasted a picturesque countryside setting, bright and elegant living quarters, and a beautiful, sloping garden. And it was all to be found merely a short train or carriage ride from central Paris, in a town already familiar to Valtesse: Ville-d'Avray.

As she signed the rental agreement, Valtesse realised a childhood dream. At that moment, something of the young Louise Delabigne stirred beneath Valtesse's gilded exterior. She became the proud occupant of a spectacular property, worth in the region of 40,000 francs (approximately £500,000 in today's money), in the pretty town of Corot's enthusiastic tales which had so enchanted her as a little girl.[23] And her new home was located just around the corner from the former residence of one of her literary heroes, the supreme Honoré de Balzac.

A short walk from the Parc de Saint-Cloud, but seemingly far away from Paris, the property was arranged over three floors. An imposing gate led guests up a sweeping drive on the right-hand side, from which the verdant garden with its pond and the graceful – sometimes erotic – statues Valtesse had installed could be viewed to their best advantage.

'I hate the dark,' Valtesse once confided to a friend.[24] Her new property catered perfectly to her taste. Enormous windows brought sunlight flooding into the ground floor spaces, with the pièce de résistance being the large reception room, which boasted spectacular views of the garden. The top floor was ideal for staff, while Valtesse selected the room opposite the stairs on the middle floor as her bedroom. Grand, light and airy, the spacious room opened out on to a long balcony at the front of the house, from which Valtesse, with her back turned defiantly away from Paris, could look down and admire her rolling garden and, beyond, the trees and hills of Ville-d'Avray.

A rumour circulated that the house was originally constructed by Napoleon III as a venue for parties when he was in residence at Saint-Cloud. It was said that the philandering Emperor had housed some of his mistresses there, and people fancied that Valtesse might have been one of the party when she was a fledgling courtesan. Such frivolous gossip made Valtesse smile, particularly when it added piquancy and intrigue to her public profile. Speculation was a powerful marketing tool. She never satisfied the stories with a conclusive response.

Thrilled with her new home, Valtesse decided to throw a lavish party to celebrate the anniversary of Napoleon Bonaparte's birthday. Once invitations were dispatched, the event became the talk of Paris. Women worried over their toilette, men made sure that they were well versed in the current affairs and politics which would no doubt be discussed. Then, on the evening of Friday 15 August

1873, a carefully selected list of guests started arriving from Paris in anticipation of a spectacular evening.

The occasion did not disappoint. Throughout the night, the hum of chattering voices and laughter emanated from the garden, while fireworks lit up the sky above the house. The police were soon alerted to the commotion.[25] Determined to stamp out such politically driven frivolity, after the party they paid a visit to Valtesse's friend, the actress Louise Mercey, and demanded that she give the names of each and every guest who had attended the party. Notes were scrupulously taken, and a record of the incident was grimly added to Valtesse's file.

Once afraid of the authorities, now Valtesse paid no attention. She was the favoured hostess, the dazzling star, and she was in her element. In any case, she slyly defended herself, were they not living in a republic now? Did the Republic not stand by the individual's right to express an opinion on their own private property? There was little the police could do, and guests declared the party a fantastic success. Basking in the glory, Valtesse eagerly resolved to repeat the occasion the following year on the same day.

But her new property was more than an extravagant fashion statement and party venue. It was Valtesse's private, sentimental gift to herself. To her delight, she had not been in residence long when the owner agreed to sell her the house. She named it accordingly: 'Rayon d'Or'.

By 1875, Valtesse was on the crest of a wave. She had the prince, she enjoyed access to his connections, she possessed her very own house in the country and everywhere she went she was treated like royalty.

Still, charming as a country retreat and a city apartment were, a queen is not a queen without a palace. Valtesse knew that – and so did the prince. So in 1875, the Prince de Sagan made an extravagant gesture. He provided the money for Valtesse to have built the most lavish, opulent Parisian home that her imagination could conceive.

The fashionable architect Jules Février was employed to design 98, Boulevard Malesherbes.[26] The boulevard had only been officially opened in the early 1860s, but already, the area had earned itself a reputation as being among the most sought-after residential quarters in Paris. Celebrated painters, writers, journalists, composers, actors and actresses clamoured to secure themselves a property on the street, and Valtesse's new neighbours would include the military painter Ernest Meissonier and later his pupil – and Valtesse's lover – Édouard Detaille, as well as the painter Henri Gervex, another of her lovers.[27]

Quite besides Valtesse's exacting standards, there were a host of practical obstacles for Février to contend with. Valtesse had set her heart on something grand, but the construction space was limited due to the site's location on the corner of the Boulevard Malesherbes and the Rue de la Terrasse.[28] Février's final design overcame the limitations with finesse. No one was more pleased than Valtesse, and when she filled the property with hundreds of expensive statues, objets d'art, antiques, exquisite furniture and walls of books, the finished result made her radiant with pride.

When a visitor arrived outside the smart, modern frontage of the sparkling Renaissance-style *hôtel particulier*, their carriage would be driven through the dark oak doors of the entrance way on the Boulevard Malesherbes.[29] Guests alighted in the courtyard, while their drivers were obliged to exit through a second gateway which led out on to the Rue de la Terrasse; the courtyard was too small for a carriage to turn around. A guest who had been deposited passed under a wrought-iron canopy before stepping into the grand entrance foyer. Here the visitor discovered a startling contrast: while the building's exterior was bright and modern, the interior was majestic, even austere, and furnished with rich, dark colours.

The effect was similar to that conveyed by Gustave Caillebotte's painting *Young Man at His Window* (1875), in which Valtesse's street can be glimpsed over the shoulder of the model.

A flight of steps led visitors immediately up to the first floor, the ground floor being reserved for domestic staff, the kitchen, the washhouse and, leading out on to the courtyard, a fine stable. Guests were then shown into the grand sitting room, an imposing space in which nearly every available wall or corner was commandeered as an exhibition space for Valtesse's growing collection of paintings, bronzes and sculptures.

For more intimate gatherings, there was a smaller reception room. Its reduced size emphasised the severity of the decor, but it was furnished with equal creativity. There were beautiful Louis XIV armchairs in cherry-coloured silk, luxurious velvet-upholstered seats from the time of Philippe II, and a magnificent table encrusted with ivory and gold. Stained-glass windows designed by Duris flooded certain spaces with light and offset the richly coloured furnishings, striking just the dramatic contrast Valtesse had been hoping to create. And although the *hôtel particulier* was small, the extraordinary height of the reception rooms (5.6m from the base of the stairs) impressed visitors with the building's grandeur.[30]

When Valtesse felt a particular gathering called for a more relaxed atmosphere, she could show guests into the bright Japanese conservatory which adjoined the large sitting room, where in addition to a host of rare tropical plants she arranged bronze statues of Buddha, miniature pagodas and lamps.

When dinner was announced, guests were shown through to the oak-panelled dining room, where they would be offered a seat at the square table in the middle of the room. It was a small table for the size of the space, but Valtesse always preferred intimate gatherings when she was hosting a dinner. The conversation was more stimulating. She rarely invited more than eight people to dinner.

Valtesse prided herself on her table and the opportunity it afforded her to showcase her gleaming silverware and Venetian glass, while she and her guests enjoyed succulent dishes prepared by her cook. Valtesse's guests were served the finest delicacies found in Paris. Poverty had taught Valtesse to appreciate the fine cuisine she could now afford. (Following the example of her former lover Offenbach, she was a loyal patron of Louis Bignon's fashionable restaurant, the Café Riche, an establishment famed for its fine wines, rich sauces and elevated prices.)[31]

The reception floor was grand – oppressively so when there were no guests. Solitude made Valtesse uneasy, so she lived principally on the second floor. It was here that the architect's skill and finesse were shown at their most superb.

Valtesse was determined that only the best would do. Obediently, the Prince de Sagan went to his savings. No expense was spared. The Opéra Garnier, designed by the architect of the moment, Charles Garnier, had just opened, sending waves of excitement rippling across Paris. Ever fashion-conscious, Valtesse decided that she would accept no other architect when it came to creating the imposing staircase between the first and the second floor.

The grand pink marble staircase showcased Garnier at his very best. It included two complicated turns, and Valtesse placed a large mirror at its base, an ingenious ploy which created the illusion that the stairs were almost twice their actual length. 'It looks like [...] the sumptuous staircase of honour in some royal palace,' one visitor marvelled.[32] That was precisely the impact Valtesse had been seeking.

Valtesse's private apartments satisfied all her requirements. There was a kitchen and a dining room (both smaller and more intimate than those on the other floors), a smart dressing room and two modest-sized bedrooms for close friends. Then came Valtesse's octagonal boudoir (which housed her favourite piece of furniture, her desk), and, finally, the most important – and secret – room of the house: her bedroom.

Everything in the *hôtel particulier* was designed to impress, and the balance between luxury and good taste had been struck in perfect harmony throughout.

Without doubt, she would require staff, and most importantly, a housekeeper for her new home. Valtesse knew just who to appoint. For all the glitter and dazzle of her new life as a courtesan, Valtesse had never lost sight of her provenance, nor did she forget those who had done her a good service. Going back to childhood, she had always been able to rely on her friend Camille. Camille had stood by her when she had nothing; now, at last, she would be able to repay the debt.

Valtesse took Camille on as a full-time housekeeper and provided accommodation for her and the man she married, Louis Meldola, of whom Valtesse heartily approved.[33] Mme Meldola, always such a loyal friend, would also prove an exemplary employee.

Valtesse was thrilled with her palatial new home, and her staff. Now, she was the ultimate *Parisienne*. But still, something was missing: no palace is complete without a throne. So, once the house was built, Valtesse immediately commissioned furniture designer Édouard Lièvre to create the most ornate, luxurious bed that her male visitors would ever have laid eyes on.

The huge Renaissance-style bed was modelled on the ceremonial beds used in the medieval period by eminent figures (often royalty) when they received visitors to their bedroom.[34] The bed was made of beech and gilt bronze and was over four metres high. The bedposts at its head extended upwards and supported a large, rectangular canopy that hovered nearly three metres above the head of the bed, atop of which sat a dome covered in luxurious blue fabric. The canopy was decorated with golden vases and intricate floral trellis work, amidst which the letter 'V' could be seen at regular intervals. Valtesse was especially fond of the figure of a faun, which she called her 'crafty little deity'. All around the top of the bed, the creatures' faces smiled down wickedly, unnerving visitors. From the support of the canopy, generous swathes of blue velvet cascaded downwards to form magnificent curtains which fell around the head of the sleeper. The ornate bedhead was topped with a flaming perfume burner. Beneath it, a circular plaque contained a pair of chubby golden cupids standing either side of Valtesse's spectacular coat of arms, in the centre of which was moulded a bold letter 'V'. The bed's circular footboard – a tantalising threshold between Valtesse and her male visitors – was decorated with a chain of flowering thyrsus, while more cherubs, fauns and flaming perfume burners completed the decoration on the bedposts.

Valtesse was elated. 'Is it not a beautifully designed piece of furniture,' she enthused, 'an example of true nobility, such as were found in the ceremonial bedchambers of times gone by, when the levees brought courtiers and supplicants together around a queen's bed?'[35]

The expense shocked even the most extravagant members of Valtesse's entourage. Friends marvelled at 'Valtesse's beautiful bed of many-coloured bronze, that famous bed which cost fifty thousand francs'.[36] This would be equivalent to just over half a million pounds in modern currency. It was an investment Valtesse considered carefully. She took her work seriously. The bed's splendour and imposing form declared, silently yet irrefutably, how she wished to be seen and treated. Valtesse had set out to be worshipped; now she had a throne from which to greet her subjects.

Once a poor linen maid's daughter on the backstreets of Paris, Valtesse had earned herself an elevated social rank, a throne and a palace. All required ongoing maintenance if she did not want to return to squalor. She needed a constant flow of generous subjects. Her craving for power was never satisfied, her passion for beautiful objects smouldered incessantly. Now, she knew exactly which circles to mix in to feed both desires.

CHAPTER 8

The Union of Artists

Since Valtesse first sat as a child watching Corot in his studio, she had been infused with respect and passion for art. Many of her early life lessons were delivered from a painter's perspective. Corot's teachings had shaped the way she perceived the world around her. He had explained the life of a painter, shown her the beauty to be found in nature and taught her the value of art.

As a barmaid, Valtesse had often served artists. They were curious characters, fascinating in their bohemianism. An artist could sit for an entire evening, absentmindedly sipping a single drink while he absorbed every detail of the smoky, bustling surroundings and busily recorded his observations in a sketchbook. Later, Valtesse's debut in the theatre reinforced her contact with painters. They lurked in the shadows of the theatre wings, their hazy silhouettes could be glimpsed sketching energetically in the orchestra pit. It was here that artists like Degas found their greatest inspiration. Courtesans and artists were alike in many respects: a courtesan used her knowledge of society to climb; an artist, to comment. But both had perfected their trade by standing on the fringes of society and observing. Artists were a familiar breed to Valtesse. They were unpredictable, exciting, dangerous – and to Valtesse, their work was compelling.

Now, Valtesse had the means to purchase art of her own. When she saw a painting or a sculpture she admired, it could be hers. To Valtesse, this was unequivocal proof of her success. With money to spend and a handsome *hôtel particulier* to fill, Valtesse set out to capture the bounty of the Parisian art world.

By the 1870s, the Paris art scene was undergoing a radical change. In the face of the archaic conventions that had governed officially sanctioned art for centuries, a controversial group of new artists had burst on to the scene and were challenging the accepted norms of representation. They were young, their ideas radical and their paintings revolutionary. The dull repertoire of uninspiring, distant historical events and myths had ruled for too long; highly finished paint surfaces, flawless physiques and unspoiled landscapes were an outrageous lie. Now was the time, the young painters insisted, to tell the truth, to show contemporary life as it really was.

At the centre of this loose-knit group of artists and writers was a notoriously rebellious painter: Édouard Manet. Manet was 'of medium-size, small rather than large, with light hair, a somewhat pink complexion, a quick and intelligent eye, a mobile mouth, at moments a little mocking'.[1] When he spoke, he was 'overflowing with vivacity, always bringing himself forward, but with a gaiety, an enthusiasm, a hope, a desire to throw light on what was new, which made him very attractive,' remarked a colleague.[2] Around Manet, the atmosphere was electric. Manet was determined to fashion a place on the cultural scene for contemporary life, and his passion was contagious. His goal was soon adopted by the comrades he gathered around him, many of whom would become part of one of the most groundbreaking movements Western art has ever known: Impressionism.

The Paris Salon was the great event of the artistic world in 19th-century France. For months before, painters would be hard at work perfecting canvases, while art enthusiasts talked of nothing else. Meeting the exacting standards of the intrinsically conservative Salon jury and having a piece accepted to the annual exhibition was the ultimate accolade, the goal of every artist aspiring to greatness. It brought the artist public recognition and the reassurance that his career would be secure for the following twelve months.

But suddenly, Manet and his colleagues had turned the art world on its head. The Salon was transformed into a battleground. Paintings became weapons.

Manet was known for ruffling the feathers of the official Salon jury. In 1865, he had rocked the art world by exhibiting his painting of a courtesan, *Olympia*, at the Salon. From her reclining position, Olympia stared out at the viewer confrontationally. She was unashamedly naked, disarmingly self-assured and daringly contemporary. The public hurled abuse in the gallery. The critics were outraged. Her body was filthy, complained one. She was 'neither true nor living nor beautiful', protested another.[3] Worse: she was a courtesan. 'What is this odalisque with a yellow belly, ignoble model picked up who knows where, who represents Olympia? Olympia? What Olympia? A courtesan, no doubt.'[4]

It was just the kind of controversy Valtesse relished. The idea of a common person – a prostitute no less – being elevated to celebrity status appealed to her. It mirrored the trajectory of her own career. Despite his close acquaintance with Manet, Valtesse's great friend, the journalist Richard O'Monroy, objected when she professed herself an admirer of Manet's work. Did she not find Manet's use of the coloured *tâche* disorientating, O'Monroy probed? Had she not observed that his paintings required the viewer to stand back and look through their cupped hand as though it were a spyglass?

Valtesse disliked being challenged on her tastes. She was resolute: she admired Manet's cause.[5] Besides, he was wildly fashionable. The excitement Manet had injected into the 1870s art scene gave it a magnetic pull for her. It was a world brimming with influential figures, new ideas, passion and excitement. An artist could appear from nowhere overnight and soar to the height of fame and fortune – just as Valtesse had. Then one disappointing canvas could bring his career crashing to the ground in an instant, and he would never be heard of again. It was an exhilarating blend of creativity and precarious fortunes. Valtesse longed to be part of it.

However, in her path lay an intractable obstacle. It was long established, woven into the very fabric of French society: the 19th-century art scene was a steadfastly masculine environment. Women artists could display works at the Salon, but their efforts were seldom taken seriously. 'Women have never produced any great masterpieces in any genre,' declared one critic in the 1880s.[6] 'There are no women of genius' was Edmond de Goncourt's view.[7] A woman had one purpose and one purpose alone: to bear and raise children.

In such a society, the female Impressionist painters were caught in a difficult position. A single woman – one who valued her reputation – could not go alone to cafés, bars, restaurants, theatres or walk in the streets. In short, unaccompanied women were excluded from all the venues that formed the mainstay of the Impressionists' repertoire. Artists like Berthe Morisot and Mary Cassatt were obliged to draw subject matter from their immediate surroundings – the domestic environment. They were never shown in the Impressionist group portraits.

Women's position in relation to the official art bodies was scarcely more favourable: there were no women on the Salon jury until 1898, and the prestigious École des Beaux-Arts only accepted its first female student in 1897.[8]

However, there remained one way for a woman to involve herself in the art world and to assert her independence and status: she could become a collector. From Queen Christina of Sweden to Catherine the Great of Russia and, particularly, Empress Josephine, the wife of Valtesse's great hero Napoleon Bonaparte, some of the most powerful women in history had been collectors.[9] So influential was Empress Josephine's patronage that she launched the careers of countless artists, and by the time she died, there were over 3,000 objets d'art (including paintings by old masters and contemporary artists, sculpture, furniture and other decorative objects) held in her collection at Malmaison. Josephine was a woman Valtesse could respect.

Collecting offered a woman like Valtesse a way to empower herself, to claim an identity. The collector must have focus, dedication, negotiating skills and an innate love of the chase – all essentially masculine qualities, currency with value in a male-dominated market. Collecting gave a woman a voice in a world cacophonous with male discourse. The possibility excited Valtesse; she wanted nothing more.

However, she first had to overcome a practical problem: that of how to gain access to the spaces in which artists moved. This was not straightforward. The most exciting artistic gatherings took place in a decidedly male environment: the café.

When the day drew to a close and the fading light made further work impossible, Manet and his friends from the artistic and literary world would patronise Paris's burgeoning café culture. From the end of the 1860s, the artist and his entourage congregated twice a week at their favourite drinking establishment, the Café Guerbois in the Batignoles quarter of Paris, where they had two tables specially reserved.[10] 'Nothing could be more interesting than these *causeries* with their perpetual clash of opinions,' Claude Monet recalled later.[11] The gatherings at the café 'kept our wits sharpened', Monet explained, 'they encouraged us with stores of enthusiasm that for weeks and weeks kept us up, until the final shaping of the idea was accomplished. From them we emerged with a firmer will, with our thoughts clearer and more distinct.'[12]

These were just the kind of lively exchanges of ideas and stimulating discussions that enthused Valtesse. Attending a café unaccompanied posed less of a risk to a *demi-mondaine*'s reputation than it might to that of a bourgeois lady. However, the meetings remained frustratingly inaccessible to Valtesse. Women were systematically excluded from these serious, intellectual debates on the role and function of art. Exclusion of any kind irritated Valtesse. Exclusion of women infuriated her.

Still, Valtesse had learned that direct confrontation was a futile response to sexual injustice. She knew she must work around it. So she followed the example of other self-aware female artists and art lovers. Using her contacts, she secured herself an introduction to another type of event, one even more to her taste: the artist's evening soirée.

Many notable artists, including Manet, hosted regular evening gatherings in their homes or studios in the 19th century. Friends and associates with connections to the art or literary world came together and joined in discussions on the serious matters of painting, politics and literature, as well as the more frivolous areas of society and current gossip. Among the most fashionable private artistic gatherings in the 1870s were the Wednesday evening soirées that the Belgian painter Alfred Stevens and his wife held in their grand home on Rue des Martyrs, just a short carriage ride from Boulevard Malesherbes.[13]

Stevens had made a name for himself with his paintings of fashionable Parisiennes, and his resulting fortune had translated into a beautifully furnished, 300,000-franc *hôtel particulier*. Guests arriving at the Stevenses could be sure of a warm welcome; the couple received cheerfully and spent liberally. Number 65 was the place to be seen, 'the very essence of good taste'.[14] With its fashionable oriental decor and the impressive display of paintings by artists familiar to Valtesse (notably her beloved Corot), Stevens' residence provided the ideal backdrop to inspiring conversations about art and literature. The magnificent view of Stevens' famous garden – an urban oasis with its pond, lush green lawn, tree-lined pathway and unusual, spherical metallic garden sculpture – merely added to the guests' sense of comfort and well-being.

The host's warmth and charm completed the evening. Stevens was a tall, handsome man, with broad shoulders and a fine moustache, which gave him an attractive, Mediterranean appearance. His face conveyed his open and kindly disposition, and with his good looks, sociability and fortune, Stevens and his wife made friends wherever they went.[15]

At a gathering like Stevens', Valtesse could sip champagne and share lively conversations with anyone from the artists Manet and Degas (who was godfather to Stevens' daughter), to the writers Gustave Flaubert, Edmond de Goncourt and Alexandre Dumas fils. In this more private environment, women were welcome; Stevens was an enthusiastic supporter of female artists. Painters like Berthe Morisot and actresses including Sarah Bernhardt appreciated these intimate evenings. They gave bright women the opportunity to participate in the stimulating conversations from which they would otherwise be excluded.

Valtesse adored artists' evening soirées. She attended more and more. As one introduction led to another, she began to expand her social network, befriending artists and meeting influential figures. Valtesse realised that valuable knowledge could be gleaned at these gatherings. She could charm her way to advantageous deals over fine works of art. Her collection began to swell. Best of all, the art scene was teeming with men. They were men of talent, the sort of men typically associated with intrigue and passion. All represented potential acquisitions – and all were potential lovers. In this pool of paintings, money and men, Valtesse saw a marvellous opportunity.

The art community warmed to Valtesse. Though cool and reserved on first acquaintance, she soon demonstrated her ability to work her way around a room effortlessly, talking easily with artists and connoisseurs alike. She proved herself well-read, versant in the current debates and artistic trends, and she knew just what to say and to whom. She had mastered the art of interspersing serious, intellectual conversation with sharp, dry humour. Her quick responses were delivered with a confident smile which lit up her face, emphasising her natural beauty. Her blue eyes sparkled brightly when she told people, laughing, that she did not seek to recreate 'modern style' in her home; she was aiming for 'Valtessestyle'.[16] People could not help but adore her.

Before long, Valtesse made the acquaintance of the landscape painter Antoine Guillemet. Of Normandy extraction and a faithful pupil of Corot, Guillemet had many points of contact with Valtesse. Tall and good-looking, with blue eyes, a square face, light brown hair and a dignified, triangular moustache, Guillemet had posed as the male figure in Manet's *The Balcony* in 1869. The young man found great inspiration in the older painter's work, and his painterly, impasto style bore the imprint of Manet's influence.[17] Vivacious and witty, yet modest and devoted to his friends, Guillemet immediately appealed to Valtesse. He was fond of society, and with his passion for literature, Valtesse found him a stimulating companion. But pleasant diversions aside, he was also a very useful contact. Guillemet's good-natured disposition had won him an impressively wide circle of friends in the literary and artistic spheres. Valtesse was delighted when, through Guillemet, she obtained introductions to even more influential literary and artistic figures.

But Valtesse saw no reason to restrict her affections to one artist. The 19th-century art world positively crackled with power, and Valtesse remained alert, never letting an opportunity pass her by.

It was by moving in these circles that Valtesse's path eventually crossed that of the successful painter of military scenes, Édouard Detaille. Tall and always elegantly dressed in smart, regimental clothes which recalled the figures in his paintings, Detaille, like Valtesse, could come across as reserved and cold to strangers. But those close to him knew differently: Detaille was bright and lively, and admired for his loyalty towards his friends. His attendance at a dinner or evening soirée guaranteed sparkling and engaging conversation, and his grey-green eyes danced playfully when he spoke, his voice quavering slightly. His brown hair and blonde moustache were always well groomed, and his fine features and healthy complexion gave him the advantage of appearing younger than his years.

Detaille's precise and meticulous nature permeated every area of his life. His colleague Gustave Goetschy recalled affectionately: 'Detaille [...] is regularity and punctuality itself [...] De Neuville calls him *The Wisdom of Nations*, and teases him sometimes for being like a housewife.'[18] Detaille's day was regimented down to the last minute. However, time was always made for leisure; the artist loved concerts, balls and the theatre. Fortunately, his circumstances meant that he need never deny himself such pleasures. His family were rich and his paintings sold easily. Financial worries were unknown to him.

Though he lacked Guillemet's impressive literary knowledge, Detaille's success, fortune and dashing appearance made him instantly attractive to Valtesse. For a woman passionate about art and with a soft spot for the military, there could be no better suitor than this smart man who had been a student of the great painter of battlefields, Ernest Meissonier. Detaille needed little persuasion to start a relationship with the charismatic red-haired beauty. He fell deeply, helplessly under her spell.

Valtesse and Detaille began to spend more and more time together. The methodical, self-controlled artist was smitten. By the middle of the 1870s, he had fallen into a pattern of paying Valtesse regular sums of money and visiting her in Ville-d'Avray. He recorded the dates – though never the details – of their encounters in the diary that he kept religiously. His visits to Valtesse (whom he familiarly referred to as 'V') became more frequent, then almost daily. As the visits increased, so did the money disappearing from Detaille's account. It was a formula Valtesse lived by. The artist paid for her coachman, domestic staff and a host of other household expenses.

Detaille's dedication was unwavering, so much so that he became a subject of light-hearted ridicule among his colleagues. Another of Valtesse's close friends, the painter Henri Dupray, delighted in cruel teasing, and urged Valtesse to join him in a practical joke. 'That cheeky so-and-so,' recalled Edmond de Goncourt, 'got Valtesse, Detaille's mistress, to send him a soaking wet shirt, which she claimed in his absence, had become saturated with Dupray's sperm.'[19]

But Detaille's love for Valtesse was impervious to public humiliation. He even painted her. Detaille only ever painted men, military scenes and battlefields, yet for Valtesse, he made an exception. She stands in the front line of the crowd in his great work, *The Passing Regiment* (1875).[20]

The illustrious courtesan and the mild, methodical artist struck some as an odd pairing. However, there was a deep understanding and respect between them. They were the same age, both sociable yet private, passionate while self-controlled. Each had something to offer the other. Valtesse was beautiful, creative and clever, and she allowed Detaille, a man whose entire creative oeuvre was dedicated to men and war, to explore the tenderness of physical love with a woman. For Valtesse's part, besides the money and the status, the power and the pride Detaille gave her, his paintings were sought after. He was pleased to offer his mistress as many works as she desired, and Valtesse contentedly added nearly 50 paintings, drawings and watercolours to her collection. Detaille's dignity touched her own reputation. But most importantly, he treated her with respect and demanded little in return. Of all Valtesse's lovers, Detaille came the closest to understanding the woman behind the myth. Their relationship continued throughout the 1870s.

With his success and reputation established, Detaille needed little assistance in his career. However, while she was seeing Detaille, Valtesse met another painter, one with whom she could play a very different role. In Henri Gervex, Valtesse saw a chance to assume a position of power.

Gervex was younger than Valtesse by four years. With dark features which betrayed his Italian heritage, he was handsome, talented and poised on the threshold of a brilliant career. Born to upper working-class parents, Gervex and his two brothers grew up in Montmartre. In 1871, Gervex was accepted to study under the prestigious academic painter Cabanal at the École des Beaux-Arts, and just three years later he won a medal when he entered his painting *Satyr Playing with a Bacchante* to the 1874 Salon. It was the start of an illustrious career.[21]

But when Gervex and Valtesse first met, the painter was still a relative newcomer on the Parisian art scene. There was much to learn. Paris was brimming with excitement and new experiences, and the young man was eager to sample them all. In 1876, he made the acquaintance of Manet, an artist he greatly esteemed, and Degas, who found the youngster's enthusiasm amusing. Before long, Gervex met a host of other avant-garde painters as well. Henceforward, his work hovered between the academic style learned during his training and the Impressionistic approach of the colleagues around him.

Gervex caught Valtesse's attention. He was young, he was exciting and he was just starting out. Valtesse had grown accustomed to older men with established reputations, and she always softened when she met newcomers trying to make a name for themselves in Paris. Her interest was piqued.

It took little to encourage Gervex to join the list of Valtesse's lovers. He was in his twenties, beguiled by the idea of women, and here before him was a sexually magnetic, clever, well-connected older female who professed herself fascinated by him and his work. Gervex found himself being invited to elegant dinners at Valtesse's home. Seated in an antique mahogany dining chair and surrounded by splendid decor, he was served succulent dishes on gleaming silverware, he tasted fine wines from crystal glasses, and he met powerful individuals, many of whom could offer him commissions. And all the while, he could stare into his mistress's eyes, content in the knowledge that he would soon be alone with her and she in his arms.

If Valtesse had little place among the subjects of Detaille's paintings, Gervex saw sensual compositions whenever he looked at her. To him, she was a vision with her hair tumbling down to her waist as she refastened her corset the morning after a night of passion. He often asked her to pose for him, and she always consented; it flattered her vanity.

Although Gervex and Detaille were the most important of Valtesse's artistic conquests, many other artists passed through the doors of her boudoir during the 1870s. She was enjoying herself. Her relationships with artists added colour and spice to her life; artists were rarely boring lovers. With satisfaction, Valtesse watched her art collection grow.

Now when guests came to visit, in addition to Valtesse's acquisitions from Detaille, Gervex and their friends, they could behold paintings, watercolours, pastels and drawings by artists as renowned as Gustave Courbet and Jean-Auguste-Dominique Ingres. There were works by English painters, established French artists like Eugène Boudin, Gustave Jacquet and Etienne Prosper Berne-Bellecour, as well as up-and-coming ones, including Jean-François Raffaelli and

Ferdinand Roybet. The collection was a perfect mirror of Valtesse's tastes and character. Traditional, academic artists sat alongside avant-garde painters, with whom she sympathised, and whom she wished to support. The former conveyed her elevated status, connoisseurship and wealth; the latter declared her perfectly in touch with contemporary fashion. And there was always the chance that one of those bright young artists would soar to greatness. It was just the kind of thrilling gamble she relished.

Valtesse was once asked why she thought it was that so many great creative talents only achieved recognition posthumously. 'You know,' she smiled in response, 'critics are gourmets and talent is a truffle that they enjoy digging up.'[22] She was determined to stake her claim before the fruit was unearthed.

Valtesse's connections in the art world meant that to her impressive collection of paintings she could add hundreds of costly objets d'art. She collected bronze statues, ceramic vases, plates, silverware, glassware and a host of other exquisite trinkets. Her most prized possession was a tall oval swing mirror (known as a *psyché* in French) in polished maple wood. It was decorated with gilded bronze, there were candleholders on either side, and on top stood a pair of winged statues representing victory. The mirror had been made for the celebrated beauty and star of the Comédie Française, Mlle Mars, and had attracted public attention when it was mentioned in Thiollet and Roux's *Nouveau recueil de menuiserie et décorations intérieures et extérieures* in 1837.[23] When she purchased the mirror, Valtesse knew she was gaining more than a beautiful object; she was buying herself an association with the famous actress, reaping the benefits of another's notoriety.

Valtesse was especially fond of Chinese and Japanese porcelain, and she purchased, and was given, superb examples of both. Few materials declared wealth and status as explicitly as porcelain. Historically, porcelain was revered and costly, and its acquisition consequently remained the prerogative of only the wealthiest aristocratic European families. The fashion for Japanese objects had taken France by storm in the 1860s, and it refused to loosen its grip in the 1870s. Valtesse's *japonaiseries* were a triumphant announcement of her awareness of fashion. However, with her ancient Chinese porcelain, Valtesse conveyed another message. Most of her pieces were the genuine, imported material, not the European imitation of the sought-after, hard-paste clay. They were bought to impress. The pieces were Valtesse's nod to France's aristocratic past, a proud testimony of her wealth and a shameless act of self-glorification.[24]

Valtesse saw her art collection as much more than a diverting hobby. It was a commerce, a business, an industry. She considered her acquisitions carefully. They shaped her identity, they gave her status – and power. Most of all, the collection brought her equality. Her lovers were always benefactors; now, at last, she had become the benefactress.

Valtesse was in her element, and her involvement in the art world did not go unnoticed. Her connections with painters led colleagues to affectionately dub her '*l'Union des artistes*' or 'the Union of Artists'.[25] Her growing collection made her radiant with pride.

Such a powerful addition to her promotional arsenal should not be wasted. She had attended artists' evening soirées and admired their collections; she coveted that glory for herself, and longed for people to be awestruck when they discovered her collection too.

Valtesse decided to start hosting a salon from her home. She made her project known in artistic circles and her venture attracted great interest, prompting contemporaries to liken her to a modern-day Aspasia.[26] From then on, every Monday evening, the rooms of her grand *hôtel particulier* would come alive, with noted individuals engaging in lively debate about painting, society and politics.

And literature. For Valtesse realised that to stand out from other courtesans, this too should form part of her cultural capital.

CHAPTER 9

Words and Wit

Valtesse knew that beauty alone would not sustain public respect. As with a portrait, so for its subject: an attractive surface must be reinforced by integrity within. A courtesan needed to be cultured, and an expansive literary knowledge was essential.

Since Valtesse had first identified the need to educate herself when she began her affair with Offenbach, she had made her own edification a priority. Her childhood had left her hungry to learn. She had a burning desire to read and vast gaps in her knowledge to fill, and her bright mind gave her a natural propensity to flourish under her own self-tutelage.

Her mental faculties impressed her contemporaries. 'She is a woman of unparalleled intelligence,' explained Valtesse's childhood friend, Jules Claretie.[1] Her admirers spotted this immediately. 'She is full of spirit,' declared the journalist Félicien Champsaur. 'To triumph, a woman must have a certain intelligence among her tools of seduction [...] Valtesse already had a rich mind.'[2] Fortunately, besides natural brilliance, Valtesse also boasted a will of iron; she was a diligent student.[3]

With practice, she had learned to write well, in an elegant, cursive style. She took an active interest in current affairs, studying the papers attentively and forming an opinion on the key issues of the day. Above all, she made a point of reading as widely as possible.

Books became her passion. She read voraciously, and the bookshelf in her boudoir reflected the same dichotomy of taste as her art collection. There were works by the classic French authors Montaigne, Rabelais, Saint-Simon and her hero, Balzac, as well as established contemporary writers including Mérimée and Alexandre Dumas fils. Valtesse was passionate about history and philosophy, and she pored over the writings of Voltaire, Michelet and Guizot. She became as versant in the works of Shakespeare and the Bible as she was in the rollicking, risqué, popular fiction of Paul de Kock.

Strong, independent women earned Valtesse's particular respect. Feminine literature had declined after 1830, but from mid-century, a wave of female authors flooded the market in an effort to forge women a place on France's literary scene.[4] However, like female artists, women writers struggled to be taken seriously. Science reinforced dominant conservative views of women, promoting the theory that females were anatomically and physiologically inferior to men.[5] It was argued that their brains were smaller, that they were intellectually deficient, and therefore emotional, sentimental and naturally predisposed to bear and raise children. Beware the woman who developed her intellectual abilities, warned conservative scientific discourse; her ability to breed would surely be impaired. Should women manifest signs of advanced intellect, 'it is by some trick of nature', concluded Edmond de Goncourt, 'in the sense that they *are men*'.[6]

Misogyny disgusted Valtesse. The independently minded, trouser-wearing George Sand claimed a revered place on her bookshelf. 'I know that my own greatest fault lies in the fact that I *cannot* submit to the least shadow of constraint,' Sand wrote.[7] 'It is liberty that I long for. I want to be able to walk out quite alone and say to myself: "I will dine at four, or seven, just as I like".' How Valtesse knew that longing. It was what drove her.

She studied the memoirs of the great courtesan Céleste Mogador with keen interest.[8] The veteran *femme galante* had invaluable advice to impart. 'I always thought that, even when a woman is wicked, it is to her advantage to seek the company of cultivated men,' Mogador reasoned.[9] 'I quickly realised that gallantry is like war; to win one must employ tactics [...] The men who obtained the most from me were the ones who demanded the least.'[10] They were wise words. Valtesse herself could have written them.

Valtesse's library gave her a complete education. She followed no structure in her choice of volumes, but prized the quantity and variety of reading matter over all else. The breadth of knowledge she acquired astounded her acquaintances.

Valtesse developed informed opinions on everything she read, and she gladly shared her views. Close friends marvelled at her ability to focus exclusively on a philosophical debate or discussion when conversation took that course. She was, one companion remarked, 'sensual and intelligent, making a distinct separation in her life between the pleasures of the body and those of the mind'.[11] In Valtesse's eyes, the salon was for intellectual sparring, the bedroom for physical pleasure. A lover might have his way with her body, but he could never alter her opinions.

Valtesse's expansive literary knowledge was showcased whenever she attended a soirée or salon. The artistic and literary spheres were intricately entwined, and the more Valtesse circulated with artists, the more writers she met.

By the middle of the 1870s, she had formed an acquaintance with the journalist, art critic, novelist and playwright, Octave Mirbeau. Born the same year as Valtesse, Mirbeau was raised in Normandy, supported the Bonapartist cause and was committed to civil matters; he and Valtesse had much in common. They also shared a close acquaintance, the actress-turned-courtesan Alice Regnault.

Alice was notorious. Augustine-Alexandrine Toulet (as she was originally named) was said to have murdered her first husband, and by the 1870s she was using her beauty to ruin a chain of wealthy men. It was even rumoured that she was guilty of the ultimate 19th-century taboo: lesbianism. 'She is a very dangerous woman for men smitten with her charms,' warned the police, 'they say she is capable of committing the most heinous crimes provided there is money involved.'[12]

Valtesse and Alice had many shared experiences. At one of Arsène Houssaye's private parties at the end of February in 1875, the two women appeared together in matching outfits, an alluring masquerade costume known as a 'domino', which comprised a hooded dress and a mask.[13] Mirbeau too was drawn to Alice; just a few years later, he would marry her in secret. But in the 1870s, the spell Valtesse cast was all-consuming.

Mirbeau found Valtesse irresistible. As they became more intimate, the writer's devotion intensified. When he spotted an article in a Belgian publication which mentioned Valtesse, he immediately wrote to her, promising to copy it out 'religiously'.[14] Mirbeau quickly recognised that Valtesse appreciated witty, dedicated men. 'I am sending two copies of this letter,' he wrote on another occasion, 'as one does an agreement of sale or a marriage contract … Would you oblige me with a little kiss? A good friendly kiss …?'.[15]

Valtesse remained reserved where her association with Mirbeau was concerned. He was not the only writer in Paris, and he was certainly not the greatest.

By far Valtesse's proudest encounter was her meeting with the celebrated author, Alexandre Dumas fils. Son of the great Dumas père, the younger Dumas initially turned to writing to pay off his debts, and he found fame in 1848 with *The Lady of the Camellias*.

With his skill as a playwright, he rose to become one of the most successful dramatists of the Second Empire.

Valtesse was a passionate admirer of Dumas's work. *The Lady of the Camellias* was published in the year of her birth. She had grown up with Dumas, so she was thrilled when her first meeting with the literary star developed into a written correspondence. To Dumas, who found the feminine mind endlessly fascinating, the erudite, red-haired beauty was an enigma just begging to be resolved. He must understand her – but Valtesse thrived on mystery. Dumas relished the deciding word, but Valtesse was adamant that she should have the last. The pair became locked in a stalemate. Like partners in an intense dance, they appeared to move together, while each focusing single-mindedly on a personal battle for power. Neither would back down.

Valtesse was both honoured and vainglorious when Dumas paid a visit to her home.[16] She willingly obliged him with a tour of the property. With Valtesse leading the way, Dumas passed from room to room, smiling politely as he listened to the descriptions of the paintings, admiring the furniture, and taking in the luxury and good taste of the surroundings. Then, when the tour concluded, he turned to his hostess: 'Now, all that remains to be seen is the most interesting bit.'

'And what would that be?' Valtesse enquired.

'The bedroom!'

Valtesse's blue eyes flashed and her lips broke into a smile. 'That, dear master, no!' she riposted. 'You could not possibly afford it!'

An account of the meeting spread rapidly, prompting smiles in literary circles. Valtesse's quick wit and self-confidence in spite of Dumas's celebrity status won her admirers.

Though novelists were important, Valtesse knew the power journalists exerted in the 19th century. They had played a central role in bringing about the falls of government in 1830 and

1848.[17] The press were a redoubtable force, and the relationship between newspaper owners, journalists and readers involved a complex game of shifting power. Collectively, the press could destroy a reputation. But used wisely, they could also propel a person's career beyond their wildest dreams. It was a spectacularly corrupt world. Journalists were a group to make your allies. Fortunately, charming intellectual men was Valtesse's speciality.

With his military background, quick humour and smart moustache, the journalist and novelist Richard O'Monroy boasted many of the attributes Valtesse admired in a man. Above all, O'Monroy proved himself a loyal friend. He was a regular visitor to Valtesse's home, and the pair could often be found talking animatedly, sharing views on subjects ranging from art and society to foreign politics. Valtesse found the journalist's company diverting; O'Monroy's regard ran deeper. When he teased her about her penchant for tall, blonde, military men, calling her 'Altesse de la Ligne' (Princess of the Infantry), his jibes were a paltry disguise for his profound attraction. A regular contributor to *La Vie parisienne* and *Gil Blas*, O'Monroy dedicated countless articles to Valtesse. He eulogised her intellect, her lustrous hair, her delightfully small breasts and her petite waist. The expression of surprise she wore whenever she greeted him was enchanting, it gave her face a naive, mysterious appearance. Her impassioned views, expressed so eloquently, endeared her to O'Monroy. At times, his interest bordered on obsession. One of his articles compiled an inventory of Valtesse's intimate measurements.[18] He recorded:

> Wrist circumference – 12cm
> Neck circumference – 24cm
> Waist circumference – 48cm
> Thigh circumference (upper) – 56cm
> (lower) – 46cm

Calf circumference – 36cm
Ankle circumference – 19cm
Chest circumference – 57cm

Readers could be in no doubt of O'Monroy's message. It was a triumphant territorial marker: a person would need to be close to Valtesse to acquire such detail. They would need to be very close.

Félicien Champsaur was another prolific journalist Valtesse always made time to see. Champsaur wrote for some of the leading papers, including *Le Figaro*, *Le Gaulois* and *L'Événement*. A familiar face in literary circles, Champsaur was a keen patron of the lively brasseries in the Montmartre district of Paris, where the most exciting meetings of literary minds took place. He revelled in Paris's vibrant social life and its diverse art scene, and he was well acquainted with the most influential literary figures of the day. Valtesse saw him as a valuable contact. It was important he adore her.

Champsaur rose to Valtesse's bait. He could not find enough words to praise her. To Valtesse's satisfaction, his admiration found an outlet in the press. Where prose failed him, Champsaur turned to poetry:

Sleep, will you take me? … I cannot … I will not
Sleep … Red golden blonde, my crying memory
sees her again this morning and, like an unsettling dream
in my kiss-starved night, her hair shines.[19]

And:

How undulating the beauty's hair
like a harvest's golden sheaf.
A poor man, a gallivanter's countess,
with her rosy lips and her wild eyes.[20]

Champsaur knew how to flatter the 'Golden Haired Beauty' of his verses. He was a useful man to know. However, few men of letters were as well-placed as Arsène Houssaye when it came to assisting a celebrity in their career. A novelist, editor, poet, playwright and literary and art critic, Houssaye had also managed the Théâtre Français for nearly ten years. His satirical *Tale of the 41st Chair at the Académie Française* (1855) typified his dry wit, and with his flowing beard and furrowed brow he looked every bit the intellectual.[21] 'Tell me what you love, and I will tell you who you are,' Houssaye famously declared. His wisdom impressed Valtesse, and his connections and authority made his acquaintance priceless.

'In the gallery of pretty and gallant ladies of the 19th century,' Houssaye affirmed, 'Valtesse is one of the most ravishing, the most delicious, the most ingenious, the most vicious, the most kind, the most tender, the most brutal, the most bewitching, the most adorable.'[22]

Such public tributes were invaluable. Valtesse knew that journalists were her lifeline.

Contemporary cynics often joked that adultery parodied marriage; and, like a stealthy wife, Valtesse had learned that men responded well to praise and recognition. It made them want to please again. She was careful that journalists were left eager to promote her. For that, they needed to see that there were the rewards to be earned.

In her accounts, Valtesse grouped together men whom she considered useful, classing them in a special category. These men could take advantage of her usual services, with one significant difference: she would waive the fee. Investments like O'Monroy and Champsaur soon paid for themselves.

Such men were also warmly welcomed to her Monday evening salon. Every week, Valtesse enjoyed opening the doors of 98, Boulevard Malesherbes to a host of journalists, writers, theatrical impresarios, artists and their associates. Against the luxurious backdrop of rich tapestries and paintings, guests sipped sherry from fine crystal glasses, while ideas and opinions on art, literature, politics and society were shared and considered. And while the company pondered the latest literary or artistic debate, Valtesse's attentive staff weaved their way between the visitors, seeing to it that every need was catered for.

The footman, Schwabb, was in place to greet guests as they alighted from their carriages. Then, assisted by Valtesse's maid, he ensured that no visitor was in want of refreshment as they admired the grand salon, or smiled at the suggestive stained-glass window Valtesse had had installed, which depicted Napoleon III visiting her boudoir. Meanwhile, the cook saw to it that the canapés never failed to meet the mistress's exacting standards. As voices hummed and glasses clinked, the staff moved about silently, each performing his or her role to perfection. And overseeing the entire operation was Valtesse's most trusted employee: her childhood friend, Camille, Mme Meldola.

Meldola's sturdy frame shuffled to and fro, slowly but surely, methodically ensuring that the household ran like clockwork. She understood her mistress's feelings and desires better than anyone, and could anticipate her slightest need. She made sure that Valtesse had no cause for complaint.

Valtesse was desperately fond of Meldola. She knew that her friend's role was not easy. It involved thinking ahead, knowing when to speak and when not. The housekeeper needed to vet the men arriving to visit her mistress. She must be ready with an excuse if Valtesse felt disinclined to see a particular suitor. And under no circumstances should the Comtesse's lovers be allowed to meet. Meldola's job demanded a fine balance of wit, foresight and a supremely unflappable nature. The housekeeper met and exceeded the criteria. Like an actress and her agent, Valtesse and Meldola formed an indomitable team. Between them, the courtesan's career was managed perfectly.

With Meldola choreographing the logistics, Valtesse adored her evening salons with their intellectual and literary discussions. Her avid reading had shown her that language could be a formidable tool, and socialising with intellectuals gave her the chance to use it. As her linguistic eloquence grew, she discovered she could manipulate words to promote or defend herself. She could destroy an adversary and be cruel when necessary. Words gave her the upper hand she had always sought.

Valtesse found language at its most empowering when she used humour and repartee. It conveyed her intellect and self-assurance. People marvelled at the Comtesse de la Bigne's sharp wit, and she was proud when it became a trademark.

A male acquaintance recalled one of his meetings with Valtesse with admiration. A self-satisfied actress from the Variétés was hosting a housewarming party, to which Valtesse was invited. At length, the hostess, whose own fortune had suspicious origins, began to criticise cheap-looking young women with seemingly no connections. Valtesse quickly silenced the speaker: 'Come now Amélie, these good ladies and gentlemen know very well that had we not been so fortunate, you and I would both be on the streets.'[23]

On another occasion, *Le Figaro* published an article that made a snide allusion to the colour of Valtesse's hair and her political opinions. Annoyed, Valtesse immediately penned a response to her assailant:

Dear Sir,

The impolite manner in which you address me should absolve me of the need to reply. However, since you take pleasure in insulting the two things that I hold most dear – my opinions and my hair – I shall reply to you as follows:

As for the political angle you believe me to have, if I am to judge by the eloquence of your attack, you are far more advanced than myself in the matter. As for my hair, which you find too red, do you not think it might be the same optical illusion that makes the grapes appear too green to the fox?

My compliments,
Valtesse

Friends recounted another anecdote which caused endless amusement. One day, a sojourn took Valtesse to the French border. When an official stopped her and enquired as to her profession, she turned to him with perfect composure and replied: 'Courtesan. And be so good as to tell the man following me, who seems not to be aware.'[24]

Valtesse's quick-witted responses were the fruit of perfect self-assurance. She was proud of her profession and the position she had reached. 'I am a courtesan,' she announced, 'and how I do enjoy my work.'[25] When invited to a gathering at Detaille's, she had no hesitation when asked to sign the guests' book: 'Valtesse de la Bigne: Lady of Letters,' she wrote.[26]

Few circumstances fazed her. She treated elegant society with the same cool reserve she might a common streetwalker, and she believed herself perfectly entitled to join their number as an equal. People could not help but admire her spirit and aplomb.

The more she read, and learned, and debated, the more Valtesse was impressed by the power of words. Privately, she marvelled at the way her contacts in the press manipulated words to shape her public persona. With delight, she watched people's reactions when her use of language showcased her knowledge and bright mind. When she attended salons and soirées, Valtesse saw writers encircled by swarms of admirers. They were revered, celebrated. She imagined how satisfying that must be.

With the linguistic eloquence she had acquired, Valtesse felt confident that she too could write and be published. So she made up her mind to write a book. It would be based on a topic about which she felt passionately and knew much: herself.

When Valtesse set to work, the field of life writing was changing. The volume of autobiographical works increased markedly in the 19th century as writers began experimenting with new forms of the genre. As literacy increased and the reading public grew, more and more authors turned their hand to autobiography. In the circles Valtesse frequented, the autobiographical and semi-autobiographical novel had become wildly fashionable. From Alexandre Dumas père to George Sand, and not forgetting Céleste Mogador, men – and, excitingly, women – of all classes were publishing works based on their lives. Mogador's memoirs had particularly struck Valtesse. The volume gave the courtesan a chance to respond to her public's perception of her. With her memoirs, Mogador had seized control.

Valtesse sensed an irresistible opportunity. Not only would writing a book earn respect and provide an outlet for her creativity, it was a chance to shape her public image. She could dispel the myths she disliked and encourage those she approved. There was another benefit, too. With her humble beginnings, her broken love affair, Fossey's return to France and her daughter's death, Valtesse's public success masked an undercurrent of personal tragedy; perhaps there was a form of therapy to be drawn from committing her experiences to paper. Gathering her thoughts, Valtesse began to write.

Isola told the tale of the beautiful, free-spirited courtesan, Isola de Freder, for whom men would fall, but whose heart resisted their affection.[27]

She had strange hair, it was red, but a very particular shade of red, in which a thousand gold sequins seemed to sparkle. Her hair was dazzling, and the long yellow and amber tortoiseshell pins could barely hold it up. Some rebellious curls escaped, caressing her temples and her neck. Seeing her like this, with a serious brow, a fine mouth, her eyes hidden beneath her heavy eyelids, one felt an overwhelming desire to approach her, to get her to speak, to assure yourself that she was a woman and not a statue.[28]

Isola is kept by a rich prince who is subject to her stringent conditions: they must never be seen out together and she will not tolerate his jealousy. Isola prizes her freedom.

One evening, there is the premiere of a new show at the Théâtre des Variétés. With experience and finesse, Valtesse describes the social battlefield of the auditorium, with its elegant ladies and its rich men.[29] During the interval, Isola is spotted by a young Breton man, Horace de Kerhouët. He is instantly smitten. Other men warn him off Isola. She is, he is told, 'a panther disguised as a woman'.[30] The men elaborate:

If she is in good humour, Isola is the most charming woman I know, friendly, cheerful, spiritual, with exquisite grace, all the grand airs of a duchess at an orgy, not at all ordinary, and a woman one leaves only reluctantly. But if by any chance a shadow falls across the beauty's soul, everyone is barred, and it is best to leave, because he who forces the door will find himself in the company of a loathsome, gloomy, sad, disagreeable, caustic woman, as sour-tempered as a usurer before a judiciary council.[31]

Isola is sly and full of 'implacable meanness', Horace is told.[32] 'She has but one accomplice: her immense pride; but one aim, one passion; herself, herself alone, always herself!'[33] But Horace is undeterred. He obtains an invitation to Isola's home, an opulent, sumptuously furnished apartment. When the mistress greets him, the golden key to her private desk around her neck, he finds her to be icy, fiercely determined – and irresistible. He becomes infatuated. Isola tells him about her terrible childhood, and shocks him with her radical opinions on philosophy and literature. Eventually, Isola banishes Horace, telling him it is for his own good, and, reluctantly, he returns to his family home to marry a girl from a respectable family. But he continues writing to Isola and she to him. Before long, Horace learns that Isola is ill. He goes to see her, and finds her dying of consumption, the fashionable illness that claimed the life of Marguerite Gautier in Dumas's *The Lady of the Camellias*. Isola finally admits that she loves Horace before dying the tragic death of a heroine.

When the last line was written and Valtesse felt satisfied with the plot and style, she deposited her manuscript with the acclaimed publishing house, Dentu. Valtesse was not a woman to refuse lightly; the editor agreed to publish. But there remained one important decision: how did she wish her name to appear? Valtesse considered the matter. A little mystery was always an advantage. Still, however, the book had valuable promotional potential. It should not be wasted. Then Valtesse realised she could satisfy both needs: the author would be Ego.

The cold monotony of February was broken that year as Valtesse waited expectantly to discover how her novel would be received – and how quickly the public would identify her as its author. She did not have long to wait.

Thanks to the promotional skills of her contacts in the press, the book generated a wave of interest before it was even released. 'Dentu has just published a little Parisian volume, which we believe is destined for great success,' announced *Le Figaro*.[34] 'It is entitled *Isola*, and it is by an anonymous author, but judging by the style and the spicy revelations, one can detect the hand of a pretty woman who is very much au courant with the fashionable secrets of Parisian high life.' The next day, an odd message appeared in the paper's personal column: 'Marquise – read *Isola*, which has just been published by Dentu, you will recognise the portrait of an actress from the Variétés [*sic*] – Robert.'[35] News of *Isola* was reaching all categories of reader.

Valtesse's diverse marketing strategies reaped immediate benefits: curious Parisians hurried out to purchase a copy of *Isola*. It was a fiction, but all those who knew Valtesse could testify to its autobiographical quality. Jules Claretie vouched for the resemblance between author and heroine: Ego could only be Valtesse. Valtesse had 'incarnated herself as the heroine of a novel she wrote to confess a little, to share her intimate thoughts', explained Claretie.[36] Like so many women, Valtesse needed people to understand that she was not like the others, her friend added. But Claretie's confirmation was unnecessary. Valtesse had long been using the epithet 'Ego'. It was embossed on her stationery, it adorned her home. *Isola*'s author was soon identified.

'I have just read a curious book: *Isola*, by a new writer who signs herself Ego,' wrote a sly Albert Wolff. 'It is the literary debut of a beautiful woman who bears an uncanny resemblance to Mlle Valtesse, a former actress in the days before she was dining out at Bignon's.'[37] Other reviewers followed Wolff's lead, pouncing on the similarities between author and heroine. 'It is Mlle Valtesse described by Mlle Valtesse,' declared one critic. 'Have you noticed how, whenever women speak of themselves, they most want to say that they are strange, bizarre?'[38] Criticisms of the book were overlooked, the flaws were far outweighed by 'spicy details, a fair bit of spirit […] and even some heart' in what was clearly an 'autobiography of a pleasant person'.[39] Albert Wolff was decided: '*Isola*, my dear, is not a book: it is a prospectus.'[40]

Parisians needed little convincing from the critics: *Isola* was a confession of Valtesse's most intimate thoughts, and judging by her colourful existence, there were bound to be scandalous revelations. Scrupulous readers combed the novel's pages for gossip and titillating disclosures as to the identity of the real courtesan's amorous conquests.

Valtesse was amused. Parisians were sorely mistaken if they thought her capable of sabotaging her most valuable asset – her mystery. Valtesse's discretion prevailed, and appetites were whetted but never satisfied.

But pre-empting the public's assumption that she had modelled Isola on herself, Valtesse used the novel to highlight her proudest features, justify her behaviour, and fuel the enigma that surrounded her. Most importantly, the novel broadcasted her intelligence. Isola's bright mind was immediately attributed to Valtesse: 'She had an ardent thirst for knowledge. The unknown, the marvellous attracted her. She would get frustrated when she did not understand something, filled with furious hatred [...] She constantly asked questions.'[41]

Just as Valtesse had hoped, the novel caused a stir and reinforced her public image. But for critics, the greatest surprise of all was the writing; it was good. Could she really have written it herself, people wondered? At first, the author of the minor literary work *Mémoires d'un décavé*, M. Fervacques, was suspected of having ghosted the novel, but to Valtesse's relief, the myth was soon dispelled. The skill was all Valtesse's own. 'She writes very well,' approved one critic.[42] 'She is a good-hearted young lady, not at all foolish,' commended Albert Wolff. 'She is one of the rare young Parisian ladies whose fast-paced lifestyle has not turned her into a perfect floozy.' Coming from Wolff, that was praise indeed. Valtesse was thrilled when Wolff's article earned her yet another nickname: the '*Sévigné des cabinets particuliers*' or 'Sévigné of private dining rooms', after the 17th-century female literary icon, Mme de Sévigné. It was a triumph.

After a flurry of excitement, the hype surrounding *Isola* died down quickly. Still, for a time, Valtesse basked in the increased attention. The novel also steered her towards yet more celebrated authors, not least Guy de Maupassant, who became a firm friend and a fascinating dinner companion. Conversation was never dull.

Nonetheless, discussion in fashionable salons inevitably followed the ebb and flow of taste. Interest soon turned to the next new novel on the market. In 1877, the year after *Isola*, Valtesse began hearing another, more established author's name. Soon, people could speak of no one else. The writer had just published a scandalous new work. It was going to revolutionise literature as people knew it. It was daring, it was shocking and it rocked Paris. How could the feat be repeated, wondered Paris's literati? Valtesse listened intently. The author was Émile Zola. The novel was *L'Assommoir*. And even before the hype had dissipated, Zola had begun planning his next landmark novel. His new book would affect Valtesse more directly. *Isola* would not be the last time she revelled in the literary spotlight: Valtesse was about to become the star of Zola's next masterpiece.

CHAPTER 10

Valtesse and Zola's *Nana*

By the end of the 1870s, Valtesse had become one of the most talked-about women on the Parisian social circuit. With her high-profile lovers, her beauty, wit, luxurious lifestyle and now the publication of *Isola*, in her late 20s, Valtesse was enjoying all the attention of a royal celebrity. Barely a week passed when her activities were not reported in the papers.

At the Opéra-Comique ball in March 1878, Valtesse made the front page of *Le Gaulois*, which dedicated a full paragraph to describing her dress, a sumptuous gown of white satin with lace sleeves, covered in turquoise net and trimmed with ribbons and Spanish lace, a tambourine giving the finishing touch to her costume.[1] A few weeks later, she was spotted at the Théâtre de l'Ambigu, perfectly at ease in the company of the celebrated author Victor Hugo and the darling of Paris's theatre scene, the actress Sarah Bernhardt.[2]

Valtesse had become an expert in using the media to her advantage. She ensured that she was seen at all the fashionable premieres, balls, dinners, soirées and concerts. She paid scrupulous attention to her appearance, and her wardrobe was constantly updated. Her dresses were ordered from the Empress Eugénie's sought-after tailor, Charles Worth. Her brooches were fashioned by Paris's most revered jewellers. Her pearls were among the finest specimens imported from the Far East. Even her choice of friends was closely vetted so that she would be shown to her advantage; she was invariably accompanied by a brunette (a suitable contrast to her red and gold locks) such as Gabrielle Dupuy or Léontine Miroy, fellow socialites whose moderate prettiness posed no threat to her own mesmerising beauty.

With her media exposure, Valtesse could hardly escape the attention of such a keen-eyed observer of society as the author Émile Zola. Indeed, by 1878, Zola's colleague, the novelist Léon Hennique, could make a passing reference to Valtesse using only her first name when he wrote to Zola, testimony that she had achieved the ultimate celebrity status.[3] As it happened, the courtesan and the novelist moved in similar circles and shared a number of acquaintances, including Gervex and, more particularly, Offenbach, Valtesse's former lover, who had often been the victim of Zola's critical pen.[4] They were both avid fans of the fashionable restaurant Bignon too, even if the reasons for their patronage differed: Valtesse went to be seen, Zola to satisfy his hearty appetite.

In 1878, Zola was furiously busy. He had just embarked on the most thrilling stage of writing: he was beginning a new novel. His focus was entirely absorbed. His latest work was to form part of his epic 'Rougon-Macquart' series, a multi-volume project subtitled 'The Natural and Social History of a Family Under the Second Empire'.[5] Zola was excited. The new novel would tell the tale of a beautiful young courtesan who held Parisian society spellbound and would eventually cause their ruin. Capitalising on the resounding success of *L'Assommoir* (1877), Zola planned to resume the story of Nana, the precocious young daughter of a pair of alcoholic parents, whom readers had met in his earlier novel.

In *L'Assommoir*, Zola had depicted the teenage Nana as a cheeky little miss and a determined flirt, who was sexually mature and whose irresistible beauty helped her survive on the street, where she won countless male admirers. Accepting gifts and treats, she could already see a route out of her impoverished surroundings. In the novel Zola was about to devote to her, he would plot Nana's continued ascent. Now an adult, she would use her looks and sexual charisma to win a role in the theatre, despite being utterly devoid of talent. Nana would cast a spell, reducing men from all levels of society to biddable servants, slaves to her slightest whim, with just a sway of her shapely hips or a flick of her long golden hair. Though essentially good-hearted, Nana would prove herself unscrupulous, even ruthless, when she had set her heart on something. She would ruin marriages and devour fortunes, making vice her profession and pleasure her master. Nana would be the very embodiment of the corruptive forces that Zola believed were rotting society from within. He had every hope that her story would inspire a similar response to *L'Assommoir*.

But in his dogmatic attachment to his plot, Zola had fashioned himself a complex creative challenge: he knew nothing of the *demi-monde*. Valtesse's world was strange and unfamiliar to him. He had heard stories, yes. He had often whiled away an evening in the company of his fellow writers, listening solemnly as they told tales of women, of dubious cafés and bars and sordid encounters. Wide-eyed, he had heard Guy de Maupassant and Gustave Flaubert chuckling as they shared colourful anecdotes of their own amorous conquests. The puritanical Zola had publicly expressed his disgust for poorly written tales of the *demi-monde*. They seemed to him crafted expressly to titillate youths. He longed to read 'the true story of the *demi-monde*' – 'if,' he conceded, 'anyone should ever dare write such a thing'.[6] With *Nana*, Zola set out to embrace his own challenge.

From the outset, Zola was determined that his novel should be different. As a journalist, he was automatically exposed to the gossip that circulated about renowned courtesans like Blanche d'Antigny and Cora Pearl. But the novelist had never encountered such women, nor frequented the places of which his more worldly literary colleagues spoke with such authority. For *Nana* to be a success, he needed accurate research material. So early in 1878, while Valtesse's attention was absorbed with balls and suppers and elegant soirées, Zola's quest began.

With his characteristically meticulous approach to research, Zola began to interrogate his closest associates to see who could shed light on to this unknown and curious world. 'Tell me, Paul,' journalist Paul Alexis recalled Zola asking, 'how does one pay a street woman? Does one settle the bill before or after?'[7] His naivety aroused sniggers and condescending looks. But passion came before pride, and his candidness reaped rewards: all sorts of tales and gossip on some of the leading courtesans of the day began to emerge. He listened attentively, his pen moving frantically as he took copious notes.

By chance, Flaubert's friend Edmond Laporte turned out to be something of an expert in such matters. He imparted a wealth of tantalising detail on the routine and habits of courtesans such as Valtesse's acquaintance Alice Regnault and Caroline Letessier. A courtesan would rise and take a bath scented with cologne while her hairdresser tended to her locks, Zola was told. She would be joined by a lover for lunch, after which she would take a nap before her afternoon promenade. Dinner and society were the order of the evening. The night – well, the night was limited only by the bounds of the imagination.[8] His mind racing, Zola noted every detail.

Novelist Henri Céard (in whose company Zola would spend many a pleasant evening in the town of Médan following his purchase of a property there that May), also had pearls of wisdom to impart. Flaubert and Arsène Houssaye came to the inexperienced novelist's aid with the names of several female contacts who could prove useful. And Alexis shared fascinating insights on lesbian activity in Paris.

But the most useful contact proved to be fellow writer and satirist Ludovic Halévy, who had made a name for himself as Offenbach's librettist, and whom Valtesse also knew well. Through Halévy, Zola won the invaluable opportunity to view actress Hortense Schneider's dressing room at the Théâtre des Variétés, where the fictional Nana would make her theatre debut. Schneider's much-discussed affair with the Prince of Wales, the future King Edward VII, provided rich material for a spicy subplot in the form of Nana's affair with the Prince of Scotland. Halévy also arranged for Zola to visit the actress Anna Judic. The primary motivation for Zola's visit was to convince Judic (ultimately unsuccessfully) to take the role of his anti-heroine Gervaise, Nana's mother, in a stage version of *L'Assommoir*. Even so, *Nana* was at the forefront of his creative mind when he accompanied Halévy to the Variétés at the end of April. He used his encounter with Judic to create Rose Mignon, Nana's rival.[9]

As 1878 unfolded, Zola's notebook began to swell. He could start to feel satisfied with his research. Visits and collated gossip were amassing to produce a pleasing dossier of material. However, too much of his research material was coming second- or even third-hand. He needed to meet one of these women in her own environment, to smell her perfume, to watch how she held herself, to scrutinise her character and to understand her innermost thought processes. And there was a further area in which Zola knew his research was painfully sparse: he sorely needed material to embellish and authenticate his description of the opulent apartment Nana would move into when she reached the height of her fame.

How could he access this vital information? Who could he meet? Once again, his friends came to his rescue. One woman, he learned, could fulfil all these requirements.

It was Halévy who first spoke enthusiastically to Zola about Valtesse. He eulogised the charms of this captivating redhead, with her milky white complexion, her piercing blue eyes, her perfectly straight nose, her sharp wit, her literary talents, her fabulous apartment and the spectacular bed she had had commissioned. Zola was eager to know more. This woman was said to be 'naturally beautiful, effortlessly spiritual, an artist with no formal training', being able to 'paint, write and play the piano quite naturally, having no tutor beside her own willpower'.[10] This mysterious comtesse, Zola learned, prided herself on being 'able to transform the first lover who came along into a docile slave with a mere click of her fingers'.[11] Zola was fascinated. He had to know more.

So Halévy recounted an anecdote. One day, Valtesse was caught by one of her highest paying lovers in the arms of a penniless young man. The rich suitor was furious. Stunned, Valtesse declared his reaction preposterous. Surely her predicament was clear: the young man's poverty made it impossible to refuse his request.[12] The story tickled Zola. Such a quick and spirited response appealed to his dry sense of humour. It was decided: he simply had to meet this woman.

With his curiosity piqued and his hunger for accuracy driving him, Zola implored Léon Hennique to arrange an introduction.[13] Hennique was a great friend of Valtesse's. He would surely be able to engineer a meeting. As Zola waited for a response, a perusal of *Isola* would be wise preparation. It might even prove a source of ideas (few of Zola's contemporaries would spot the striking similarity between the opening scene of *Nana* at the Théâtre des Variétés and the first chapter of Valtesse's earlier novel).

Valtesse knew that her ability to engage in intelligent, well-informed conversation gave her the edge over women deemed merely 'pretty'. Together, intellectual capital and beauty provided the key to her security. And there was always more to learn; her knowledge must continue to expand. Her self-education was an ongoing project that required her to read as often and as widely as possible. Despite that, Valtesse had never considered Zola's novels a necessary part of her education. His books had no place on her shelf.

Nonetheless, when Valtesse learned of Zola's desire to meet her, she could not help but be impressed. Zola was one of the leading French novelists of the day. He was a literary celebrity. Valtesse's quick mind and ironic sense of humour drew her towards those who exhibited the same. Zola had made a name for himself with just the kind of devastating critiques which entertained her. And quietly, secretly, Valtesse glowed with the flattery of Zola's interest.

Valtesse's media profile was of the utmost importance to her. Here was the chance to become the star of the famed novelist's next work. She could flaunt her wealth and her tastefully furnished home, yet remain shielded behind the protective veil of fiction. She could enjoy all the attention without having to reveal too much of herself, and so tease her public's curiosity. It was an irresistible opportunity. She promptly agreed to Zola's request, and dispatched a formal invitation to Hennique and Zola to attend a supper at her apartment, to which Gervex and the artist Dupray, as well as her lawyer friends Émile Strauss and Lucien Jullemier, were also cordially invited.

Zola could not have hoped for a more favourable response. The evening would provide rich material on which to base Nana's luxurious home, the dinner party he intended her to host there and most importantly, her bed. It was a thrilling prospect.

Valtesse was renowned for her perfectly choreographed dinners, where carefully selected dishes were presented on Oriental porcelain and silverware and accompanied by expensive wines served in her prized Venetian glass carafes. The dinner designed to greet Zola demanded her usual degree of care and dedication. But the cook would have to be given especially meticulous instructions: Zola was a notorious gastronome. Everyone knew that this novelist could eat for three men. When abroad, it was the food Zola complained about most bitterly. 'God sent us food,' he grumbled to his publisher, 'but the devil invented English cooks.'[14] Certainly, this dinner required careful planning. The novelist must leave with the best possible impression – Valtesse's reputation depended on it.

So it was that one evening in 1878, Zola's carriage drew up outside 98, Boulevard Malesherbes and its passenger stepped out into the courtyard, as he prepared to dine with one of the most celebrated courtesans in Paris. Following the footman up to the salon on the first floor, the introspective, puritanical novelist's beady eye darted around, his senses heightened, as he absorbed every detail.

Finally, he was witnessing for himself the palatial surroundings those exotic creatures, the courtesans, inhabited. The rooms were grand, solemn and richly furnished – self-consciously so. The artwork and sculptures were undeniably impressive; yet they reflected such a melange of different periods and styles that the overall effect was one of confusion. In Zola's view, the decor betrayed an amateur artistic eye. Every room was overfilled with objects, so that the sounds throughout the house were muffled. And what was that potent floral smell that permeated the air, Zola wondered? The novelist felt certain he recognised the intoxicating scent of violets.

At last, having made his way through the palace, Zola finally came face-to-face with its queen. The woman standing before him challenged all his preconceptions.

As Valtesse and Zola beheld each other in the reception room, the dinner guests knew that they were witnessing the meeting of two of the most dynamic minds in Paris. Both were intelligent, both were masters of linguistic eloquence – and both could use words as an instrument of destruction. It promised to be a spectacular show.

But a crucial difference divided the novelist and the courtesan: their attitudes to sex. Valtesse's sexual energy was expended daily, and in the most experimental of ways. Meanwhile, Zola's remained carefully contained, jealously guarded, finding an outlet only in food and in his novels. His childless marriage perplexed his colleagues, particularly when he insisted so publicly on the importance of children. Then his single-minded pursuit of the family's maid, Jeanne Rozerot, some years later, and the swift appearance of two children, strengthened adversaries' accusations of sexual repression.[15] Valtesse's dinner guests were in no doubt: the atmosphere in the dining room was going to be charged that evening.

Once the guests had taken their places around Valtesse's dark wood dining table, service could commence. As the scent of the different dishes announced the arrival of each course, and the sound of cutlery on china accompanied their consumption, the diners had ample topics of conversation. But Valtesse's admirers reported witheringly that Zola's contribution was minimal.[16] With unwavering self-interest, he busied himself taking a sheaf of notes, interrupting the discussion only to enquire how high the ceilings were before attentively recording the response. Valtesse would neither confirm nor deny the tale. On the other hand, since Zola had only dined at the home of one courtesan while researching his novel, his impressions of Valtesse and her *hôtel particulier* were soon known, and in the most public of ways. Through *Nana*, nosy Parisians were treated to a guided tour of Valtesse's home.

Not only did Zola decide to locate Nana's mansion just a few streets away from Boulevard Malesherbes, but his fictionalised description provided a startlingly accurate portrait of Valtesse's living quarters. The novelist found the space in which he ate to be 'magnificent', a 'very high-ceilinged dining room hung with Gobelin tapestries and having a monumental buffet graced by antique faience-ware and wonderful old silver'.*[17] The table was 'resplendent with gleaming silver and cut-glass'.*[18] The guests at the small dinner party Nana decides to give in chapter ten of the

---

* © By permission of Oxford University Press.

novel dine on the kind of fine dishes Valtesse approved of, beginning with soup, then moving on to roasted meat, truffles and finishing with fruit for dessert, with plenty of champagne being enjoyed throughout.

But if Valtesse and Nana's home environments were alike, the hostesses differed markedly in character. After his evening at Valtesse's, Zola was inspired to depict Nana's guests discussing literature, politics, society, horseracing and crime. Valtesse could converse knowledgeably on any one of these topics, and she adored the races. However, when Nana participates in the intellectual sparring that takes place at her dinner party, she exposes her ignorance. By contrast, Valtesse was widely considered to be a woman of 'rare distinction, remarkably intelligent, highly cultured, possessing an exquisite taste in art and literature, great wit and a fine literary skill'.[19] The idea of showing herself up as Nana does would have horrified her. In Valtesse's world, it simply never happened – she made sure of it.

Frank exposure of social inferiority, as exhibited by Zola's fictional hostess, also shocked Valtesse to her very core. Overwhelmed by the wealth – and debt – that now surrounds her, Nana takes comfort in nostalgic reminiscences of her past with her childhood friend Satin. Over dinner, the women speak openly about their poverty, and Nana's father's alcoholism, causing the other, socially superior diners much embarrassment. No dinner party of Valtesse's would compel guests to shift uncomfortably in their seats. The thought of her past sullying the self-image she had worked so diligently to fashion appalled her. Throughout her life, Valtesse remained vehemently 'controlled, self-contained, reserved'.[20] An intensity and a magnetic inner strength flickered behind her bright blue eyes whenever she fixed people with one of her penetrating stares. 'I am myself,' she insisted, 'without a past, without a history, having come strangely into the world which I find strange.'[21]

Even Valtesse's closest friends still had no idea that their companion had had two children.[22] Mystery was an essential part of Valtesse's image and she was a master at retaining it.

But if she valued discretion, Valtesse attached as much importance to etiquette. Nana's approach to her evening is careless, setting her worlds apart from the woman Zola dined with. Valtesse prided herself on receiving guests in perfect style. In *Isola*, Valtesse described a dinner party thrown by the elegant Capucine de Vidouville. The scene was not written by a woman inclined to disregard accepted etiquette. Valtesse was profoundly sensitive to a hostess's responsibilities.[23] From the invitations and the flowers to the place settings and the menus trimmed with silver leaf, it was not in Valtesse's nature to neglect her guests' requirements.

For Valtesse's closest friends, such differences provided unequivocal proof of Zola's ignorance. The red-haired beauty had entirely perplexed him. Valtesse simply failed to conform to his mental image of the typical courtesan. He did not understand her charm, her subtle complexity or, friends insisted, her intelligence.[24] 'She has depth,' Félicien Champsaur explained, 'and that is precisely where M. Zola got it wrong.'[25] If Zola had been seeking a neat confirmation of a predetermined checklist of character traits, he would be bitterly disappointed by the woman he found in Valtesse.

Still, once dinner was complete, the novelist was finally able to satisfy the real hunger that had led him to 98, Boulevard Malesherbes. Valtesse offered him a tour of the rest of the property. Zola did not waste a moment. As he followed his hostess around her home, every detail was recorded, each fine painting closely inspected, and all the sights and smells and muffled sounds duly noted. Zola's colleague Paul Alexis revealed that his friend 'was able to see everything, the layout of the sitting room which joined onto a greenhouse, the bedroom, the expansive space of the dressing room, even the stables, so that he could give an informed description of Nana's home'.[26]

Among the observations that were absorbed into *Nana* was Zola's description of the house as 'a palatial, Renaissance-style building with a fantastic interior arrangement of rooms and furniture, modern comfort in a setting of rather studied originality'.*[27] He examined the 'wonderful Oriental hangings', with the 'antique sideboards, and huge Louis XIII armchairs'.*[28]

Furthermore:

the steps under the grand glass awning in the courtyard leading up to the front terrace were carpeted, and once in the vestibule you were assailed by a scent of violets in the warm air trapped between the heavy wall hangings. The staircase was wide and lit through a pink-and-yellow stained-glass window which cast a pale, flesh-coloured golden light. At its foot, a carved wooden blackamoor stood holding out a silver tray full of visiting cards; there were four candelabra, each supported by a bare-breasted marble female, while the vestibule and landings were furnished and decorated with bronze figures, Chinese cloisonné vases full of flowers, divans draped with antique Persian rugs, and armchairs covered in old tapestry, forming a sort of entrance hall on the first floor.*[29]

As Valtesse led the tour through the apartment, an unspoken question played on everyone's minds: would Zola enjoy the privilege Dumas was denied? Would Valtesse take him into her bedroom? There was no predicting how she would react, and Valtesse knew it. She relished the power that brought.

The prospect of fame and public attention, the thought that her bedroom might feature in the latest top novel, were powerful incentives to be more generous with Zola than she had been with Dumas.

* © By permission of Oxford University Press.

Besides, on one point at least, Valtesse and Nana heartily agreed; concessions could always be made 'when a work of art's involved'.*[30]

Thus the real star of Zola's trip to 98, Boulevard Malesherbes, the object that soon had the whole of Paris talking, was Valtesse's fabulous bed.[31] There could be no better model for his character's grand throne. People described it as the 'vessel of Paris', and the comparison between boat and bed appealed to Zola.[32] He did not forget it. (Not long afterwards, he named his own rowing boat 'Nana'.) Zola was determined to make Valtesse's bed the star of Nana's boudoir.[33]

His hostess's enthusiasm for her favourite piece of furniture was contagious. Zola decided that Nana too should gain as much satisfaction and empowerment planning the great commission as she will the finished item. Taking Valtesse's bed as inspiration, but allowing his imagination to roam untamed, Zola described the bed as:

> utterly unique, a throne or altar where all Paris would come to worship her in her naked, equally unique, beauty. It would be made entirely of embossed gold and silver, like some gigantic jewel, golden roses hanging on the silver trellis; along the bed-head a band of laughing cupids would be leaning forward, surrounded by flowers and peering at the voluptuous delights concealed in the shade of the curtains.*[34]

Delighted, Zola left Valtesse's dinner party with both his spiritual and physical appetites satisfied. He had everything he needed to make Nana's home recognisable as the spectacular residence of a leading courtesan. His notes collated and his creative juices flowing, Zola returned home to assimilate what he had seen. Now, the real work began.

While Zola drafted, reread and altered his text, Valtesse was left wondering how her dinner party and her cherished home would be shown in writing. She disliked uncertainty. It made her uneasy. Fortunately, Zola worked quickly when inspired and the reading public were clamouring to begin his next book. Within months, the publication of *Nana* was announced.

Nana whipped Paris up into a positive frenzy. Never before had a novel been hyped as fervently. It became the fashionable topic of conversation long before it appeared in print in October 1879. 'The name is plastered on every wall in Paris,' Henri Céard informed Zola, 'it is verging on obsession and nightmare.'[35] Paris's reading public were growing impatient. On the day before it was finally released as a serial in *Le Voltaire*, *Le Gaulois* dedicated a massive quarter-page advertising slot to the novel.[36] 'Nana' was printed in large letters across the paper's back page, and on the front, readers could enjoy a celebrity feature on Zola and his preparation for the novel. The next morning, *Le Gaulois* proudly announced on the front page that they too would be serialising *Nana* at the same time as *Le Voltaire*. Such a move was extraordinary. Finally, on page two, readers could at last begin the first instalment of the long-anticipated novel.

Paris's reading public rushed to buy their copy of *Le Voltaire* or *Le Gaulois*. Familiarity with the story became a necessity in social circles. Everyone was talking about it.

Zola fully expected a backlash. The subject matter was undeniably risqué.[37] However, the novel's steamy reputation worked in his favour: sales of the serial rocketed, exceeding Zola's wildest hopes. To hit sales of 4,000 copies was considered a great success at the time; when *Nana* appeared in book form, it sold 55,000 copies overnight.[38]

Soon, the critics' responses flowed forth. Naturally, the subject matter was far from salubrious, but the damning responses centred more on Zola's inaccuracies and naivety. Many seconded Aurélien

Scholl's view: an hour in the wings of the Variétés and a dinner with Valtesse hardly qualified the author to cast judgement on the *demi-monde*.[39]

Zola's earnest hunt for models for Nana had not gone unnoticed by the eagle-eyed public. People immediately spotted Blanche d'Antigny and Cora Pearl. How insulted the late Blanche would have been, exclaimed Georges Ohnet, to be cast as the foolish Nana.[40] Nana was not modelled solely on Blanche, *Le Gaulois* wisely countered: she was a composite creation.[41]

Still, for many readers, there could be no doubt: Nana was Valtesse. Valtesse was the only courtesan Zola had met and dined with in her own *hôtel particulier*. Word spread rapidly.[42] The reading public immediately began combing the text in search of parallels.

Those who knew Valtesse did not have to look far. Nana and Valtesse's pasts were uncannily alike. Both had an impoverished upbringing with flawed, promiscuous maternal role models. Valtesse's close and influential associate Jules Claretie would have recognised the significance of Nana's First Communion in *L'Assommoir*, which establishes her anticipation of gifts and love of material things.[43] Claretie had never forgotten the moment he first set eyes on Valtesse at her own First Communion.[44]

But there were further, more profound similarities, too. Readers of *Isola* would remember how quickly the work environment robbed the anti-heroine of her innocence.[45] Similarly, Nana owes her streetwise nature to the experience of her first job. The resonances between Valtesse's debut in Offenbach's *Orpheus in the Underworld* and Nana's first performance at the Variétés as the star of *The Blonde Venus* struck many as more than a coincidence. Like Valtesse, Nana's looks were all critics could find to recommend her.[46] Sharp readers were bound to make the link.

From Paris, Henri Céard wrote to Zola who was staying in Médan: 'there is ridiculous gossip circulating here about *Nana*,' he fumed.[47] 'I was in a Franco-Russian salon the other evening where a gentleman, with absolute sincerity, claimed that Nana was Valtesse, and he cited the names of three or four other well-known Parisian ladies who are expected to appear in your next novel.' 'All the stories are untrue,' Zola insisted publicly in *Le Voltaire*.[48] His statement made no difference. The rumours continued.

Meanwhile, at 98, Boulevard Malesherbes, Valtesse scoured the pages of *Nana* to locate the material she had supplied. She began to read. And as she did, she grew angry. How dare Zola? Her confidence had been grossly betrayed, and she was filled with remorse for having lent her property to such a classless novel. She was particularly incensed by the remark that the *hôtel particulier* had been embellished by 'a few silly, sentimental touches and a bit of gaudy magnificence' which recalled 'the tastes of the flower-girl who once used to stand day-dreaming in front of the shops in the arcade'.*[49] The liberties Zola had taken infuriated her. They made her nervous, too; her reputation was at stake. The public must not believe that she shared Nana's poor taste or stupidity.

Valtesse observed the commotion surrounding the novel. She was no stranger to public attention and gossip: she relished being in the spotlight – she had, after all, agreed to Zola's request in the first place. But this attention was different. It posed a serious threat to her reputation. Valtesse knew that she must consider her reaction carefully. But time was of the essence; all eyes were on her.

Valtesse made sure that her feelings were known. Publicly, her response passed from open disdain to derision. She would have no more to do with the deceitful novelist she had so cordially welcomed into her home. Zola was very naive, Valtesse told people, if he thought that a girl could become a sophisticated woman, an

---

* © By permission of Oxford University Press.

irresistible seductress, by employing such low means as Nana. She vented her anger to writer Harry Alis:

> These novelists, they used to think all courtesans were fallen women who wanted to redeem themselves ... now they are all foolish women, beautiful and stupid as a lump of marble, who pass by like a curse, destroying, dissolving everything in their wake. How naive.'[50]

With her friends, Valtesse laughed at the gross inaccuracies in Zola's story. And she had plenty of support. 'He knows nothing of the *demi-monde* which he talks about,' Georges Ohnet complained. 'He has never seen what he describes, so he describes it badly [...] He insults all present-day courtesans.'[51] The condemnatory reviews were encouraging. To Valtesse's relief, her reputation emerged intact and she unscathed.

∽

As the next year, 1880, unfolded and the excitement surrounding *Nana* started to dissipate, Valtesse could finally relax back into her routine of dinners, soirées, afternoon teas and dances. Once the autumn drew to a close and Parisians started anticipating the festive season, the frequency and number of these events seemed all the greater. There were invitations to reply to and outfits to be chosen, and tending to her social diary provided Valtesse with a full-time occupation. But then some news reached her: Zola, the papers announced, had decided to adapt *Nana* for the stage. It would open in the new year, in just three months time.

Excitement began to mount. Who would be playing the title role? Conversation in salons hummed with the question. One name was on everyone's lips. The speculation reached a climax when François Oswald mischievously remarked in *Le Gaulois*:

'M. Chabrillat has just engaged Mlle Valtesse to play the role of the pretty young wench in *Nana*.'[52] At lightning speed, the story travelled across the Channel, where news of Valtesse's imminent appearance was reported in the *Morning Post*.[53] When she heard the gossip, Valtesse knew an immediate response was required. She quickly composed a letter to the author of the jest:

Dear Sir,

To play a main part in *Nana*, I would need to be an actress; I am not, nor do I wish to become one.

Be so good as to rectify this error in your paper to set my mind at ease.

Yours, Valtesse

Valtesse was determined: the public should be under no illusion that she endorsed her association with the foolish Nana. She was better than that. But curiosity is a powerful emotion, particularly where reputations are concerned. Not even Valtesse was immune. The public could yet interpret the play as a dramatisation of her life. It made her uneasy; it was too much to disregard as a trivial pest.

With only a week until the opening night, Zola was immersed in correspondence and discussions involving the performance, when he received a note from Hennique:

I have just received a message from Valtesse, who, not wishing to write to you herself, has asked instead if I could request from you two first-class seats in the dress circle for the opening night of *Nana*.

Would you be so good as to offer these to this charming… young lady?

A quick message to confirm would be greatly appreciated.[54]

Suppressing any sense of self-satisfaction, Zola good-naturedly dispatched two tickets to Valtesse. On 28 January 1881, Valtesse's carriage drew up outside the Théâtre de l'Ambigu, and she stepped out to take her place among a host of Paris's most fashionable elite for the premiere of *Nana*. She saw her attendance neither as an endorsement of the play nor an admission of defeat; rather, this was her chance to prove her superiority.

As the curtain rose and the play began, Valtesse could feel encouraged. The audience around her were not enjoying themselves, and the scene in which a fire broke out in one of the characters' properties caused genuine alarm. Mme Zola was reduced to tears. The last few scenes were better received, but Valtesse felt relieved. The tale appeared even more ridiculous on stage than it did in the novel, and she delighted in openly expressing her amusement. When the curtain fell, Valtesse left with her curiosity satisfied, content that an unbridgeable chasm separated her from Zola's anti-heroine.

In the long run, light-hearted gossip about her link to *Nana* did Valtesse's reputation no harm; if anything, it helped publicise her self-image. She soon returned to a life of soirées, social engagements and brilliant salon conversations. A courtesan had to ensure that she put herself where the public would see her. Valtesse was bright enough to approach that goal creatively – and she knew just who could help her achieve it.

CHAPTER 11

A Picture Speaks a Thousand Words

ana brought Valtesse a flurry of attention, but she remained stoical. She was under no illusions: public curiosity would soon turn to something – or someone – else. Her image needed constant attention if she were to hold her position as one of Paris's leading courtesans.

The written word was not the only promotional tool available to a cultured courtesan. As she circulated in the art world, Valtesse was increasingly struck by the power of the visual image, and by the time she reached her late 20s, she had learned how to make it work for her. Harnessing its power depended on maintaining excellent relations with painters.

Throughout the furore surrounding *Nana*, Valtesse continued her relationship with Édouard Detaille. Their affair had lost something of its original intensity, but in Valtesse's eyes, the painter's companionship, prestige and renown made the connection worth maintaining. However, she kept her natural impulses carefully in check and insisted that she was respected at all times. It was a delicate balance to strike.

While Valtesse was not the only woman Detaille pursued, his devotion remained firm. He showered her with gifts, painted canvases for her and dined with her as often as he could. Just a few months after *Nana* appeared, he was busy working on a watercolour which he intended for Valtesse.[1] Detaille realised that his mistress's affection must be earned. He had learned the hard way that she would not tolerate a man's neglect.

Nor did Valtesse have patience where competition was concerned; Detaille found he was seeing less of her in the months preceding *Nana*'s publication when he began an illicit affair with another woman.[2] Still, Detaille's enigmatic 'Mme X' turned out to be merely a passing folly, a fleeting irritation. Shortly afterwards, Valtesse found herself facing a far more serious rival for the artist's affection: the actress Réjane.

Daughter of a director and a box office assistant, Réjane had the theatre in her blood. With her cherubim features, sultry eyes and arched eyebrows, which animated her face with a curious blend of confidence and surprise, Réjane won admirers when she first stepped on to the stage at the tender age of fifteen. Before long, she had established herself as one of the darlings of the Parisian theatre scene and was heralded as the next Sarah Bernhardt. Her star continued to rise as the final years of the 19th century approached. Réjane was attractive, charismatic and, born nearly a decade after Valtesse, she also had youth on her side. Réjane caught Detaille's attention – and Valtesse noticed.

Detaille started spending more and more time with Réjane from the spring of 1880. When he took a trip to Brussels later in the year, true to his punctilious nature, Detaille wrote to the actress every day. On his return to France, he made plans to see Valtesse, and on 6 July 1880, the pair met for dinner. However, Detaille's evening did not end when he left Valtesse; he spent the rest of the night with Réjane. Valtesse watched the couple's relationship unfold. She had sworn never to commit herself to just one man, and she knew she could not expect monogamy in return. But Detaille was one of her most reliable benefactors. The actress was threatening her resources.

Valtesse knew Réjane. The women mixed in similar circles. Both had enjoyed the company of Offenbach, and they were often spotted at the same opening nights and soirées.[3] Valtesse had a great deal of knowledge about her rival. She also knew just how to keep a man when she considered him worth keeping. The time had come to put those skills into action.

Valtesse noticed that Detaille and Réjane fought often, and she made sure that she was there to soothe the artist's troubled mind whenever the couple had an argument.

'Very stormy scene with R,' Detaille reported in his diary on 17 July.[4] He immediately turned to Valtesse for consolation. Her commitment reaped handsome rewards: for all the attraction he felt towards the actress, Detaille could not bring himself to sever contact with Valtesse. His love ran deep. Réjane had good cause to fume with jealousy.

The tension was finally broken on 23 July, when the two women confronted each other. The showdown took place at Detaille's home.

> Met V with whom I was meant to have lunch at my place. R had installed herself in my bedroom. I did not go in. V insisted on coming into the house. I did not know what was going on. V and R had a conversation! V came to find me and we went for lunch together at Payot's. R took V's letters away with her… Thank goodness today is over![5]

Just what Valtesse said to her rival remained a mystery. But she had marked her territory and emerged victorious. The painter spent no more time with the actress that day – he spent it with Valtesse. Valtesse was determined not to be displaced by the younger actress. And now, having philandered, the artist would have to prove his commitment to her.

Detaille was only too keen to comply. His visits to Ville-d'Avray became more frequent towards the end of the month and the sums of money he lavished on Valtesse grew even greater. He ensured that she wanted for nothing. His dedication was unshakeable, and all his friends could see. Fellow painter Alphonse de Neuville was sure to send his greetings to Valtesse when he wrote to Detaille after the confrontation between the artist's mistresses: 'My regards to Mlle Valtesse who I presume is still the reigning sovereign. It would be hard to find better.'[6]

Valtesse could appear demanding and even spiteful. She loved dogs, and when she decided to buy a pair of sleek white greyhounds, she named one of them after the artist. But the relationship was far from one-sided; Valtesse found Detaille attractive and interesting. His profession brought other, practical advantages, too. A painter could create a world. He could choose what it included and shape how viewers perceived things – and people. That was a powerful skill. Valtesse saw that it could be used to a person's advantage.

'The role of painting is first and foremost to assist history,' was the wisdom Detaille's tutor, Ernest Meissonier, had sought to instil in his protégé.[7] The obedient pupil seldom painted civilian subjects or women, and made a name for himself as the painter of the French army. This aversion to female subjects worked in Valtesse's favour. It made her appearance in *The Passing Regiment* (1875) all the more noteworthy. When she agreed to pose, Valtesse made a quick calculation: as one of only a few civilian women among military men, she would be noticed. Viewers might even recognise her. Those who did would be impressed by her patriotism and her association with such a prestigious artist.

The painting brought Detaille attention and acclaim. His 'deep love of precision and sincerity in execution' were praised; the same 'meticulous and solid qualities' that people admired in his tutor were commended.[8] Many declared it the artist's finest work, and Valtesse's presence in the painting was a source of immense pride.

Still, however, she remained one of a number. Valtesse knew that if a woman truly wished to make a bold affirmation of her status, there was a more powerful way of achieving it: portraiture.

Portraiture remained a popular artistic genre throughout the 19th century.[9] As an awareness of individual identity filtered down through the class hierarchy, more and more people felt compelled to make their social position manifest. Capturing an image of the self proved an effective way for a person to make a visual statement of their identity. Photography made the portrait accessible to the masses, but it had one frustrating limitation: it 'shows you as you are, not as you should be', exclaimed one horrified journalist.[10]

The painted portrait could create a flattering yet believable fiction, and it continued to adorn the walls of the Salon during the second half of the 19th century.[11] Having a portrait painted declared power, status and wealth, and the greater the artist, the more prestigious the subject appeared.[12] Through careful selection of portraitist, venue and time of exhibition, a portrait could act as a powerful marketing tool. The fact had not escaped Valtesse's attention.

Conscious that she was often seen mixing in bohemian circles, Valtesse realised that commissioning a portrait by the esteemed Salon artist Gustave Jacquet would flag her respect for traditional values and officially sanctioned art too.

Jacquet had trained under the revered William-Adolphe Bouguereau, and his early works reflected his master's classic, highly finished style.[13] Once he began exhibiting at the Salon, he made a name for himself with his anecdotal, romantic period scenes and his painstakingly observed costumes. Jacquet's lightness of touch sometimes brought him criticism, but he enjoyed the support of some loyal admirers. As a critic observed of one of his canvases, 'do not look at it as a painted canvas: it is the most gracious decorative vision.'[14] By the time Valtesse sat to have her portrait painted by

Jacquet when she was in her 30s, he had already won his first medal. Jacquet was an estimable artist.

Jacquet's representation imbued her with all the elegance and class she hoped to convey. Facing the viewer, Valtesse smiles gently. With Jacquet's feathery brushwork, her skin appears soft and her eyes inviting. Her hair is scraped back, and wispy streaks of gold and white capture where the light catches it. Valtesse's pale décolletage and shoulders melt into the background, and with her elegant posture, a single, rich gold choker gives her a lofty, aristocratic appearance. But for all the refined dignity of the finished piece, Jacquet still succeeded in making his subject appear gentle and approachable – quite the opposite of the cold, reserved persona Valtesse usually enjoyed projecting.

It was certainly different from Gervex and Detaille's representations of her, but Valtesse was full of praise for Jacquet's work. It showed 'such grace', she found it so 'bewitchingly seductive', that she could only enthuse about it.[15] Why, she exclaimed, it flattered the artist nearly as much as it did the model.

The academic-style portrait filled her with gratification. However, scandal still served a purpose – and what's more it thrilled Valtesse, for her mischievous streak was incorrigible. The controversy that helped propel another portrait of her to prominence was just to her taste.

In 1878, the same year Zola had visited her in the course of his research for *Nana*, her other dinner guest, and lover, Henri Gervex, had outraged the Salon jury with his painting *Rolla*. The work may have shocked, but it firmly established Gervex's reputation. The following year, two of his paintings were accepted by the jury. One of them was a portrait of Valtesse.[16]

In a sun-drenched summer garden, dappled light animates verdant foliage and illuminates a single female figure. Valtesse stands demurely clutching a blue parasol, and from beneath a chic white bonnet, her hair tumbles down her back – just as Gervex preferred. Coyly, confidently, her eyes fix firmly on the viewer. Borrowing the lighter palette and looser brushwork of the Impressionists, Gervex made a bold move with the portrait of his beloved, for it was the first *plein air* canvas he produced. His efforts impressed the critics.[17] 'It is actually easier,' observed one reviewer, 'to paint interior scenes, however complicated one might think them to be, than to paint a full-length figure outside.'[18] People found it reminiscent of Claude Monet's *Women in the Garden* (1866–67). It was a comparison to be proud of.

Gervex's renown brought Valtesse instant attention. '*Mlle V*... is a blonde with fiery hair,' commended one reviewer.[19] Her elegance was remarked on, and the way the background foliage highlighted her beauty impressed critics.

When the painting was shown again at a later exhibition, Gervex post-dated it, flattering Valtesse by ten years. But any fashionable Parisienne would have spotted that her costume, a pretty lilac afternoon dress with fitted bodice and a ruched skirt which restricted leg movement, was typical of the late 1870s.[20] Valtesse was careful that she always remained abreast of fashion. So to the original Salon viewers, the painting confirmed Valtesse, the epitome of the modern courtesan, to be an arbiter of fashion. Valtesse was delighted by the accolade.

When the painting was shown in the exhibition *Portraits of the Century* in 1883, it firmly established Valtesse's place among the greatest faces of France. 'A hundred years ago, artists painted politicians, great ladies,' Jules Claretie wrote in his review of the exhibition. He went on:

Under the Empire, soldiers with shaven chins and well-trimmed sideburns appeared [...] between pretty pink creatures in gauze dresses. With the Restoration and the reign of Louis-Philippe, men of state [...] literary figures and poets [...] Under the Second Empire, it was pretty women painters fought over. Today it is actors and actresses [...] This is very significant. M. Gervex has even given a place among these *Portraits of the Century* to a beautiful person with golden hair, Mlle Valtesse de la Bigne, who seems to smile spiritually at these great, official honours. A sign of the times, a philosopher or a cynic might complain. I do not frown upon it, but I note it as a curious symptom of our times.[21]

Claretie was right: times were changing. For centuries, a Frenchman's status had been determined by birth. Now, Valtesse, a courtesan, took her place alongside kings and queens. She was thrilled with her likeness, and when she acquired the portrait, it was hung in pride of place in her grand sitting room, where all her guests could admire her lover's homage to her.

⤜∞⤛

Gervex had an important acquaintance he especially wanted his favourite model to meet: Édouard Manet.

Valtesse was impatient to be introduced to the great artist. Manet's very name resounded with excitement and modernity. He was known by all and criticised by many, but to Paris's artistic avant-garde, Manet was a hero. For an image-conscious Parisienne, having her portrait painted by Manet was the ultimate fashion statement. With his charm and vivacity, the painter set female hearts fluttering. He suffered from a condition known as locomotor ataxia, which involves a gradual deterioration of the spinal column and nervous system. In Manet's case it had been brought on by syphilis. By the 1870s, this malady (which would prove fatal) had already affected his legs, rendering movement difficult. But Paris's female population were undeterred; they simply came to him. A constant stream of women of all classes flowed through the doors of his studio to have their likenesses captured.[22] Manet was magnetic. 'Once one has come to Manet's studio,' remarked his cousin René Maizeroy, 'even for a casual visit, one cannot make up one's mind to leave.'[23]

Like Gervex, Manet too had caused yet another scandal in 1877 when *Nana*, his painting inspired by Zola's fictional character, was rejected by the Salon jury. While rumours circulated that the anti-heroine of Zola's *Nana* was based on Valtesse, she agreed to an exhilarating proposition: the great Manet himself, the creator of the painted *Nana*, wanted to paint her portrait.[24]

It was deeply flattering. Valtesse now felt confident that her reputation had not been tarnished by her connection to Zola's novel, and she could never resist teasing the public's appetite for gossip once she felt secure. She was excited by the idea.

A day for the sitting was agreed upon, and when it arrived, Valtesse carefully selected the outfit she wished to be shown in. Manet was both an admirer of contemporary female fashion and a master of representing it; Valtesse wanted to be seen at her best. She settled on one of her most flattering, tight-bodiced blue dresses, with a high lace collar, which recalled the dignified clothing of latter-day royalty. She ensured her russet hair was perfectly styled, held back from her face in a neat, braided bun – she liked the rather severe, serious edge it gave her. However, a few stray curls of her red-gold locks escaped, betraying her less inhibited side. Finally, in her ears, she fixed a pair of dazzling gold earrings, a nod to royalty and a symbol of power. The effect was striking. Valtesse looked the very essence of a contemporary monarch.

Satisfied with her appearance, Valtesse prepared herself to receive the famous artist. She waited patiently for his arrival. The agreed time came and went. Manet did not appear.

Then all at once, Valtesse realised in horror that there had been an embarrassing misunderstanding: Manet was expecting her to visit him.

Anxious that she might have annoyed the great master and jeopardised her chance of being immortalised by his brush, she quickly penned a letter to be delivered immediately.

'I am a goose,' she confessed. 'I thought that you wanted to paint me at my home, and I waited. Would you be so good as to grant me another day, sir? I will come to you. I really am the silliest thing. A thousand apologies, yours, Valtesse.'[25]

To Valtesse's relief, Manet made light of the confusion and agreed an alternative day. She was careful not to miss the opportunity a second time. When the day arrived, Valtesse, accompanied by Gervex, travelled to the painter's studio in the Rue d'Amsterdam and the sitting began.

Examining the subject before him, Manet decided that a side-on, head and shoulders view would be the most flattering composition, and he selected soft pastels, increasingly his medium of choice as his failing health reduced his strength.[26] Using bold sweeps of blue pastel, Manet's sure hand traced the sharp contours of Valtesse's bodiced waist, changing to swift, loose, vertical zig-zags to create the ruffles of her collar. Confident, undulating strokes of sand, brown and red depicted her trademark hair. But her skin, with its smooth, pale complexion, demanded a different handling. Under Manet's skilled hand, it appeared flawless, with the rosy hue of Valtesse's cheeks blending seamlessly into the pale peach of her jaw. Against her milky skin, Manet's depiction of her pink rosebud lips and bright blue eyes with their heavy lids made her likeness all the more compelling.

The sitting complete, Manet felt content with his efforts, and Valtesse was elated. Never one to compromise her position with excessive flattery, Valtesse conceded that in Manet's case, she must make an exception.

'Dear master,' she wrote to the painter when the work was presented to her, 'I cannot tell you how happy I am that you have created my portrait, nor how much I like it. Thank you with all my heart, it was most amiable and gallant of you. I say gallant because you have flattered your model. In short, I feel immensely proud to have posed for a master such as yourself. Yours, Valtesse de la Bigne.'[27]

A firm friendship blossomed from Valtesse's sitting with Manet. Manet lived close to Boulevard Malesherbes, and Valtesse began to join Gervex and the host of other artists, writers and fashionable members of society who would call on Manet at the end of the day for stimulating conversation and an aperitif. And just as Valtesse admired Manet, he too warmed to her. The painter was impressed by her quick mind and entertained by her bold repartee. Valtesse was refreshing. As he grew to know her better, Manet felt qualified to start using an affectionate nickname: the 'Châtelaine of Ville-d'Avray', a playful reference to the tragic heroine from the 13th-century French romance, *The Châtelaine de Vergi*, who takes her life when she believes her lover has betrayed her trust.[28]

Manet and Valtesse often dined together and shared ideas. 'I was meant to take lunch yesterday at Montelais with the beautiful Valtesse,' he informed his close companion, the actress-turned-courtesan, Mery Laurent, at the end of September 1880. 'But the gathering was postponed,' Manet went on, explaining: 'the Châtelaine of Ville-d'Avray already had someone over for lunch.'[29] Even a celebrity of Manet's calibre had to be viewed in perspective; a star-struck courtesan was a sorry creature indeed. She neglected other connections at her peril.

Still, Valtesse was only too happy for Manet's portrait to be exhibited at the Galerie de la Vie Moderne a few months later.[30] It was a public testimony of her link to the celebrated artist and for such a man to have painted her portrait it led viewers to the inexorable conclusion that Mlle V must be an important figure in society.

Not long after Manet exhibited his portrait, Gervex asked Valtesse if she would pose for a very important commission. She had grown used to her lover's requests to sit for him. But the painting Gervex now had in mind was to be different. He had been asked to produce a decorative painting for the Salle des Mariages of the Mairie in the 19th arrondissement of the city. The piece was to be a glorious visual celebration of Republican ideals, and to ensure that it met the brief, Gervex's work would be scrupulously monitored.[31] But the artist already had his own ideas about the piece's composition. And on one point he was certain: he wanted his mistress to appear in it.

The theme of the piece was matrimony. Following the Revolution, marriage had been secularised. Since then, couples had been obliged to have a civil marriage at the mairie before the traditional religious ceremony which would take place a day or two later.[32] However, for many, civil marriages were unsatisfactory, ill-attended events void of all the sentiment one should expect of a wedding.[33] But Gervex felt sure he could challenge such criticism. He simply had to sell the civil ceremony to his modern audience.

Gervex began making sketches of a civil wedding ceremony taking place in the very room in which the painting was going to hang. He called on the son and future daughter-in-law of the mayor Mathurin Moreau (who was also a sculptor) to model a couple in wedding attire.[34]

Gervex positioned the couple in the centre of his canvas, standing before Moreau in his role as mayor, to take their vows. Then, behind a large desk, he placed a pair of officials busying themselves with paperwork. The couple's family were seated in the front row, and behind them, Gervex painted his pièce de résistance: the congregation. In among the fashionably dressed gathering of people, Gervex included some of the most popular celebrities of the day.[35] He turned the civil wedding into an unmissable social occasion.

Gervex was determined that his civil wedding should have all the visual appeal, pomp and grandeur of the traditional religious ceremony. In her elaborate white wedding dress, the bride still looks radiant.[36] The desk takes the place of an altar, and the mayor, that of the priest. The Bible is replaced by his lofty tome, while the usual ecclesiastical stained-glass window illustrating a distant religious story is exchanged for a transparent window providing a familiar, up-to-the-minute view of Paris. Every aspect of *The Civil Marriage* had been carefully considered – so it was with dismay that Gervex discovered his efforts had failed to impress.

Critics railed against the use of an oversized genre painting to decorate the town hall. The Catholic Church was particularly ferocious in its response.[37] The piece was denounced as cold and ridiculous, lacking in all religious sentiment.[38] 'If M. Gervex claims to have conferred prestige on the lay ceremony,' wrote the reviewer in *La Défence sociale et religieuse*, 'he has failed in the attempt.'[39]

The virulent critical responses brought one pleasing advantage, however: swarms of curious viewers came flocking to the Salon to see the painting everyone was talking about. And it was Gervex's star-studded congregation that provided the greatest interest. When viewers beheld the painting, they could indulge in a diverting game: how many stars of the 19th-century social scene could they recognise?

There in the crowd was Zola, and close to him, Manet. People spotted the notorious socialiser, the Prince of Wales, and the future Tsar Nicolas II. There was the journalist Richard O'Monroy with his trademark moustache. And there, next to him, a single figure stood out. One woman looked straight back at the viewer, confidently, defiantly: it was Valtesse. Surrounded by royalty, lovers past and present, and sworn enemies in the sacred matrimonial ceremony, Valtesse held her head high and stared her viewer in the eye. The work was a triumphant testimony of her success: here she was, a courtesan, playing a starring role in a painting about marriage. Conventions no longer impeded her. And how comfortable she looked alongside her fellow models, the Prince of Wales and the future tsar. It was almost as though they were intimate.

Paintings were a vital form of personal propaganda for Valtesse. Through art, she was securing her place among history's most memorable figures. She had won the heart of Paris, and that support was to prove invaluable; Valtesse's next battle would have international ramifications. Now, she would ensnare one of the country's leading politicians and conquer France's overseas territories.

CHAPTER 12

A Political Affair:
Gambetta, Annam and Tonkin

here was far more to Valtesse than her appearance, social astuteness and cultural flair. Her bright mind needed constant exercise, and France's fast-paced political scene provided the perfect material.

Valtesse's staunch Bonapartism had earned her the doubtful honour of close police surveillance. Her response to the intrusion was defiant: she ensured that the authorities' suspicions were never disappointed. Her social calendar was liberally punctuated by intimate gatherings which she hosted for her Bonapartist friends in Ville-d'Avray.[1] Meanwhile, her spectacular annual fireworks display on the anniversary of Napoleon's birthday had become one of the big social events of the summer.

The world of politics was intoxicating. Valtesse loved the heady combination of power struggles and principles. It stretched her curious mind and nurtured its growth. She saw no reason – and harboured no desire – to conceal her political views. The press were constantly reporting her latest political activities, and the authorities' outrage amused her.[2] She had no intention of refusing such an exhilarating drug.

One of the causes that particularly captured her interest was France's colonial position. The country's hunger for colonies mounted after 1870 as France struggled to rebuild herself in the aftermath of the Franco-Prussian war and the Commune. Valtesse had learned a great deal about one of these areas of colonial interest, the Indochinese territories of Tonkin and Annam.

Her knowledge was yet another gleaning of her affairs. Valtesse's weakness for uniforms had left her with a ponderous backlist of military lovers. One of these was a naval officer who bore the weighty name of Alexandre-Camille-Jules-Marie Le Jumeau de Kergaradec.

Kergaradec was a highly regarded member of the French navy. After enlisting in 1857, Kergaradec's career path had carried him steadily up the ranks, so that by the time he met Valtesse he had secured himself the distinguished position of ship's lieutenant and enjoyed a salary to match.[3] He became *Chevalier de la Légion d'honneur* (Knight of the Legion of Honour) in 1864 and later *Officier de la Légion d'honneur* (Officer of the Legion of Honour). Official honours and military prowess always impressed Valtesse, and with his smart naval uniform, long face, dignified moustache and beard, and neatly groomed hair (even if it was thinning), Kergaradec boasted all the qualities she found attractive in a man.

With their semi-nomadic lifestyles, soldiers and officers were notorious seekers of uncomplicated carnal pleasures. They provided courtesans with a ready source of clients. Valtesse had enjoyed a close relationship with Kergaradec when he was in Paris, during which time she basked in the air of distinction that surrounded him and enjoyed the approving looks he received whenever he entered a room. Friends insisted that it was on Kergaradec that the character of Horace in *Isola* was based. But while Horace is forced to leave Isola and travel to Brittany, Valtesse and Kergaradec's affair was terminated by an even greater journey: in 1875, Valtesse's lieutenant was posted to Indochina, where he became the French consulate in Hanoi.

The loss of a suitor was always concerning for a courtesan. Still, Valtesse was never short of admirers; she felt confident that she would not want for material possessions in Kergaradec's absence. Besides, the idea of a great expedition to such a faraway land intrigued her. When she began receiving letters from Indochina, she was eager to learn more. Kergaradec was happy to oblige his curious mistress.

Kergaradec's work required him to familiarise himself with the territory, its people and the political situation and to report back to France.[4] Few men were better qualified to teach Valtesse about Indochina, and Kergaradec's vivid descriptions of the territory captured her imagination.

There were attractive bays, not least the vast and spectacular Bay of Along with its boats and ships, and the Bay of Tourane, famed for its beauty, its depth and the marble rocks which the Annam people believed sacred.[5] There were sandy mooring points, and the coastline was dotted with pretty rocky islands. Inland, there were mountains, forests, and stretches of plain which would become flooded in the rainy season.[6] With such varied geography, it was no wonder that the territory offered such a rich source of goods desirable to the West, such as coal, lead and zinc. Then there were the people. An Annam woman ranked below her man, but she enjoyed better living conditions than her Chinese counterpart. It was she who prepared the family meals, food that seemed strange next to the typical French diet. How much rice they ate! And even in the very poorest families, it was unheard of to celebrate a special festival or a feast day without tea.[7]

The territory struck Valtesse as exotic, fascinating – and valuable. Before long, parcels from the East began to arrive at her home in Paris. She unwrapped them to find fine plates with delicate floral decoration, elegant porcelain vases, miniature pagodas and statues of Buddha, and all manner of exotic trinkets. Valtesse was elated.

Her collection was already immense, but she made space for all the intriguing pieces her former lover sent her.

In his letters, Kergaradec explained the French position. The French had been making their presence felt in Indochina throughout the second half of the 19th century, and by 1867 they had colonised the southern third of the Indochina peninsula. In 1873, Tonkin and Annam became the new targets. After a year of confrontation with the French, Emperor Tu Duc of Annam agreed to sign a treaty. However, correctly assessing the incompetency of the French representative, the Emperor seized the opportunity to get France to agree to conditions which set her at a disadvantage. This injured French national pride, but of greater concern was that the Emperor was ruling his people under a dictatorship. Shops were being pillaged, innocent civilians were being attacked – and the French seemed unable to extend their protectorate to Annam and Tonkin.

Stirred by her own sense of patriotism and moved by the terrible suffering of the Annam people, Valtesse decided something must be done. The French government must take decisive action. If only she could gain access to the men who wielded power, she felt certain she could steer the government's approach for the country's benefit. She needed to speak to a politician with influence, someone who could convey her ideas to the top of the political hierarchy. Valtesse believed she knew just the man – as luck would have it, he was her next-door neighbour.

By the 1880s, Léon Gambetta was a revered figure on the French political scene. Ten years older than Valtesse, Gambetta's ambitious nature had spurred him to quit his provincial home town of Cahors in his teens and travel to Paris to study law.[8] Once installed in the capital, the stocky, olive-skinned southerner was quick to publicise his strong Republican opinions, surprising people with his confidence and his mastery of rhetoric. Though an unsuccessful lawyer, Gambetta's charisma and linguistic fluency impressed, and in 1869 he was elected to the Legislative Assembly. Becoming one of the principal activists for the defence of France during the Franco-Prussian war, Gambetta's most memorable feat came when he took off from Paris in a balloon at the end of 1870, soaring triumphantly over the German lines before establishing himself at Tours. He was instrumental in persuading the National Assembly to vote for the formation of the Republic in 1875, and by 1880 he had become President of the Chamber of Deputies, the legislative assembly of the French parliament.

With his bear-like physique, booming voice and personal magnetism, Gambetta seemed to overcome any political obstacle that was laid in his path. If ever there was a politician with influence, it was Gambetta.

But if he lived his professional life in the public eye, Gambetta kept a closely guarded veil of privacy over his personal affairs. And that was the aspect that most interested Valtesse. It was the channel through which she hoped to reach him.

In 1872, Gambetta had begun an affair with the captivating and intelligent Léonie Léon, whom he adored. The daughter of a French colonel, Léon had dark hair and piercing eyes which would fix those she met with unnerving intensity.[9] She was the same age as Gambetta, she was attractive, charming, and she too was passionate about literature; in many respects, Léon was Gambetta's intellectual equal. It would have been a perfect match, were it not for an irascible stain on Léon's reputation: she was a courtesan.

After her father died, Léon had been forced to seek employment in an upper-class house, where she was seduced. She was left with little choice but to become a mistress. In 1865, she bore a son, and by 1874, the police had been alerted to her activities. From then on, her movements were tracked. 'She was wearing jade earrings,' observed one police officer when he spotted her, 'a straw hat with blue feathers, a velvet beret, astrakhan cape, fur trimmed kid boots.'[10] Léon's painstaking efforts over her flamboyant appearance were a clear indicator of her lowly status.

In the eyes of society, Léon was dishonoured and ruined. Ironically, given that Gambetta was leading the opposition to the Catholic party in France, she was also a devout Catholic. Marriage was impossible. If they wanted to be together, they would have to live as concubines, betrothed but unmarried. It was a state both were willing to accept.

Gambetta needed to be in Paris for work, but he found it impossible to keep his personal affairs private in the city. Moreover, it was tedious to be always surrounded by work. So in 1878, Gambetta decided that he needed a more comfortable venue for his affair with Léon to flourish, somewhere his mind could escape the heavy business of politics. The location must be picturesque, romantic and untouched by the crude hand of modernity, but it still needed to be close to Paris. Gambetta believed he knew just the place. He settled on a charming town he had passed through many times on his carriage rides back to Paris from Versailles: Ville-d'Avray.

With its forests and peaceful country walks, Ville-d'Avray was the ideal spot for a couple fond of walking to make their love nest. To begin with, Gambetta rented a small house, but by the end of the summer of 1878, he had become the satisfied owner of a portion of the property formerly owned by the writer Honoré de Balzac, Les Jardies.[11]

Gambetta was delighted with the property and with Ville-d'Avray. He wrote to Léon when he was there alone:

> How I love the pleasures – new for me – of solitude, this great and beneficial silence, these wonderful wooded refuges, these calm and sleepy waters at the foot of perfumed heaths, and above all the voluptuousness of reflecting, of thinking, of meditating at one's ease, without hubbub and recriminations from outside![12]

Léon was invited to join him whenever she could.

Word of the town's new arrival spread fast in Ville-d'Avray, with Gambetta's cook proving the most efficient purveyor of gossip. 'M. Gambetta is a man,' the cook confided when asked about the politician's affair with Léon, 'and he's not married. I can tell you, just between us, this person who is passed off as his relative is not a relative. So, you see, he can't receive anyone, and he couldn't care less what people might say about him.'[13]

Valtesse listened to the gossip with interest. Les Jardies was in the next road to hers. She had often passed the home of her literary hero and wondered what it must look like inside. Besides, a courtesan was always well advised to watch the movements of powerful politicians, and the task became more interesting when the man concerned had a secret to conceal. With the information she had received from Kergaradec playing on her mind, Valtesse realised that an opportunity was being presented. If she could win Gambetta's confidence, she was sure she could persuade him to secure France's colonial hold in Indochina. She, a woman and a courtesan, would be playing an active role on France's political stage. The prospect was thrilling. Valtesse began to plot.

Gambetta was known for his unwavering determination once his mind had settled on something. Popular account held that when his father sent him to a religious school as a boy, he became so miserable and fixed on leaving that he wrote home in fury: 'If you do not remove me from this place, I will gouge out my own eye.'[14] The father laughed and dismissed the threat – until he was summoned to the school. The young boy had done as he had promised. Curiously, the father insisted that his son remain at the school. But before long, he received another letter. The boy was planning to remove his second eye. This time, Gambetta got his way. His father removed him immediately.

Gambetta had a glass eye fitted as a replacement, and as his political career blossomed, he learned to use it as a weapon during his speeches. When discussion became animated, he would slowly close his real eye, fixing his terrified adversaries with his immobile, gleaming glass replica. The tactic won him many a debate.

There was no doubt: winning Gambetta's trust was not going to be easy. Valtesse knew that success demanded stealth and patience. Neither fazed her. She was amused but undeterred when her first attempt to speak with the politician failed. She gleefully recounted the incident to Félicien Champsaur.

One morning, Valtesse explained, she was taken by the idea of visiting the home formerly occupied by Balzac.[15] Harnessing her handsome grey stallion, Néro, to her fine mahogany-trimmed carriage – both gifts from admirers – Valtesse made her way across the wooded ground that separated her property from the former home of her literary hero, with her prized greyhound, Detaille, trotting beside her. As she neared Gambetta's house, Valtesse stopped a local man to ask the way to the entrance.

'Which way to Les Jardies please, Sir?'

'Go down the hill, then go back up the other side of the Chemin Vert. That is where it is.'

'Tell me,' Valtesse continued, 'is M. Gambetta there?'

The countryman grunted, 'Perhaps … Maybe.'

'Does he live alone?' Valtesse pursued.

'Alone?' the man repeated.

'With family then?'

The man smiled. 'There are only female cousins in that family, and they change all the time,' he chuckled, before replacing his pipe in his mouth.

Valtesse continued on her way and finally reached the entrance to Les Jardies. There, as if he had been expecting her, was Gambetta.

He was small, pot-bellied, and wore a grey suit. Valtesse thought his pince-nez rather affected; a monocle would have sufficed in his condition. A soft black hat covered Gambetta's bushy grey hair, and he leant on a walking stick. Valtesse approached him.

'Might I be able to visit Balzac's house, Sir?' she enquired, adopting her sweetest tone.

'Why?' the politician snapped. 'No ... No ...,' he growled, shaking his head like a bad-tempered child.

Valtesse could see that she would not be able to win him round – at least not that day. Undeterred by the frosty reception, she returned home and made up her mind to try another tack. She decided to write the politician a letter, hoping that a more formal approach, one which reduced the chance of a confrontation with Léon, might gain her the interview she desired.

> Dear M. President,
>
> I am writing to you to request a meeting. I am addressing my correspondence to M. the President of the Chamber first of all, and then to M. Léon Gambetta.
>
> Yours sincerely, Valtesse de la Bigne

This time, Gambetta relented.

> Dear Madame,
>
> If you would care to come to my office in Paris tomorrow, Wednesday 1 September, I shall be available to grant you the meeting you request.
>
> Yours sincerely, L. Gambetta

Valtesse needed no further invitation. The very next morning, she arrived at the station at Ville-d'Avray and boarded the 10.30 train to Paris.[16]

After lunch with one of her artist friends, Valtesse travelled to the Palais Bourbon. On arriving, she was immediately taken to meet Gambetta. Valtesse turned on all her charm. She excused her appearance, which she laughingly dismissed as quaint country attire. The politician surely understood: how difficult it was for a lady to remain lovely when she was obliged to travel by train, with all that dust and heat! Gambetta was caught off guard. Valtesse was working her magic.

As she spoke, Valtesse's observational skills worked quickly. She tried to get a measure of the man before her. He was 'very friendly', she remarked, though 'a little dirty'.[17] And privately, she regretted having agreed to an early afternoon meeting: the scent of garlic from a hearty lunch lingered on Gambetta's breath. But these were trivial grievances; the important point was that the President of the Chamber of Deputies was listening to her.

Gambetta invited her to take a seat, but Valtesse noticed that he looked uneasy. It was to be expected: he was a Republican; Valtesse was a Bonapartist. She was also clever, well-read and an expert at manipulating social situations to suit her purpose. And she was known to be bold. In the back of his mind, Gambetta recalled the case of Charlotte Corday, the infamous female assassin of Jacobin leader Jean-Paul Marat.[18] He watched Valtesse suspiciously. Caution was needed with this woman.

Valtesse sat firmly back into the chair she had been offered. Gambetta watched in earnest. Valtesse began to speak.

She outlined her connections in Tonkin and Annam and described the content of the letters she had received from her lover. Gambetta listened attentively.

He was startled. This bewitching female spoke eloquently. She understood the intricacies of the situation in the Indochinese territories, could talk knowledgeably about the area's history and its people, and was confident that she knew exactly how to ensure that France triumphed. Gambetta was intrigued. He explained that the matter was of great interest to him and that the Chamber planned to address it in due course.

Valtesse insisted that, truly, Tonkin was a very small territory. How glorious it would be if it belonged to France. Gambetta smiled. His speaker was persistent. Slowly but surely, Valtesse was breaking down his defences. With mounting satisfaction, Valtesse realised that the old politician's wariness was subsiding. Her beauty and charm were winning him over.

Why, surely a man of Gambetta's intelligence and standing must see how favourably he would be regarded if he secured France such a territory? His popularity would soar. And of course, the value of a territory as rich as Tonkin to France need hardly be stated.

Gambetta considered his speaker's powerful argument. Could she elaborate on the points she had made? She could.

'Madame,' Gambetta said at last, 'I am afraid that I cannot examine all the material in your dossier today.'[19]

For a moment, it looked as though Valtesse's efforts had been in vain. But Gambetta explained: 'I have agreed to a meeting which I cannot postpone.' He continued: 'would you be so good as to write me a report on the matter?'

Valtesse was triumphant. She wanted nothing more.

Gambetta paused briefly, before adding: 'I have heard much about you, Madame. I know your house, your villa. We are neighbours …'

Valtesse had cause to smile. She had achieved what she had set out to do. Agreeing, with all the sweetness and gentility she could summon, that she would compose the report immediately, she bid Gambetta farewell. Valtesse returned home and set to work.

Gambetta did not have long to wait. In less than a fortnight, Valtesse's report arrived on his desk. Gambetta began to read – and the further he read, the more he was impressed by what his pretty neighbour had to say.

With perfect eloquence, Valtesse outlined the geography and history of the kingdom of Annam, with its nine southern provinces of Annam and its sixteen northern provinces of Tonkin.[20] She gave an informed account of the kingdom's language and its economy, and laid particular stress on the dictatorial nature of the Emperor Tu Duc's rule.[21] 'Tu Duc exerts absolute power over this population,' Valtesse explained, and she described how jobs were distributed unfairly among the people. A French protectorate would redress the balance. The country's industry was undeveloped, and yet there were resources that France could exploit. She advised that France should not attempt to conquer the territory, a move which would be costly and difficult, but to expand its protectorate across all areas of the kingdom.

Valtesse presented her argument clearly, she gave reasons, she provided examples. And her conclusion was firm: a French expedition to Annam and Tonkin was not only advisable, it was essential. Gambetta was impressed.

Just days after Valtesse deposited her report, a crisp white envelope arrived at her home in Ville-d'Avray. The official stamp on the front was full of promise: 'Chamber of Deputies'.

'Madame,' the enclosed letter began, 'I find the report that you were good enough to write me excellent in both form and structure, and you should publish it, unless you would rather I do so.'[22]

Valtesse could glow with pride. It was a magnificent accolade. Gambetta was one of the leading politicians in France. His stirring speeches had been known to rally even the most reluctant of men. His articles had earned him a reputation as one of the most articulate Republicans in France. Now, this revered figure considered her political treatise to be 'excellent' and publishable. It was a tremendous coup.

Still, Valtesse knew that the situation was delicate. If France wanted to make real progress, the ruling powers in Indochina must not be alerted to her campaign. But the temptation of having her political essay published – and her intelligence showcased – was impossible to resist. Valtesse agreed to have a version of her report printed in *Le Journal Officiel*. But dare she allow her views to appear in a daily paper with as high a circulation as *Le Figaro* too?

On Wednesday morning on 22 September 1880, readers of *Le Figaro* opened their papers to find a curious article on page four by an unknown contributor who went by their initials only: V. de la B.[23]

'His Majesty Tu Duc is without a doubt the most disillusioned ruler imaginable,' the mysterious author began, 'he governs his subjects according to his whims, and his sceptre is a cane, which he uses to issue tens or hundreds of blows wherever he pleases on those who dare break the rules that he invents each day.'

Valtesse described how the Emperor denied his subjects basic necessities to satisfy his own flights of fancy. She explained that whenever Tu Duc wanted to go fishing, whole stretches of water were cordoned off, and local inhabitants were forbidden to fish or sail until his Majesty grew tired of the sport.

But her most horrific revelation was the form of punishment in force in the territory. Tu Duc's brother thought nothing of shaving a woman's head and parading her through the streets when his pride had been injured. Then, when a minor military captain failed to show him due respect, the same prince killed him with his bare hands, congratulating himself that the gesture would serve as a warning to others. Tu Duc himself issued punishment on a different principle: the culprit must suffer and his own bank balance must increase.

If only there were not so many princes, Valtesse lamented; alas, there were three generations' worth, perhaps 1,000 or more, all of them enjoying shamelessly decadent, unproductive lifestyles. Princes spent the whole day smoking opium, indulging in leisurely pursuits – and marrying. Some princes had as many as 30 wives; one had more than 100 children. Could inhabitants not draw consolation from the possibility that one of these rich princes might want to do business with them? Hardly: princes thought it laughable that they should be expected to pay for goods in shops.

Valtesse was desperate to imprint the urgency of the situation on the French conscience, and turned her attention to the other dangers faced by the Annam people. What terror would the French people understand? What terrified her? She considered for a moment. Then the answer came to her: tigers.

'There are no fewer tigers in Annam than there are princes,' she warned readers, 'and they live primarily on the inhabitants.'

Valtesse recounted an anecdote whereby some locals had gone to sleep in a forest at the end of a long day gathering berries. After a while, one of the men was awakened by a tugging on his leg. He realised in horror that it was a tiger. As the animal's courage mounted, it began to drag the man away from the group. His comrades woke to hear the ghastly cracking of their colleague's bones between the tiger's ferocious jaws. The men spent the rest of the night frozen in silent terror. When daybreak finally came, they hurried back to their village. As they left the clearing, they passed a chilling sight: there, not far from where they had been sleeping, lay the remains of their companion. Only his skull was left.

Satisfied with her colourful description of the dual threats of royalty and tigers to the Annam people, Valtesse felt sure that the extracts of her report would make the desired impact on the people of Paris.

Between *Le Journal Officiel* and *Le Figaro*, Valtesse caught the public's attention. Paris began to respond. 'Through this report, Valtesse has grown considerably and takes the lead among modern courtesans,' conceded an otherwise sceptical reviewer.[24] 'This streak of genius flatters her enormously [...] It justifies her elevated position. Valtesse is a national treasure.'

Édouard Manet, *Mademoiselle Lucie⋆ Delabigne, called Valtesse de la Bigne*, 1879,
pastel on canvas, 55.2 × 35.6cm, The Metropolitan Museum of Art, New York,
H.O. Havemeyer Collection, bequest of Mrs H.O. Havemeyer, 1929.
N. inv.: 29.100.561.

⋆ Valtesse is referred to as 'Lucie' in certain gallery records.
I have retained this reference where appropriate.

Lucie Emilie Delabigne aka Valtesse de la Bigne, *c.* 1880, photo Anatole Pougnet.

Henri Gervex, *The Civil Marriage*, 1880–81, oil on canvas, 83 × 99cm, Salle des Mariages, Mairie of the 19th arrondissement, Paris.

(BELOW) Close-up of *The Civil Marriage* showing Valtesse.

Henri Gervex, *La Toilette*, 1878, oil on canvas, 55.5 × 38.2cm, private collection. Experts are now confident that the model in this painting is Valtesse.

Valtesse's bed.
Designed by Édouard Lièvre, *Lit de parade* belonging to Valtesse de la Bigne,
c. 1875, Paris, gilt bronze, beechwood and velvet, 410 × 260 × 200cm,
Les Arts décoratifs – Musée des Arts décoratifs, Paris.

Two photographic portraits of Valtesse.

Henri Gervex

Édouard
Detaille

Liane
de Pougy

98, Boulevard Malesherbes, 1877 drawing by M. Huot.

Jean Rostand (1894–1977), the biologist and philosopher, and subsequent owner of Valtesse's home Rayon d'Or in Ville-d'Avray, pictured in front of her former property.

Henri Gervex, *Portrait of Madame Valtesse de la Bigne*, 1879,
oil on canvas, 205 × 120.2cm, Musée d'Orsay, Paris.

Valtesse's tomb at Ville-d'Avray.
Only the square base and the first circular mounting remain in place today.

Valtesse knew that she had taken a dangerous risk. The successful expansion of France's protectorate depended on maintaining the utmost discretion. But for the moment, Valtesse's articles were harmlessly garnering her respect and admiration. Few people made the link between the politically astute courtesan, the Republican politician and the government's strategy for addressing the problems in Annam – apart from one. Just weeks after Valtesse's text appeared, *Le Figaro* published another article. It took pride of place on the paper's front page and the author was a man Valtesse knew only too well: Émile Zola.

The piece launched a vicious attack on Gambetta. To Zola's mind, the politician was ineffectual and his approach outmoded. Turning his attention to Gambetta's speeches, he inquired, 'What? Is that all?' They were 'no more eloquent than those of two or three hundred equally ambitious lawyers who had simply not been as lucky'.[25] But then something in the second column gave cause for Valtesse to sit up and take notice: 'M. Gambetta is not passionate about our modern world. [...] He is a Greek or Roman in disguise. He clearly thinks himself in Athens or Rome; his Republic is 2,000 years old, and when he thinks about rebuilding it, he sees himself crowned with roses, a crimson cloak about his shoulders, drinking wine in the company of Phryne and Aspasia.'

It was difficult to ignore the thinly veiled allusion to Valtesse. The reference to the ancient Grecian women had been carefully considered. The bright and beautiful Aspasia was said to have been a courtesan, and her Athenian home became a hive of intellectual activity, attracting some of the greatest thinkers and writers of the day. Phryne too was a courtesan, and was famed for her complexion, while her beauty inspired countless works of art. Both figures had become fashionable with artists in the 19th century – and both had been compared to Valtesse in the press.

Zola's powers of perception were finely tuned. Valtesse's interest in Annam had indeed established a firm, if unlikely friendship between the statesman and the courtesan, one founded on mutual respect and acceptance of their political differences. Gambetta liked to tease Valtesse, and she enjoyed responding with quick repartee. Alerted by the sound of explosions, Gambetta would stand in his garden and watch the fireworks lighting up the sky over Valtesse's villa every 15 August.[26] The light show was an irresistible invitation to confront the display's pretty choreographer. A quick-fire exchange became a tradition that both parties relished.

'You sent another rocket into my garden!' Gambetta would roar.

'If it was up to me, I would send bombs!' Valtesse would retort. '*Badinguiste!*'[27]

'Jacobin!'

They would both laugh.

'Now, my beautiful neighbour,' he would say, composing himself, 'there is an evening that you cannot refuse me.'

'Oh really? And when would that be?'

'The evening of 2 December!'

The suggestion was an outrageous tease; Gambetta knew full well that the symbolic date was fixed in Bonapartists' calendars, being both the anniversary of the 1805 victory at Austerlitz and Louis Napoleon's 1851 coup d'état.[28]

Valtesse's article on Annam was a triumphant proof of her intellect. But if people thought that the government were actually acting on the advice of a woman – a courtesan no less – there would be an outcry. Would Zola's article alert the public to that scandalous possibility? Everything hung on what now happened in Annam.

But Valtesse had little opportunity to worry about her political profile for the moment. There was trouble brewing. Her previously secret personal life was about to burst on to the public scene in one of the most sensational court cases of the decade.

CHAPTER 13

The Thickness of Blood

With her political acuity showcased and her public profile glittering, Valtesse should have felt quietly relieved. Her social prestige had always deflected attention away from her past. Parisians were far more interested in the whispered names of the notable men who had been spotted pulling up outside – and furtively leaving – 98, Boulevard Malesherbes. But behind her public face, Valtesse was haunted by her past. She assured people that she was uncomplicated, that she had no past.[1] But this was not true. The contact she maintained with her mother, her daughter's guardian, was a constant reminder of the life she had left behind, the life she had felt she must erase to succeed as a courtesan. The revelation of her humble origins and her vice-ridden youth could sully – or even destroy – her carefully constructed public image. It was an appalling possibility, the kind of niggling fear which could consume the mind in quieter moments. She was successful, renowned, secure – why should she worry? But then finally, in 1881, her greatest fear became reality: her past and present collided.

When Valtesse had given birth to Julia-Pâquerette in 1867, she was still a teenager and quite unprepared for motherhood. She had lacked the maternal instinct women were supposed to find natural, and besides, experience had taught her to distrust close, affectionate ties. At the time, she had believed her most promising career path to be rooted in the theatre, a profession whose lifestyle was incompatible with motherhood. Entrusting her daughters' care to her mother was at once professionally shrewd and personally liberating.

Valtesse did not sever her link to Pâquerette, her remaining daughter, once she became a courtesan and her career began to blossom. However, she was cautious; she ensured that a comfortable distance was maintained between them. She retained only indirect contact with the little girl, through letters and the monthly allowance which she supplied for her maintenance.

But when Pâquerette became a teenager, Valtesse suddenly changed her mind. At the beginning of 1881, just months after she visited Gambetta and her report on Annam and Tonkin appeared in the papers, she announced she wanted sole custody of her daughter. Her reason was simple: she had begun to doubt her mother's trustworthiness. In fact, she now feared that her little girl's safety might be in serious danger – and she was determined to do everything in her power to protect her child.

Mme Delabigne's refusal was steadfast. She would not give up the little girl to whom she had become a surrogate mother. Valtesse was furious. She confronted her mother in a heated dispute. Each was as stubborn as the other. So in February 1881, Mme Delabigne turned to a tribunal in Mantes and arranged to have a family pact drawn up.

The pact set out that Pâquerette would be placed in Saint-Joseph's school for girls in Boulogne-sur-Seine, where she would be a boarder until she was eighteen. Mme Delabigne would take her during the holidays and if she fell ill, and Valtesse would cover all expenses. Valtesse would be allowed to write to her daughter and to visit her if she liked. But she could not take her out of the school or involve her in her decadent lifestyle.

Valtesse inspected her mother's proposal closely. She disliked restrictive rules. But agreeing to them would enable her to stipulate a proviso of her own. It was a condition born of a paralysing terror – the very fear which had prompted her demand for custody. On no account was Pâquerette to be taken to spend time with one particular woman, a woman Valtesse despised and whose influence filled her with dread: her own sister, Emilie Tremblay.

Of Valtesse's six siblings, only two were still alive by the 1880s. Valtesse had a younger brother, but there is no evidence to suggest that the siblings maintained contact. That left her sister. Emilie had watched her older sister's rise to fame. Any pangs of jealousy she felt would have been justified. But there was little point competing: Valtesse's position held firm – she reigned over Paris. Perhaps, though, Emilie reasoned, her sister's success could be tapped into and channelled to the rest of the family's advantage. Following Valtesse's lead, Emilie assumed the name Marquesse. She set herself up as a madam, establishing a brothel in the Rue Blanche which soon became notorious. As her enterprise began to prosper, she realised that she could flaunt her connection with her older sister to secure clients. What did it matter if the sisters did not get on? There was money to be made.

To Valtesse, Emilie represented everything she had sought to eradicate from her life: her past, the sordid world of low-level prostitution, unbridled corruption and classlessness. This woman embodied her deepest fears.

Mme Delabigne was only too aware of the tension between her girls. She could see that this was a condition on which the obstinate Valtesse would not yield. Keeping Pâquerette depended on her agreeing to it. Mme Delabigne and Valtesse both signed and the pact came into force.

Valtesse was ruled by her meticulously timetabled schedule of clients and social appearances, but she would visit Pâquerette when she could. She was a great letter writer too, and the little girl would often receive a letter written in her mother's elegant hand. Curiously, Valtesse always began her correspondence addressing Pâquerette as 'my little sister', never 'my little girl'. 'She thought it made her seem younger,' Valtesse's critics scathingly affirmed.[2]

But Valtesse's relationship with her daughter was more complex than journalists allowed. Valtesse was not immune to affection. She never failed to respond to a letter or to make every possible provision for the little girl's material needs. But she had suffered great hurt. Genuine closeness and intimacy unsettled her. And she simply had no personal experience of a flawless maternal role model, and still less a conception of how it might feel to be one. The very notion was mysterious to her. Her letters to Pâquerette are those of a woman torn, a woman longing to express affection, yet wary, anxious that the recipient should not get too close. It was an approach to potentially intimate relationships that Valtesse would replicate throughout her life.

However, Pâquerette was under no illusions. She knew Valtesse was her mother. And much as the arrangement subverted traditional family roles, all parties seemed content with its terms – until the summer of 1881.

Through her correspondence with her daughter, Valtesse learned of some alarming news: the child had been making visits with her grandmother to see Marquesse and attending flamboyant evening soirées. Sometimes, it would get so late that they would be obliged to spend the night there, Pâquerette innocently told her mother. As Valtesse read her daughter's words, the truth began to dawn on her: Pâquerette was being led towards a life of prostitution. To her horror, Valtesse could see her own past replaying before her eyes.

Valtesse knew she must act quickly. There was not a moment to spare. She immediately demanded that a tribunal be brought in to resolve the issue. As the child's natural mother, Valtesse had the odds stacked in her favour and, to her delight, she won. Armed with the results of the appeal, she set off triumphantly for the boarding school one day in the summer term of 1881. Upon arrival, she demanded her daughter, and Pâquerette and her belongings were hurriedly gathered together. Valtesse promptly removed her from the institution and enrolled her in another boarding school in Seine-et-Oise. When the news reached Mme Delabigne, she was enraged. Now, she was going to fight to win the child back – and she would do so in public, so that everyone would be able to see the great wrong she had suffered.

When news of the forthcoming hearing was made public, the papers pounced on the story. What a scandal! One of the most prominent courtesans of the day was not a countess after all, but a commoner. What would all those distinguished gentlemen who had listened to Valtesse's touching tales of her noble father and her honourable mother say now, Albert Wolff asked maliciously?[3] 'I have always been told that Valtesse was of noble birth,' wrote another bewildered journalist.[4] 'She is a mother,' exclaimed *Le Figaro*.[5] She had been keeping two children secret, 'young fruit born of a young love'.[6] So why would an unmaternal *demi-mondaine* suddenly decide to embrace her maternal instinct? What appeal could this long-neglected child now have for her? Clearly, the press riposted, the courtesan had seen that the young girl was blossoming into a ravishingly beautiful teenager. Valtesse must have mercilessly calculated her daughter's beauty to be a marketable asset. She was grooming her to become a courtesan.

But best of all, this renowned beauty with aspirations of grandeur was going to fight her own mother in public, where all the sordid family history would no doubt be exposed. It was a journalist's dream. Word quickly spread across the city.

Paris was charged, and Valtesse's name was splashed across the front pages of all the newspapers. This publicity threatened her very livelihood. Valtesse knew she had an onerous challenge ahead of her if she were to keep her reputation intact and at the same time safeguard her daughter's future.

⌒∞⌒

As dawn broke on 15 November 1881, the sky over Paris was grey and overcast, and there was an icy nip to the air. It was the day of the hearing.

The cold was not the only factor Valtesse needed to consider as she selected the outfit she would wear that morning. As usual, her appearance must please her supporters. But it was vital that she look dignified, sober – as though she were a worthy mother. And as she dressed, with these requirements in mind, there was every reason for her feelings to be mixed. Here she was, preparing her toilette to make yet another public appearance, where she would be looked at and admired, where she must once again use her charms to cast a spell over an expectant audience. It was familiar territory. But the intrusive exposure of the past she had worked so hard to erase was a new experience. It was unknown and it was frightening. Anything could happen.

The prospect justified a torrent of emotions as Valtesse stepped outside into the unforgiving cold. Standing outside her home on that crisp winter morning, Valtesse would have seen her breath on the air in front of her as she prepared to board her carriage. Then, having climbed into the vehicle and settled back into the leather seat, she began her journey through Paris's familiar streets, passing swiftly along Haussmann's sparkling new boulevards, the freshly painted modern apartments flashing past the window in quick succession. In a smart horse-drawn landau like Valtesse's, the journey would have taken little more than 30 minutes. Still, it was precious time to reflect and compose herself. At last, the city's imposing Palais de Justice came into view.

Undeterred by the sombre weather, flocks of curious Parisians had also wrapped their coats and scarves around them more tightly than usual that morning. And then, bracing themselves against the biting cold, they hurried briskly through the streets to take up their seats at the hearing all of Paris was talking about.

As spectators arrived at the *première chambre*, the magnificent, high-ceilinged courtroom quickly took on the appearance of a fashionable soirée. Once Valtesse had taken her place and began to look around her, she could see the audience brimming with artists, politicians and courtesans. They filled the room, jostling, all talking at once, trying to catch a glimpse of her as she knew they would. The event had become a veritable social occasion.

As silence was called, the room fell into an anticipative hush, broken only now and then by an ill-timed cough or the creak of one of the dark mahogany pews as a viewer shifted to get comfortable in his seat. Everyone was watching with bated breath to see what the verdict would be and how the courtesan would react. The tension was almost palpable. The hearing began.

Mme Delabigne's lawyer was Maxime Napias, a familiar figure on the Parisian legal circuit. He was the first to speak. Pâquerette, he declared firmly, should be restored to her grandmother's care according to the terms of the original agreement. His case was built on one simple argument: Valtesse was unfit to be a mother. He began his attack.

Valtesse was not 25 or 26 as she claimed, but 34, Napias objected. (Some papers would later report this as 33.) With her beauty and her fortune, she had become a well-known figure in the art world. To think that she was even known as 'The Union of Artists'! Napias pointed out that she owned not one, but two extravagant homes. She had failed to impress in her theatre performances – at least as far as her acting ability was concerned. And furthermore, she had a penchant for radical politics. Did the court not remember the outrageous scandal caused by her Bonapartist fireworks display in Ville-d'Avray only a few years earlier, when the words 'Long Live the Emperor!' were shamelessly spelt out in glowing colours across the sky? They should. This woman was dangerous. A woman who dabbled in politics was not to be trusted. And her reputation as one of the most notorious courtesans in Paris went before her.

Then came the most absurd – and alarming – part of Napias's defence: did the jury know that this woman had published a novel using the pseudonym 'Ego', a name which could be seen on all her stationery? He produced a copy of *Isola*. 'Isola is Mme Valtesse,' he proclaimed. 'To know Mme Valtesse, all one need do is read her portrait written by her own hand.'

Incredibly, Napias proceeded to quote passages of *Isola*, presenting them as hard evidence of Valtesse's character.

'Isola is a monster. She has mastered the art of seducing, charming, captivating anyone fascinated by her beauty. Defenceless, he becomes her slave; she forces him into submission, […] Beware he who looks into her feline eyes'.[7]

Napias paused for a moment, allowing his words to make their impact. 'Further on,' he continued, 'we find this:'

'Give me your word of honour that you have never loved.'

'The most beautiful girl in the world can only give what she has; I have no word of honour.'

'Look now, be frank.'

'In my situation, frankness is a capital fault which leads to ruin.'[8]

Napias was now in his stride:

'I do not love and I do not get bored. I live alone, *ego* is my motto and I am effortlessly true to it.'[9]

It was enough to make the pulses of Valtesse and her lawyer race. They sat helplessly in silence as Napias's accusations echoed round the courtroom. Surely the court would not base their decision on the behaviour of a fictional character?

But Napias was not finished with the novel. There were other characters he sought to assassinate through its pages.

'In this volume,' he pursued, 'there is a woman to whom attention must be drawn. In the novel, she is called Clairette. In reality, she is named Mme M., and we shall have more to say about her shortly.'[10]

Napias was talking about Camille Meldola. He had carefully selected passages from *Isola* which described how Clairette managed the debauched ways of her mistress. This 'friend', Napias concluded, was responsible for introducing Valtesse to Pâquerette's father. 'Today,' he pursued, 'M. and Mme. M. live under the same roof as the opulent Isola.'[11]

His character assassination under way, Napias realised that he must account for the behaviour of his own client as well. There was much to criticise. It was important to pre-empt the opponent's attack.

Mme Delabigne's life thus far, the lawyer insisted, had been one of martyrdom and hardship.[12] She was now 61. Back in 1844, she was unwittingly seduced by a teacher named T. at the school where she worked. This despicable character fathered her seven children despite being married to another woman. When she finally severed contact with him, Mme Delabigne continued to live a life of poverty, admirably raising her seven illegitimate children single-handedly.

Napias explained how Pâquerette had been the fortunate recipient of his client's natural instinct for maternal nurturing. When the little girl's mother selfishly abandoned her, Mme Delabigne generously took care of her as though she were her own daughter.

Still, the lawyer knew that powerful words needed supporting evidence. And he believed he had just the proof he needed. He unfolded a piece of paper and began to read. It was a letter from Mme Delabigne to Meldola, warning her to stay away from Pâquerette and accusing her of corrupting Valtesse when she was a little girl. 'I loved my daughter as today I love hers,' Napias finished before returning his attention to the audience.[13] Mme Valtesse, he concluded firmly, was as unfit to be a mother as his client was worthy of this post. With that, he returned to his seat.

Throughout his appeal, Valtesse had been listening quietly and watching closely. The criticisms were harsh, but she maintained her composure. This was essential, however much turmoil and anxiety she might be suffering inside. She had been planning her defence with her lawyer and friend Lucien Jullemier for weeks. It was a delicate situation. Her very livelihood was at stake. She needed to play it carefully. But then performances were her forte.

Valtesse's whole case hinged on eulogising motherhood and the mother–child bond. But in so doing, she would be challenging her own mother, thereby scuppering her own defence. It was a fine line to negotiate.

Jullemier rose to his feet. The challenge before him was significant, but he was prepared. He began his defence, delivering carefully-chosen phrases in a solemn, matter-of-fact tone.

The woman sitting before the court today was one of the most excellent people – and mothers – he knew. He pointed out that Valtesse had generously bestowed thousands of francs on her mother for the sole purpose of raising Pâquerette. If his client had left her daughter in the grandmother's care, it was because she had sincerely believed her mother to be too old to repeat the dubious acts which had so scarred Valtesse's childhood. Clearly, Jullemier continued, his client had been grossly deceived on this account. Mme Delabigne had not dedicated the time she should have to surveying her daughters when they were young; how could she now criticise her child's conduct when she had been the one to encourage it?

Jullemier's defence was gathering momentum.

Before the hearing, Valtesse had firmly instructed him that reserve was of the utmost importance. She had been just as adamant that this request should be made known to the court from the outset. But after such a scathing character assassination of his client and friend, it was difficult to remain composed. 'I should like to point out,' Jullemier fumed, 'that the appellant may well have decided not to marry, but she did a fine job of embracing maternity. She had seven children! [...] She called my client 'The Union of Artists', but you could just as well call her 'The Union of Bankers'.[14]

The case was heating up. Valtesse sat listening attentively. She did not utter a word, nor did Mme Delabigne. But the mother and daughter were destroying each other nonetheless through the mouths of their lawyers. The audience was gripped.

Jullemier continued:

this cautious and pious grandmother was taking Pâquerette to visit her daughter Marquès [*sic*] whom my esteemed colleague assures us was a simple laundress. A strange kind of laundress who writes her letters on scented blue paper – like this – decorated with birds opening their beaks as they prepare to leave the nest![15]

A murmur ran round the courtroom. If this was reserve, what might the results of a full-scale attack have been? The audience sat on the edge of their seats.

That, Jullemier declared, was the reason Valtesse had taken her daughter back. This grandmother's conduct was shameful. And, he added emphatically, she had no right to prevent a mother from exerting her *natural* rights.

As Jullemier uttered these words, the foundations of Napias's defence suffered a potentially fatal blow. Mme Delabigne and her lawyer knew that this line of attack posed the ultimate threat to their case. It was a shrewd argument, for it tapped into a very contemporary concern.

The natural quality of the mother–child bond was the aspect most eulogised by contemporary discourse promoting motherhood. People enthusiastically approved sociologist Paul Janet's view when he wrote that nature had established between a mother and her child 'a bond so precious that nobody would think to question its validity'.[16] These ideas had secured a strong hold on the public's imagination. Maternity had become fashionable. Jullemier knew exactly what he was doing. Why, this *natural* mother merely wanted her daughter to receive the good education that she herself had been denied. Could she be refused such a *natural* request?

And this novel that his honourable colleague insisted was an accurate portrait of his client? 'I have no way of confirming whether my client is the author,' Jullemier ventured slyly, 'but in any case, can we condemn her based on the actions and conduct of her heroes? If that were the case, no novelist would be able to keep his or her children.'[17]

Jullemier's defence was becoming stronger by the minute. But had his outburst been too much? Had he gone a step too far?

Valtesse need not have worried on this account. She had a trump card. Now, it was time to use it.

It came in the form of a letter she had asked to be read. Resuming his composure, Jullemier began. It opened with a response to a crucial question: was Valtesse's mother responsible for her daughter embarking on a life of prostitution?

'Sir, I should like to give you the answer you request, and it is true I cannot, I am embarrassed.'[18]

As her words resounded round the courtroom, Valtesse brought her delicate hands to her face and hid her eyes. When she uncovered them again, onlookers were startled; her huge blue eyes were moist with tears and she swayed a little, as though she might be about to faint. The court was transfixed, moved by her emotion. As the lawyer continued, people looked from Valtesse to the speaker and back to Valtesse again. With Jullemier narrating, Valtesse was free to perform to her own script. It was a masterfully acted scene.

'My mother may accuse me, treat me badly, insult me, if she wishes [...] But if she forgets that I am her daughter, I cannot forget she is my mother, and a mother is sacred [...] As for my conduct towards my daughter [...] In the irregular situation in which I find myself, never, outside this hearing, has her name been mentioned. I have friends I have known for ten years who do not even know that I have a daughter. I raised her. My daughter is twelve today. If I have removed her from her grandmother's care, it is because I have discovered things concerning the child which have made me afraid. That is to say, that if as a daughter I cannot judge my mother, as a mother I must protect my daughter.

'Do not ask any more of me Sir, and if, in front of the judges you require material proof, tell them this: that the grandmother, who has a secure existence and is not needy, was going to spend days and nights with my daughter with Emilie Tremblay, otherwise known as Marquesse, in Rue Blanche.

'Tell the judges this too, Sir: my daughter is in a convent, saintly, innocently; please ask that they do not disturb her. She is my daughter, I want her and her grandmother is not fit to look after her. I implore you to give her to me. Save her, I beg you.'[19]

A murmur rippled round the courtroom. Valtesse was back on familiar territory and she was working her magic. 'The title *mother* is so sacred, and from the lips of a woman, it becomes so moving,' commentators observed.[20] All that Jullemier need do now was cement its effects with some final, hard evidence against the opponent. Mme Delabigne's continued contact with her granddaughter's objectionable father was the perfect source of material.

Richard Fossey had failed to impress either lawyer, and his name, a homophone of the French word *fossé* or ditch, made him an easy target for ridicule in the press.[21] When he learned of the forthcoming trial, his priority had been to ensure that his name be kept out of any ensuing scandal. A few letters sufficed to illustrate the surprisingly familiar tone Fossey took with his daughter's grandmother and his shortcomings as a father.

'Dearest Maman, I am counting on you for 400 big ones. Oh, do not get yourself worked up, I need them! Say hello to my little Pâquerette.'

The lawyer was determined that his defence should have a powerful conclusion. And so in the final minutes, he took a dangerous gamble which could have cost Valtesse the case. If the court would not give the natural mother custody of her child, they were implored to designate someone else – anyone but the grandmother – to care for her.

It was a risky closing shot. But Jullemier had already disproved Fossey's paternal capabilities. Valtesse only hoped that they had done enough to convince the court of Mme Delabigne's unworthiness.

The jury retired to deliberate. As she sat in that chilly courtroom, dressed in her restrictive court attire, waiting to hear the verdict, Valtesse could only feel tense. Which way would things go? All around her, the spectators sat expectantly, transfixed.

Eventually, the verdict came. Prosecuting attorney Robert began to speak.

Pâquerette, he announced, was to be entrusted to the woman most fit to care for her, the one to whom nature had assigned this role: Valtesse.

The audience drew breath, the unbearable tension finally broken. To Valtesse's relief, her performance had worked: she had won the case. Mme Delabigne was incensed, furious – and distraught. She broke down in tears: tears of genuine despair, sympathised some papers; tears of fury that she had lost, according to others. But as Valtesse had hoped, her fierce determination, her ability to command an audience and her linguistic eloquence gave her the advantage over the child's grandmother.

Robert had some final cautionary words for the grandmother, too. Mme Delabigne had been seriously misguided when she had accused her daughter of being a fallen woman, incapable of raising her child in a moral environment. With elation running through her veins, Valtesse had cause to radiate one of her quietly confident smiles when Robert issued his closing observation: 'Courtesans, for the most part, give their children an even stricter upbringing than other women.'[22] Now she knew for sure: she had won.

The case might have been over, but the following days were critical. The repercussions of the hearing in the papers would determine the state of her reputation. For all the self-assurance she projected at the hearing, once safely home at 98, Boulevard Malesherbes, she could surrender to her natural anxiety as she waited for Schwab, her footman, to bring the morning papers up to her the next day. What would the impact be?

As she opened the papers, at least one of her expectations was immediately confirmed: all of Paris, it seemed, had an opinion to give.

Her professed maternal instinct was viewed with suspicion. 'What day, at what time and why was Mlle Valtesse taken with this sudden desire to see her little Pâquerette and have her close to her?' one journalist asked maliciously. 'No one knows. The writer presumes, however, that it was a rainy day, when her closest acquaintance of the moment had declared that thanks to her, his pockets were now as empty as his mind.'[23]

But such comments missed a crucial point: in allowing her past to be made public, Valtesse had risked the very thing she considered most precious – her reputation. For the sake of her daughter, the mother in her had compromised the courtesan.

Valtesse found that much of the press coverage maintained that she and her mother were as culpable as each other. Valtesse was not wrong to seek custody; she should only have done it sooner. 'I would issue her with a substantial fine for having agreed to separate from her daughter in her tender youth,' one journalist complained.[24]

Mme Delabigne might have lost the case, but for many, there could be but one ultimate loser: Pâquerette herself. With such a family, another critic exclaimed, 'this little girl has much to complain about!'[25]

The reports can hardly have surprised Valtesse. She knew that the tabloids were always going to be her harshest critics. But her plight received support as well, and from the most unexpected sources. Albert Wolff's biting irony was renowned, but his acerbic remarks paradoxically worked in Valtesse's favour. She could not be blamed, he declared. She was the product of her background. Of all those involved in the case, it was 'undoubtedly the courtesan' who emerged the most worthy figure.[26]

A journalist like Wolff carried weight among the public. And it was the public's opinion that mattered most to Valtesse. People had seen that she had behaved with dignity and decorum. She had been careful to remain cool-headed in court, proved how articulate she was and had given the impression that her critics' snide remarks were of no consequence to her, that she was above idle gossip. For all the criticisms, Valtesse's public could not help but admire her. She felt increasingly reassured, as the following weeks confirmed that her reputation had emerged untarnished. At last, she could relax. She still wore her crown.

The court hearing would be valuable preparation, too. She had rallied Paris to her cause and defeated her mother. But there were further problems in store. The hearing would not be her last brush with the law, nor had her involvement in the government's dealings with Indochina passed unnoticed. Within months, Paris was to witness the mysterious death of a high-profile public figure, an embittered legal battle, a revolutionary art exhibition and a scandalous novel – and Valtesse was to be at the centre of them all.

CHAPTER 14

Slander, Scandal and Sun Queens

The courtesan was a creature with a limited lifespan. Culture could be acquired and etiquette learned, but physical appeal was essential. A tired and aged body was an indisputable obstacle to the profession. But if old age formalised the end of a career, infinitely more difficult was the transitional phase that preceded it. It could break a woman if she resisted it, secure her future if she embraced it. Eventually, every courtesan found herself there: middle age.

In the early 1880s, Valtesse was approaching her 35th birthday. She knew she was considered beautiful, but she entertained no illusions: before long, her looks would fade. Fresher, younger faces were appearing all the time. 'Valtesse,' *Gil Blas* reported, 'whom people have baptised the Union of Artists, because she has been pleasing the laureates of the Salon for more than 25 years, has just encountered a rival in the beautiful Anna Vauthier, who a breakup with a high-ranking Egyptian has just put in circulation.'[1] Competition was everywhere.

A courtesan's security depended on more than her appearance. She must profit from her looks while she could, and nurture her reputation and investments in anticipation of when she could not. With foresight and pragmatism, Valtesse had always saved diligently while making a trademark of her more durable, non-superficial qualities: her cool reserve, her wit, her intelligence and her impressive cultural knowledge. The public were receptive to her efforts.[2]

Now that she was no longer in the first flush of youth, it was time to capitalise on these intangible assets to ensure her continued sovereignty. Valtesse needed Paris's respect and support more than ever, for as the 1880s unfolded, a chain of unexpected events was going to test her in public as she had never been tested before.

The first challenge arose at the start of 1882, just weeks after Valtesse's triumph over her mother in court. One crisp January morning, Valtesse's usual routine was interrupted when an anxious Meldola came to her, insisting that they speak. The women were sworn confidantes, so when Meldola announced that a horrific incident had befallen her, Valtesse urged her friend to explain what had happened. Meldola began.

She told her mistress that she had been out walking with her husband on the outskirts of Montmartre, when she had had a terrible shock.[3] As the couple made their way, Meldola spotted a pair of figures approaching them. She felt sure she recognised the women, and as the two sets of walkers neared each other, Meldola's suspicions were confirmed: it was Emilie Delabigne, and beside her, Valtesse's sister, Marquesse.

Meldola realised that her enemy had seen her.

The old woman's demeanour flushed first with recognition and then with rage. 'You sold my daughter!' she screamed.[4]

Gripping her husband's arm, Meldola quickened her pace. Only a few weeks had passed since the court case. Emotions were fresh and wounds were raw. Catching up with the couple, Mme Delabigne seized M. Meldola's walking stick and passers-by watched aghast as she raised her arm above her head. With a horrifying swish, the stick swiped through the air, and came crashing down just millimetres from Meldola's head, catching her earring. The piece of jewellery clattered to the ground, and the terrified couple began to run.

As the housekeeper's story unfolded, Valtesse grew furious. Were there passers-by, witnesses who would corroborate Meldola's tale? Meldola confirmed that there were: a young man named Georges had witnessed the attack. He was only nineteen, but he would surely support her. Valtesse felt doubtful. Young men were easily swayed when there was a tempting incentive – a favour from the madam of a brothel, for example.

But Valtesse saw her friend's distress giving way to healthy determination. She could probably claim for damages. The earring alone was worth at least 300 francs.[5] Meldola was decided: Mme Delabigne had insulted her in public – she must be made to pay in public, too.

So it was that that March, Valtesse's personal life resumed its position on the front page of the Parisian newspapers, as Meldola and Mme Delabigne found themselves face-to-face in court once again.

On the day of the hearing, the lawyer, M. Lébre, arrived to defend Meldola, while a familiar face appeared in defence of Valtesse's mother: Napias. And he was determined not to be beaten a second time.

Mme Delabigne had been seen holding the walking stick, denial was impossible. So the lawyer's argument was pragmatic: she had seized the stick in defence. It was Meldola who had issued the insult, and the old lady had grabbed the walking stick off M. Meldola to prevent him hitting her.[6]

'Old Mme Delabigne resented my client,' Lébre countered, 'because of her ongoing friendship with her daughter, Valtesse.'[7]

'Mme Meldola is still bitter that the role she played and continues to play in the house of the famous courtesan known as

"Valtesse" and "The Union of Artists" was exposed during the last hearing,' Napias shot back.

All Meldola's hopes were pinned on the young witness, Georges. He stepped forward to speak, but seemed confused. What was his profession?

'My profession? Son of a landlord,' he retorted.

Laughter rippled through the audience. Silence was called for.

No, he did not recall seeing anything. Was he certain? No – perhaps he saw a cane raised. He could not say who held it. He certainly did not hear the insult that was supposed to have been issued. But other witnesses had.

'Tarts!' people insisted they had heard Meldola call out when she saw the mother and daughter.

It looked as though victory was slipping through Meldola's fingers. Napias reminded the court of the passage from *Isola* which he had quoted in the previous hearing.

Meldola grew angry. 'The proof that I am not Mlle Valtesse's maid is that I do not live with her,' she snapped.

'Really?' probed Napias, amused. 'Well, of the two pieces of correspondence you sent us, the first states that you live at number 1, Rue de la Terrasse, while the second gives your address as number 17 of the same road. On my advice, my client sent you a letter to the second address requesting a receipt of delivery. The letter was returned to her with the following advice: "Mme Meldola is unknown at number 17". You do not live at number 17, but you and your husband live at number 1, Rue de la Terrasse, in Mlle Valtesse's sumptuous apartment.'[8]

Lébre leaped to his feet and began to protest. The judge silenced him and demanded that he be seated.

The tribunal began to deliberate, but their decision was quickly reached. The scenario was a familiar tableau of Parisian street life: two working-class women, each bearing a grudge, had bumped into each other and a quarrel had broken out. The older woman deserved compassion. Mme Delabigne was acquitted.

A woman's pride was a precious commodity. Valtesse understood that better than anyone. Still, the case resolved, it was hard to suppress a wave of relief. Her media profile could now regain its former sparkle.

But Meldola would not let the matter rest. She called for the case to be reviewed, and was pleased when she was granted a second hearing in June. This time the housekeeper could walk away satisfied; her adversary was ordered to pay a 25 franc fine and a further 25 francs in damages.[9]

Valtesse knew that her mother's defeat would only embitter the already fractious relations between them. However, Meldola's loyalty deserved payment in kind. Besides, a happy and triumphant housekeeper was easier to live with – and more obliging – than a disgruntled one. Valtesse needed Meldola. She felt sure that the drama would pass and that daily life would resume its normal pattern. Edmond de Goncourt's request for assistance in providing research material by way of a female perspective on adolescence for his novel *Chérie* (1882) was a flattering interlude in what Valtesse hoped would be an otherwise calm rest of the year, spent in the usual manner: socialising, enjoying art and literature and tending to her public profile.[10]

But then at the end of 1882, something unexpected happened. A horrific accident took Parisians by surprise – and it scuppered Valtesse's plans for serenity, thrusting her into the spotlight once again.

One morning towards the end of November, a shock report appeared in the papers: Léon Gambetta had shot himself.[11]

Parisians were plunged into disbelief. Was the great statesman dead, people asked? No, but he was badly injured. Gambetta had been handling his gun at home in Ville-d'Avray when suddenly the weapon had gone off and a bullet had penetrated his right hand, exiting just below his thumb and injuring his forearm. Four of the best doctors and surgeons in Paris rushed to the politician's bedside.

The nature of the injury was incredible. Surely the unshakeable statesman had not tried to take his own life? It must have been an accident – or a skilfully covered assassination attempt. Press and public alike buried themselves in hypotheses.

'Was M. Gambetta responsible for his own injury?' asked a journalist in *Le Gaulois*.[12] 'His friends say so, but the way they say it gives cause to doubt. Firstly, these gentlemen do not agree among themselves. Some say that the accident took place in Gambetta's bedroom. Others claim that it happened in the garden.'

Theories abounded: Gambetta had shot himself; no, the gun really had gone off accidentally, while he was cleaning it; and maybe Gambetta had not been alone.

> It has been pointed out that the weather was frightful, certainly too bad for the attractions of country living alone to have brought Gambetta to Les Jardies. It is supposed, therefore, that he had company.[13]

Every street corner in Paris buzzed with speculation. Had Gambetta been with Léonie? Was it true that she had sold sensitive government information to the fiery courtesan La Païva who had connections with Bismarck? Was Léonie now being blackmailed and, distraught, had she tried to take her own life, only for Gambetta to injure himself in intervening?

Then within the closed confines of private salons one more, scandalous theory began to circulate. Savvy society men muttered knowingly, fashionable ladies spoke in whispers behind their fans: perhaps Léonie had become insanely jealous of her lover's association with the famous courtesan Valtesse de la Bigne, and shot Gambetta in a fit of rage.

Valtesse observed the commotion from the sidelines. She made no comment on the hypotheses. She did as she had so often done: she watched.

Valtesse was not alone in refusing to act. Public curiosity remained unsatisfied because, injured and bedridden though he was, on one point Gambetta remained firm: there would be no official enquiry.

Proponents of the 'crime of passion' theory had cause to smile knowingly. Less cynical Parisians were bemused. But that was Gambetta; it was promising if his hot-headed temperament was returning.

Then, at the end of December, an announcement appeared in *Le Gaulois*:

> Yesterday afternoon, M. Gambetta had a violent attack and for
> quarter of an hour, doctors thought their efforts were going to
> be in vain. After half an hour of suffering, the invalid picked up
> a little. The rest of the day passed without incident.[14]

The relapse came as a surprise, but everyone knew Gambetta to be made of strong material. He would surely recover before the New Year.

But it was not to be; the wound that had got the whole of Paris talking, about conspiracies and crimes of passion and Valtesse, had gone gangrenous. On 31 December 1882, Paris awoke to some shocking news: Léon Gambetta was dead.

After the dramatic headlines came articles, reviews and reports scrutinising every aspect of the statesman's life, career and mysterious death. For the last few months, Gambetta had been busying himself with matters in Tonkin, promoting the value of the territory for France and attempting to consolidate the country's position in Indochina. When Commander Rivière was sent to conquer Hanoi with 500 men in April, media attention turned with renewed fervour to Gambetta and Tonkin. Within days of the statesman's death, all matters concerning Tonkin – including Valtesse's article – were scrupulously re-examined. Finally, the revelation that Valtesse had influenced Gambetta's political strategies came spilling out on to the front pages of the Parisian daily papers.

'Do you know where the idea of the expedition to Tonkin was born, that controversial project which was interrupted by Gambetta's death?' stirred the journalist Dandeau. 'In an elegant private apartment, which is located at number 98, Boulevard Malesherbes, and is inhabited by a pretty woman, whom you will almost certainly have spotted at the theatre, in the Bois, at the races, and wherever fashionable society goes: Madame Valtesse de la Bigne.'[15]

The journalist detailed everything that had taken place between the 'golden blonde with white skin' and the President of the Chamber of Deputies. Their meeting was discussed, Valtesse's report was transcribed in full, and the paper even went so far as to print Gambetta's letters to Valtesse on its front page.

Where had the journalist uncovered such sources, people wondered? It was almost as though Valtesse had fed him the information, that she had wanted her association with the revered statesman to be made public.

'That is the true story of the collaboration between Mme Valtesse and M. Gambetta,' the journalist concluded triumphantly. 'It is not the first time that a woman and a statesman have collaborated in public affairs. But one must admit that there is something particularly spicy about the circumstances of this collaboration.'

The public agreed. Suddenly, the whole of Europe was talking about Valtesse's relationship with the statesman and the scandalous possibility that France was in the hands of a politically powerful, real-life Nana.

'Mlle Valtesse is the lady who, it appears, has inspired the Tonkin expedition,' an English journalist exclaimed.[16]

'She means to bargain France a piece of Tonkin as she used to do a deal over a landscape painting at the Hôtel Drouot,' marvelled the French press.[17]

'Statesmanship is often influenced by wire pulling,' spat one Scottish journalist, 'but it is scarcely credible that in our day the wire should be pulled by a woman, regarding whom it can be said that she did hold a high position in French society.'[18]

In June, *La Réforme* published an article that exposed the full extent of Valtesse's communication with Gambetta, her relationship with Kergaradec and her involvement in the Tonkin expedition. The media backlash was unprecedented.

Valtesse had long been a Parisian darling, but now the press were watching her every move. People spoke about 'her' war in Tonkin, and she was compared to historically influential consorts, including Mme de Maintenon, Mme de Pompadour and Empress Eugénie. Meanwhile, the most innocuous letters or texts bearing her name were of the utmost interest.

'Anything written by this eminent female artiste is an object of curiosity,' declared a journalist in *Le Gaulois*.[19] Suddenly, notable figures in society were appearing in press offices with letters that Valtesse had written. In those humble sheets of paper, the editor of *Le Gaulois* saw banknotes. Here was a way to increase circulation.

'Mlle Valtesse has addressed some precious notes to a number of esteemed figures on some of the principal questions which concern our contemporary society,' the paper announced.

There was a letter to Republican politician Gustave Rivet on paternity searches:

I have known lots of fathers. I have hunted for several on other people's behalf. I must tell you, Sir, that these hunts have always proved fruitless. In our troubled times, no creature conceals itself as artfully as a father. [...] In the great social fishbowl, it is difficult to catch a father, even with the best lines. [...] When you have lost a father, it is pure madness to chase after him. The father is, as you say in legal speak, inaccessible and uncatchable. Perhaps you understand what that means.

There was a report written to the *préfet de police* about what Valtesse perceived to be a gross injustice in the card game of baccarat. She insisted that the matter demanded his immediate attention:

Nobody has yet found a way to win at baccarat, other than to cheat. [...] I have found no solution, have you?

On one occasion, Valtesse wrote to the Lord Chancellor:

Magistracy is divided, as I am sure you will know, into two classes: judges [*magistrature assise*, literally 'seated' magistrates] and state prosecutors [*magistrature debout*, literally 'standing' magistrates]. People want to reduce one to the detriment of the other. This is wrong. If all the magistrates were 'standing' they would be exhausted after two hours. I have known many magistrates. They do not need that.

Finally, the paper included a witty letter Valtesse had written to the Minister of Agriculture, declaring her firm belief that what the country needed was more stud farms:

I have visited several stud farms ... They are very interesting places, particularly at lunchtime. I have always left the yard feeling cheerful. I therefore believe we should increase the number of stud farms. There should be one in every road. The stud farm is man's friend. There is a direct link between stud farms and the question of paternity searches. The stud farm is the triumph of paternity. If one is searching for paternity, look no further.

Valtesse's sparkling wit brought a smile to people's faces. Her quick humour danced off the page and Paris adored her for it. Some of the greatest courtesans had watched glittering careers crumble when they reached their 30s, or even earlier. Blanche d'Antigny was just 34 when she died, Marie du Plessis barely 24. At nearly 35, Valtesse was in her supremacy.

'The whole world resounds with the sound of Valtesse's name,' gushed journalist Fernand Xau:

> The newspapers talk only of Her and if this continues, we will speak of the century of Valtesse as they do that of Pericles or of Louis XIV. History, impartial history, will burnish her name on its bronze tablets.[20]

'She is no longer The Union of Artists,' declared another journalist. 'She is The Union of People.'[21]

The mystery of Gambetta's death remained unsolved, and the gossip columns eventually fell silent. But one thing was clear: Valtesse had been instrumental in laying the foundations for France's actions in Tonkin.

Drama could be exhilarating, but it was exhausting, too. After the court case and the scandal of Gambetta's death, Valtesse craved some light relief. She had been toying with the idea of publishing another book. In May 1883, a new pet project, *Lettres à Nana*, which included a selection of letters she had received from various love-struck suitors, enabled her to reconnect with her creative side.[22] Valtesse never intended to repeat the bold literary statement made by *Isola*; she decided that only a few copies should be made available to a very privileged handful of readers. And her love letters, like her body, came with a hefty price tag: each book sold for a staggering 1,200 francs – people always prized more highly that which was unique and costly. Some might have read an ironic undertone in Valtesse's dedication to her mother, but any gesture of filial recognition stood to dilute Emilie Delabigne's bitterness.

The book was a diverting, if temporary project. Still, by the middle of 1883, Valtesse's creative appetite was not yet satisfied. More than anything, she yearned for some harmless fun. That autumn, her wish was granted.

Over the preceding few years, Valtesse and her fellow Parisians had witnessed some incredible scientific advances and social transformations.[23] The Exposition Universelle of 1878 had firmly re-established Paris as a great European city, and the 1880s announced themselves as a spectacular period of change and progress. At last, the political landscape appeared stable and industry was booming. With the spread of steam power, the iron, chemistry and automobile trades were prospering. So was the electricity industry, which had a direct impact on communications. A Parisian could now take a train to most far-flung corners of rural France, and as travellers gazed out of carriage windows, they could see canals being built where previously only cattle had grazed. The Third Republic's reverence for science and technology was rewarded by the emergence of public telephones in Paris from the 1880s. Citizens relished the novel luxury of flooding their homes with electric light at the mere flick of a switch, while the circulation of newspapers increased in response to growing literacy levels and improved printing technology.

Whether conscious of wider industrial advances or not, men and women of Paris noticed a measurable change in their everyday lives. The poor were still poor, but the middle and upper classes had more money in their pockets at the end of the week, while the rise of mass consumerism and the ever-expanding entertainment industry offered an outlet for those spare francs. Women's fashion became a matter of popular, not just elite, concern. That supreme wonderland, the department store, bewitched the Parisian housewife, while an eruption of café concerts, balls, music halls and sporting events served pleasure-hungry Parisians a gluttonous spread of entertainment possibilities. Paris was heaving with new and extraordinary wonders, while the city sparkled and shimmered with the hypnotic glow of electricity. It was a time of excitement, prosperity and optimism. It was the dawn of the Belle Époque, and it seemed it would last forever.[24]

That such a climate should influence the arts was inevitable. Jules Lévy, a former member of the avant-garde literary club Les Hydropathes, was sensitive to the atmosphere of change. When a gas explosion left residents of the Rue François Miron injured or homeless in 1882, Lévy decided to organise an unprecedented exhibition.[25] Humorous, satirical artworks would be created exclusively by amateurs and exhibited at a fundraising event intended to parody the official Salon. Works' titles played on words, and were jocular and deeply ironic. Delighted with his initiative, Lévy baptised his radical new art movement 'Les Arts Incohérents'. After a first exhibition in July led crowds of curious Parisians to discover the new group, Lévy repeated the event in October. The show was a resounding success, and plans were soon under way for the first official exhibition in twelve months' time.

Early in September 1883, a newspaper announcement caught Valtesse's eye.[26] It was a call for entries for the next exhibition of 'Les Arts Incohérents'. Valtesse studied the requirements with interest. The exhibition was open to all. She could exhibit a sculpture, drawing or painting. The only conditions were that the work she presented should not be pornographic, and, most of all, should not be remotely serious. If accepted, her piece would be on show for the whole of Paris to see for precisely one month. Valtesse's creative imagination began to race.

For all her respect for tradition, the concept appealed. Painting was a favourite hobby of hers, and she loved parody and wordplay. Taking up her brush, Valtesse set to work. In the first week of October 1883, she sent her finished canvas along to the Galerie Vivienne.[27]

On 15 October 1883, the doors of the gallery opened to a bustling crowd of visitors. Viewers made their way through the four rooms of the gallery and up the staircase, stopping to admire paintings and sculptures by amateurs as well as those by seasoned artists like Henri Pille.[28] A corner of the gallery was even set aside for works guaranteed to be originals by eminent personalities, including the Comte de Chambord and Louis-Philippe. And as visitors flicked through the catalogue, they came across an intriguing entry:

> Bigue (Mlle de la) [*sic*]
> First name: Valtesse
> Qualities: all
> Student of Émile Élu
> 98, Boulevard Malesherbes
> 30 – *Lézards cohérents* or *Coherent Lizards*

The title of Valtesse's canvas was a humorous play on the wording of the movement's name. Despite the organiser's stipulations, her painting was playfully risqué. It showed 'two little animals playing a game which the artist seems to understand,' exclaimed C. Chincholle in *Le Figaro*.[29] 'This pair of reptiles assume a pose that my pen could not describe without the ink turning red,' wrote a titillated Félix Fénéon in *La Libre revue*.[30] Still, Valtesse managed to elude the sign 'concealed for reasons of morality' that Lévy placed over certain of the more offensive pieces. And the critics agreed that her cheeky painting was one of the most original exhibits on show.

Over the course of the month, more than 20,000 of Paris's trendsetting elite swarmed to the gallery to see the works. Journalists rhapsodised over the event, which was declared an extraordinary success.[31] 'What would Paris become if we could not laugh, even at the great painters!' *Le Figaro* commended.[32] 'Long live jolly people,' seconded the journalist in *L'Europe Artiste*.[33] 'Let's celebrate them, they are a rare breed.'

'Les Arts Incohérents' soon fixed itself in people's minds as the most forward-thinking and witty art movement of the day.

Drunk on its own success, the group began to organise fantastic burlesque balls, which quickly became the fashionable event of the spring. Paris's fun loving artistic crowd flocked to the parties, intent on dancing away their troubles. At the first ball, the walls of the venue in the Rue Vivienne were decorated with earnest signs:

'Melancholy not permitted.'

'Please do not spit on the ceiling.'

'Boredom prohibited at the penalty of a fine.'

'Never pick up a fallen woman! You might pick up your mother-in-law.'[34]

Two orchestras installed at opposite ends of the room struck up polkas and quadrilles, as a colourful sea of guests arrived wearing fabulous masks and costumes.[35] There were clowns, bearded ladies, men dressed like Bonaparte, women disguised as chambermaids and even a golden man. By midnight, every corner of the room was bustling, yet still a steady stream of enthusiastic latecomers flowed through the doors. At two o'clock, the most spectacular masks were paraded and the grand entrance of courtesans took place. Only at five in the morning was dinner announced, and as guests squeezed around small, preset tables, or arranged themselves cross-legged on the floor, the food that appeared was as fantastical as the costumes.

Valtesse and her friends, like fellow courtesan Léontine Godin, danced and laughed and sang late into the night, for no fashionable Parisienne discarded her champagne glass before six the next morning. This was what Valtesse had yearned for; this was real fun. Here, she could flaunt her wit, her artistic talent and her contemporaneity.

Among the fashionable faces dancing alongside Valtesse and Léontine at the Incohérents' events was journalist and writer Jules Hippolyte Percher, better known by his pseudonym, Harry Alis. When Alis had come to Paris as a teenager, he had begun frequenting popular circles of fashionable young writers, and was immediately welcomed into the fold. His career path decided, he had pursued his dream to write while maintaining a day job as an administrative employee for the highways department. Within a few years he had founded a monthly journal, formed intimate acquaintances with esteemed literary personalities like Paul Bourget and Guy de Maupassant and written a handful of short stories and novels. With his literary connections and his passionate commitment to France's colonial expansion, Valtesse and Alis shared many points of contact.

Valtesse fascinated Alis. Where did her culture and self-composure come from? This ethereal red-haired beauty radiated purity and light. And yet what strength of character and determination it must have taken to drag herself from the cesspit of Parisian society – apparently unscathed – and scale her way to its summit. Could ruthless blood really flow beneath such a porcelain-white complexion?

Léontine was happy to supply the answers to the questions Valtesse dismissed. She was even more compliant when the girlfriends had had a dispute, as sometimes happened. Léontine had been heard to call her friend a 'man eater' after a drink or two.[36]

Valtesse's tale captured Alis's imagination. It was a novel begging to be written. He could not resist answering the call.

In 1884, *Reine Soleil, une fille de la glèbe*, or *Sun Queen, A Country Girl*, was published. It told the tale of a young girl from the rural Savoy region of France who comes to Paris to work, only to have her innocence shattered by heartbreak and the cruel reality of working life in the city. Deceived by love, Reine falls into a life of prostitution, developing a stoical approach to human relationships, flaunting her beauty and educating herself with the aim of amassing as much wealth as possible from her lovers (many of them painters).

The novel was fast paced and exciting – and it was unashamedly based on Valtesse. Readers were told how Reine could captivate an audience with her intelligence and spirited conversation. She is 'viciously desirable', with her 'superb body of a peasant who glows with the health of her ancestors and a childhood spent outdoors'.[37] She has 'long golden hair' that, when loose, gives her the appeal of a 'mystical virgin'.[38] Cold-blooded and practical, Reine keeps 'an exact account of her income and expenses, increasing one, forcing herself to decrease the other, all the while observing her strict, self-imposed rule never to touch her accumulated fortune'.[39] Alis described Valtesse perfectly.

Readers soon believed they had cracked Alis's code. In November, a *Gil Blas* report on the activities of 'a pretty and flamboyant *demi-mondaine* with flavescent hair' was able to describe her as 'this young lady who is now referred to as the character in the book by Harry Alis, Reine Soleil', confident that readers would make the link to Valtesse.[40]

The model for the main character was clear. However, for readers, the fun began when it came to identifying the men concealed behind the secondary characters. It became a gripping detective game, and the prize was scandalous gossip.

There was the undemanding Souterre, the painter of panoramas and portraits, who was an Officer of the Legion of Honour and whose payments were made with military punctuality. Painfully aware of his mistress's sexual magnetism, Souterre takes an apartment near Reine for fear of losing her. Everybody spotted Detaille.

Then there was the modernist painter Morris, 'who passed for Reine's *amant de coeur*. Not that she truly cared for him; he simply amused her, and made her other lovers wildly jealous.'[41] Reine helps promote Morris and his work by presenting him in artistic circles and exhibiting his paintings. The likeness to Gervex was uncanny.

Reviews of the book were mixed. 'It would be unfair to deny M. Harry Alis's talent; his talent for detail, at least, and his talent as a writer. He clearly aspires to create a work of literature and succeeds; but a work of art, no.'[42] Critics agreed that the writing showed 'great powers of observation', but that it remained 'a second-rate novel'.[43]

Reine Soleil did not generate the controversy *Nana* had, and Valtesse greeted the interest with cool reserve. Steered in the right direction, public curiosity had always been her faithful friend. The thinly veiled identities of Alis's characters turned the book into an unexpected, but welcome, promotional tool.

Valtesse had proved that she could adapt to life's ebb and flow with dignity. The public's support was reaffirming. But by her late thirties, Valtesse was growing restless. Paris was glorious, but it could be tediously safe and predictable, and society tiresome. Valtesse decided that she wanted something – somewhere – different. And as the 20th century drew closer, an exciting new project began to take shape in her mind.

CHAPTER 15

The Thrill of the New:
the Comtesse in Monte Carlo

s Paris looked towards the new century, Valtesse remained spirited, lively and, for many – as Jules Claretie observed – 'always beautiful'. But she did not grow complacent. Valtesse knew she could not afford to waste the last years of her youth. Time was running out. Soon, her earning capacity would dwindle to nothing. Driven and determined, Valtesse made her future material and financial security her priority. She sought out opportunities that would bring comfort, attention, and, wherever possible, intellectual diversion. In a city as rich in entertainments as Paris, such occasions could always be found.

The summer was the best time of year to enjoy an open-air concert. The Thursday and Sunday afternoon concerts at the Jardin d'Acclimatation came highly recommended by guidebooks, and were a wonderful opportunity to exchange gossip with friends while being admired in public.[1] Meanwhile, in June, the world-famous Grand Prix at Longchamp brought together wealthy men and the adrenaline rush of horseracing in one delightful package, while offering Valtesse the perfect chance to show off her chic summer wardrobe. When Valtesse's smart victoria drew up at the 1884 races, heads turned;

she was positively 'resplendent' in a becoming mauve dress with a pearl grey overcoat and a soft, Rembrandt-style hat decorated with pink ribbons.[2] Conversing as easily with a group of high-ranking dignitaries as she did with her close female acquaintants, Valtesse's seemingly effortless ability to please impressed her fellow racing enthusiasts. But then mastering the art of conversation was one of the courtesan's first lessons, and Valtesse had graduated with distinction.

During the autumn, Parisians could be sure of ample exhibitions, plays, concerts, balls and circuses. And whenever Valtesse found her week to be lacking in pleasant diversions, Ville-d'Avray was only a short train journey away. The town was superb when the trees burst into warm clouds of russet and orange, and she could invite just whom she pleased.

In the springtime, the streets and boulevards of Paris exploded into avenues of colour, as fashionable men and women paraded freshly painted carriages and wardrobes of crisp new clothing. As one journalist observed, the arrival of spring was undoubtedly 'the Parisian event *par excellence* ... Let the glorious symphony of light clothing commence!'[3]

The Association of Dramatic Artists' annual ball was one of the most keenly anticipated social events of the spring season, where 'all the elegant women from the big and small theatres in Paris' competed for the unofficial title of the city's most glamorous female.[4] Valtesse never failed to appear. She would plan her costume weeks in advance to ensure that she looked her best, and the 1885 ball in March was no exception. However, that year, Valtesse had something rather different in mind. With her 40th birthday ever closer, she wanted to create a sensation. To achieve that, she required the compliance of three of her friends.

On the evening of the ball, crowds of established celebrities, aspirational newcomers and fashion-conscious socialites flowed through the doors of the Opéra-Comique. Class boundaries disintegrated as *monde* and *demi-monde* rubbed shoulders, united in their common goal to see and be seen. Diamonds glittered, chandeliers sparkled, perfume and laughter lingered in the air, and with the light and cheerful melody of Johann Strauss's *Blue Danube* resonating through the theatre, the evening promised to be the social highlight people had come to expect.[5]

Valtesse arrived surrounded by six of her girlfriends, like a queen with her ladies, and all eyes followed them as the chattering party made their way to the box Valtesse had taken. The box would be 'one of the picturesque curiosities of the ball' if the beauty and costumes of its occupants were anything to judge by.[6] Valtesse, Mme Faure, Mme de Benard and Mme de Bornay had been enchanted by the idea of appearing together as the four seasons, and Valtesse had elected herself to be the radiant summer. Guests agreed that she looked ravishing in 'a cream tunic made of Indian crêpe and transparent gauze, tied at the waist by sprigs of willow'.[7] The base of the tunic was a witty testimony to Valtesse's sense of fun. It had been adorned with a garland of baby artichokes, potatoes, cabbages, tomatoes and Brussels sprouts, and her shining red-gold locks were crowned with a headpiece of Morel mushrooms. The costume suited her to perfection.[8]

Gossip at the Association of Dramatic Artists' ball invariably turned on the events that had taken place during 'the season' (generally agreed to comprise December through to April) in the south of France. For in spite of all the entertainments Paris had to offer, Valtesse was not alone in finding herself bored during the winter months; nowadays, as soon as the monotony of winter restricted outdoor activities, curtailing the capital's usually busy social calendar, every fashionable Parisian with means packed their bags and headed for the Riviera.

Ever since rail links had opened up the country mid-century and the Treaty of Turin saw Nice annexed to France in 1860, the

Riviera had been drawing expedient, sun-seeking Parisians.[9] With its balmy climate, cloudless blue sky, lush flowered gardens and array of entertainments, from theatres to concert halls and sporting events, the Mediterranean coastline had become a magnet for tourists – and sovereigns – across Europe. 'The Riviera is certainly one of the loveliest spots on this fair earth,' commended an English travel guide, and thus 'visited by streams of human beings, lovers of nature and students of art' as well as 'thousands of sick invalids'.[10] Press coverage of the royal sojourns of the Russian Empress Alexandra Feodorovna, the Grand Duchess Marie Alexandrovna, Queen Victoria, her notoriously fun-loving son the Prince of Wales, and countless European princes gave France's southern coastline added prestige. By the late 1880s, the Riviera had firmly established itself as the favourite tourist destination of the Parisian elite. In fact, the area soon to be baptised the Côte d'Azur grew so fashionable that, one weekend, *Le Figaro* saw fit to replace its popular weekly literary supplement with a special illustrated number on Nice and Menton.[11]

The rail company Chemins de Fer de Paris à Lyon et à la Méditerranée were quick to respond with a host of special deals. A privileged few passengers could even travel in luxury on the overnight train from Paris, in a carriage fitted with a private salon, bathroom and toilet. The rich, pleasure-seeking Parisian could board a train leaving the capital at seven o'clock on Tuesday night and be sure to arrive in Menton at 3.15 the next morning, in time for a hearty breakfast and a day of uninhibited pleasure.[12]

Valtesse adored the Riviera. She had long been a convert to the attractions of Nice, having holidayed there often. The Riviera was colourful and vibrant in the months Paris became grey and dull. In January, Paris felt empty and tired, like the morning after a party which had gone on just a little too long; by contrast, Nice and Monte Carlo were the dizzying climax of a perpetual celebration, where all the guests were friends and the champagne glasses never ran dry. And with the soothing lap of the ocean in the background, the feeling of warmth on her back and the fresh, citrus scent of lemon trees, to Valtesse, the Riviera felt worlds away from the grey drudgery of winter in the capital.

Valtesse's mind was made up. Bored with Paris, yearning for change and anxious to keep up with emerging fashions, Valtesse decided that she would like her very own property on the Riviera. She could join the aristocracy and the fashionable elite during the winter months. She could entertain guests and impress her girl-friends with her charming holiday retreat. It would be immense fun. And where better to spend the final years of her youth and beauty than the favoured holiday destination of the richest, most powerful men in Europe?

But deciding where to have the property built was less straightforward. Cannes was the favoured winter haunt of her old acquaintance the Prince of Wales, with whom she had posed for Gervex's *The Civil Marriage* (1880–81). But people in Paris had begun to snigger: the area was becoming self-consciously British. Nice was certainly charming, but Valtesse was acutely aware that she lacked sufficient local knowledge. Perhaps there was somewhere beyond Nice that she had not considered, a town that would soon soar to the height of popularity. She did not want to miss out. Wary of making a mistake, Valtesse wondered how she could be sure of choosing wisely. She needed someone she could trust, a person familiar with the southern coast, sensitive to the movements of fashionable society, and dedicated to pleasing her. Gervex fitted the job description as though it were designed for him.

In 1886, a letter arrived for Valtesse in Paris from the ever-dutiful painter. The previous year, Gervex had travelled along the Mediterranean coast in the company of Maupassant, a memorable trip which furnished the bachelors-in-arms with countless tales of gripping adventures. Gervex was well placed to advise on the area that interested Valtesse, and his appearance in Cannes that January was enthusiastically reported by the local press.[13]

But by the second half of the 1880s, Gervex was growing exasperated with Cannes. The weather was miserable and so was he; he pined for his former mistress. Valtesse had cooled towards him, yet professionally, Gervex was on the crest of a wave. It was bewildering, almost as though her interest had expired as the artist ceased to struggle and need her help. The intimate studies of young women he was producing did little to alleviate his longing for the tender touch of Valtesse's skin.[14] And society on the Riviera made Gervex incredulous: people paid visits, entertained, and gossiped about others' wealth, breeding, relationships – in short, anything and everything. Life was just as it was in Paris. Still, laying his grumbles aside, he had some useful information to impart.

Valtesse had wanted to know about the prospects of the area along the coast from Nice towards Sainte-Maxime and further inland. Gervex urged her to reconsider. The location was far from desirable. 'To begin with, Rochebrune is an hour and a half from Cannes by train, and the area does not seem at all likely to become fashionable, it is isolated and deserted.'[15]

Valtesse abandoned the stretch of land to the west of Nice as a potential site for her new home, mentally moving her search closer to the city itself. But as she listened more attentively to conversations in Paris, a clearer picture began to form; for many, Nice was a mere adjunct to the celebrated, more glamorous city of Monte Carlo in the principality of Monaco.

'Of all the winter seaside resorts on the Mediterranean,' Parisians were informed, 'Monaco occupies the top place by virtue of its climate, its diversions, and the elegant pleasures that it offers its visitors who have turned it into the meeting place of the aristocracy.'[16]

Monte Carlo's varied offerings meant that the face of the typical tourist varied considerably. Invalids coming to benefit from the health-giving properties of the famed waters of Nice and Menton often ventured along the coast to Monte Carlo to marvel at the breathtaking scenery and enjoy the free concerts. Then every year, pilgrims travelled to the little Gothic chapel of Sainte-Dévote to pay their respects. But the elegant crowd and the aristocrats – the society Valtesse enjoyed – came with a different itinerary in mind. It centred entirely on pleasure.

Ever since the English introduced the vogue for sea bathing in the early 19th century when they began visiting the northern French coastal town of Dieppe, the practice had ingrained itself in the French mindset as a pastime which was at once restorative and fashionable.[17] By the 1880s, Monte Carlo's seafront was lined with luxurious hotels, each unique in character, alike in elegance, and catering to the most demanding tourist's slightest whim. And at whatever hour a visitor like Valtesse chose to step outside her hotel, she could be sure of finding entertainment and pleasure.

The great opera house had been designed by none other than Charles Garnier, the creator of Valtesse's imposing staircase, and when it opened in 1879, the venue quickly earned itself an unrivalled position as the place everyone went to see first-class plays and operas performed by some of the greatest theatrical names in Europe. There was the bustling flower market, a feast for the senses, with its colours, fragrances and the sound of lively chatter as gossip passed between elegant shoppers. Tourists could stroll along the seafront, pausing in one of the busy little cafés to rest their feet, quench their thirst and watch the world go by.

But the irresistible draw for the more daring visitor was the city's glittering casino. An adrenaline-charged haven of pleasure for some, a breeding ground of 'deadly evils' and a 'plague spot' for others, the casino was undoubtedly the two-sided jewel in Monte

Carlo's dazzling crown.[18] The ornate, columned frontage of the grand building commanded reverence. Once inside, and beyond the imposing gilded vestibule, men and women could relax in the plush salon or install themselves in the reading room. But the anterooms were merely a polite precursor to the main attraction: the gambling saloons. When a visitor felt that fortune was smiling on him – or he could merely wait no longer – he could venture across the vestibule, present his visiting card to the doorman and try his luck in one of the games rooms.

No room was more awe-inspiring than the grand games room, with its beautifully painted walls, Moorish ceilings, and polished floors.[19] Inside, drawn blinds and curtains reduced the lighting to a sombre glow, and there reigned an eerie silence. Around the tables sat men of all ages, old women, young women, and, as one appalled English visitor observed, 'even *ladies*'.[20]

The atmosphere was intense. 'You cannot fail to be struck by the extreme quiet among so many people,' marvelled one visitor. 'Everyone speaks in whispers. There is a certain solemnity about it, the same as that felt in a church.'[21] For a courtesan hoping to attract benefactors, it was indeed something of a pilgrimage. The casino was a rich hunting ground, teeming with wealthy, important men; all had come eager to spend money and hoping to win more. Every *horizontale* arrived dressed in her most flattering, head-turning outfit and her finest jewellery, with the sole objective of upstaging her competitors.

The casino's critics held it responsible for all manner of social ills. Their argument was strengthened by the high concentration of prowling *lionnes* like Valtesse, as well as the staggering number of suicides reported in Monte Carlo each year. But for its patrons, the casino was an institution, and for every tale of ruin and destitution, there was a success story of some lucky soul whose financial prayers had been answered at the gambling tables.

Still, when the charged atmosphere around the tables grew too intense, gamblers could step outside into the bright sunshine and meander around the casino gardens, or perhaps listen to one of the free concerts that were performed nearby. Tourist guides eulogised the gardens, 'a true marvel by virtue of their layout, the care with which they are tended, the varied scent of the trees, the quantity and beauty of the flowers and their magical appearance.'[22]

On the beach just beyond the casino, a vast space was dedicated to Monaco's famous pigeon shoot, which every year drew crowds of sporting enthusiasts to the edge of the ocean. Along with the races in Nice, the pigeon shoot was one of the highlights of the winter season, and its progress was closely followed back in Paris. The enterprising Chemins de Fer de Paris à Lyon et à la Méditerranée offered Parisians an open-ended return train ticket to attend both events.[23] The ticket was valid for twenty days; a traveller could take up to 30kg of baggage, and, for a supplement, even upgrade to a luxury carriage complete with bed and private salon. A first-class ticket cost 190 francs, just over £2,000 in today's money.[24]

Monte Carlo buzzed with fashionable people and entertainment, while its proximity to Nice meant that, if she were based there, Valtesse would still be able to attend the famous flower festival and visit friends like socialite Blanche Duvernet who had purchased holiday retreats in the town.[25] Monte Carlo's casino was especially tempting. Many a courtesan had made her name there. The stakes were high, the men rich and powerful and the adrenaline rush addictive. Valtesse was decided: if Monte Carlo was where Europe's aristocracy and trendsetting elite went, then that was where she must go too.

Valtesse had plans drawn up for an ostentatious luxury villa on the Avenue Monte Carlo (now the Avenue d'Ostende), just a few minutes' walk from the casino and the seafront.

The villa began to take shape, but it was a ponderous project:

perfecting a building that met Valtesse's lofty standards would take time. Valtesse wrestled with her impatience to move into her new home, which she felt certain would be spectacular. In an effort to distract herself, she divided her time between Paris and Ville-d'Avray, making the occasional foray further south, to the fashionable spa town of Bagnères-de-Luchon on the Spanish border, for example, which offered a tantalising reminder of the southern way of life and a taste of the pleasures to come. A short stay in Bagnères-de-Luchon a week after her 40th birthday was a pleasing antidote to a landmark that made Valtesse uncomfortable.[26]

In the first few weeks of 1889, Valtesse began her usual preparations for her annual trip to the Riviera. However, this year there was added excitement in the air as she selected the clothing she would take with her on holiday; now, Valtesse was closer than ever to possessing her very own property on the Riviera.

She returned to Paris in April satisfied, and in plenty of time for the usual spring line-up of races and opening nights. She was content, having completed her Mediterranean stay in Nice with her friend Léontine Miroy.[27] But friends' homes and grand hotels, however luxurious, could not equal the thrill of being the chatelaine of one's very own villa.

When Pâquerette, now in her twenties, announced her engagement to a respectable young railway company employee, Paul Jules Auguste Godard, Valtesse's hunger for the excitement of the Mediterranean only intensified.[28] Now, she could leave Paris and enjoy herself, content that society would no longer hold her responsible for another's well-being. She was more anxious than ever to start spending her breaks on the Côte d'Azur in her new seafront property.

Fortunately, from May, a new diversion presented itself, gripping Paris's attention and sweeping Valtesse along with it: the Exposition Universelle of 1889.

The exposition was not the only world fair Paris had hosted, nor was it the first to take place under a Republican regime. But it was symbolically important: 1889 marked the 100th anniversary of the French Revolution.

The public commemoration of that notorious period of social unrest alarmed certain European countries still ruled by monarchies, reducing the anticipated number of participants. Nevertheless, as preparations came together, everything boded well for a successful, innovative exposition and Parisians eagerly awaited the grand opening.

The exposition was established at two sites, with fine arts and industrial exhibits on show at the Trocadéro and the Champ de Mars, while the Esplanade des Invalides housed a colonial exhibit and several state-sponsored pavilions. There were sensational displays of artistic skill, architectural dexterity and scientific genius, and as national and international visitors flocked to the city to marvel at the wonders, Paris basked in its own glory. And of all the exhibits, by far the city's proudest was the awesome iron structure that, for months, Parisians had been watching creep up the skyline of the Seine's left bank: the Eiffel Tower.

Though vehemently criticised, few could deny that Gustave Eiffel's bold architectural statement commanded respect. At over 300m high, in 1889 the tower was the tallest metal structure in the world. It took two years to build once the Burgundian engineer Eiffel won the state-run competition for its design. At the monument's inauguration, Eiffel climbed on foot to the top of the tower and raised an enormous Tricolore flag, while Parisians gazed up in wonder as the great masterpiece of engineering glittered and twinkled with the glow of over 20,000 gaslights.

As soon as it was opened to the public, millions rushed to see Eiffel's awe-inspiring achievement and witness the unprecedented views over Paris for themselves. Among the celebrity visitors were

Sarah Bernhardt, the Prince of Wales, the Shah of Persia and even William F. Cody, alias Buffalo Bill. Everyone wanted to admire the great structure and Valtesse was determined to be among their number.

Valtesse made sure that her visit was recorded in the official register. On the day she ascended the tower, she signed the book triumphantly with a witty verse she had composed for the occasion:

> Every pleasure passes;
> Seize it while you might.
> It is always an advantage
> When you are caught off guard at night.[29]

Valtesse's visit to Eiffel's grand edifice would be valuable preparation. At long last, towards the end of 1891, she received the news she had been waiting for: her very own feat of architectural genius was nearly complete and ready for her to move in.

'The beautiful Valtesse de la Bigne [...] has gone to oversee the construction of a villa which is said to be spectacular,' *Gil Blas* informed its readers as the building work was in its final stages.[30]

Villa les Aigles was a masterpiece of design and decorative finesse.[31] Valtesse's new winter retreat recreated all the luxury of her home in Paris, with the addition of fabulous sea views. Like an exotic, Far Eastern palace, the sparkling white villa boasted a grand, columned entranceway with an enormous Bonapartist bronze eagle stretching its wings above those who passed beneath. The windows to either side opened out on to column-fronted balconies, while the tall, dome-roofed turret on the right infused the building with all the romance of a fairytale castle. Valtesse had requested that her personal coat of arms be visible at regular intervals throughout the building. Inside, there were spacious reception rooms and bedrooms, and huge glass doors ensured that guests were never far from a breathtaking sea view.

Villa les Aigles was everything Valtesse had hoped. This season, when she graced the Riviera's social scene with her radiant presence, she could do so in the knowledge that every evening she would be returning to her very own luxury seafront property.

Back in Paris, the villa was causing a stir. People were impressed and Valtesse glowed with pride. Villa les Aigles was declared 'the most charming love nest, perched in a rock face'.[32] It was the property Valtesse had 'reserved for winter sojourns and sun-seeking expeditions when winter has donned its first coat', *Gil Blas* reassured Parisians curious about the movements of their favourite politically minded *demi-mondaine*.[33] Its 'proud turrets dominate the permanently azure sky of Monte Carlo', eulogised another journalist.[34]

As the chatelaine of a smart new, palatial villa in one of the most fashionable tourist spots in Europe, Valtesse was in her element. Now, all that was needed to turn her house into a home was people and laughter. Valtesse set to work, inviting all her friends to come and sample the delights of the Riviera with her. She had perfected the art of events organising, and nothing gave her more pleasure than hosting lavish parties and magnificent dinners in her new property.

Valtesse's girlfriends could hardly wait to see their companion's holiday home and taste the exotic Mediterranean lifestyle for themselves. Gabrielle de Guestre, Eva Mégard and Gabrielle Dupuy eagerly packed their suitcases, and the proud hostess arranged for the guest rooms to be made up.

It was the first of many fabulous Mediterranean holidays. Valtesse had reasoned that the coastline's popularity could only increase, and her inkling was soon confirmed. Throughout the 1890s, doctors' conviction that a change of climate was an unparalleled preventative for tuberculosis brought health-conscious city dwellers flocking to the Mediterranean coast. Then in 1895, Queen Victoria's visit to Nice propelled the already fashionable Riviera to the very height of popularity. The Queen arrived in Cimiez in great state, bringing with her her own mahogany bed, her favourite Chinese porcelain crockery, a tea service, a writing desk, black toiletry bags, sheets and tablecloths (sent specially from Balmoral), and a grand entourage of personnel, which included her private doctor, five ladies in waiting, two grooms, and a fleet of domestic staff.[35] Locals marvelled, while Valtesse and the fashionable elite studied the sovereign's movements approvingly. That was how a dignified person should travel; that was real style.

By the time the electric tramway to Cimiez was installed ahead of Victoria's arrival, Valtesse's Monacan winter sojourns had become a fixed part of her annual routine.[36] The Comtesse's departures from Paris were ceremoniously announced in the newspapers. Valtesse invariably timed her stays to coincide with the races and the flower festival in Nice, and she made sure never to miss the pigeon shoot in Monte Carlo. When in residence in the villa, her days were spent enjoying the town's multiple diversions, while in the evenings, Valtesse would take in the delights of the opera, the theatre and concerts. The casino was a permanent temptation, but unlike so many courtesans before her, Valtesse never allowed the excitement of a bet to trounce her financial common sense. Her attachment to security prevented such an error. When she entered the casino, she intended to win – and success at the gaming tables was a narrow-minded interpretation of victory.

Wherever they went, Valtesse and her girlfriends turned heads. When they were not enjoying all that the town had to offer, the women could be spotted on Valtesse's sun-drenched balcony, surveying Monte Carlo, sipping coffee, smoking and laughing as though they had discovered the reflex for the very first time. Passers-by were charmed by their childlike enjoyment: the women were clearly close – very close.

It was true. Valtesse found the presence of her female companions reassuring. Her girlfriends understood her better than any man could. But after a while, stories began to circulate and questions were asked. Why had Valtesse not married one of her rich suitors now that she was past her prime? She seldom appeared without a posse of her girlfriends these days. *Gil Blas* joked that only a eunuch could arrest Valtesse's attention.[37]

But it was not until Valtesse started to be seen out with a new, much younger female friend that public speculation turned into a more serious questioning of her sexuality. The woman concerned was a recent addition to Paris's array of courtesans. She was young with a striking, androgynous beauty and she was heralded as the up-and-coming star of the *demi-monde*. That fresh face was Liane de Pougy. Valtesse was her friend, her mentor, her idol – and then, her lover.

CHAPTER 16

❧❧❧

The Feminine Touch

As the new century drew closer, women were enjoying more power and opportunities than ever before. The 1880s witnessed the introduction of secondary education for girls and the reintroduction of divorce (forbidden since 1816), and for the first time, a married woman was allowed to open a bank account without her husband's authority.[1] Women had never known such liberty. Then, with the rise of the safety bicycle, the first two-wheeled vehicle suitable for women, freedom became a reality and female emancipation seemed an achievable goal.

According to the popular stereotype, the 'new woman' rejected domesticity; she was educated and went to work. She had her hair cut short, she smoked, and she abandoned her corset and petticoats for knickerbockers and bloomers – the bicycle demanded it. Times were changing and male anxiety mounted.

But for partisans of the conventional gender templates, by far the most unexpected and alarming twist in this tale of female empowerment was the rise of lesbianism.

Parisians were first called to consider the practice of lesbianism in their midst in 1836, when Alexandre Parent-Duchâtelet published his groundbreaking *Prostitution in the City of Paris*.[2] However, while it exposed the issue, the work, which was to become a sociological bible, remained limited as a reference source on lesbianism. Undiscriminating, society placed unwavering faith in the writer and drew what seemed a logical conclusion: lesbianism was the depraved and monstrous vice of prostitutes.

For more than half a century, that view held firm, stimulating the imagination of novelists and titillating their delighted readers. From Adolphe Belot's *Mlle Giraud, ma femme* (1870), to Zola's *Nana* (1880), lesbianism was the theme of the moment, at once food for male fetishism and a sugar-coated vehicle for a moral.

Only in 1889 was lesbianism revisited in a serious sociological study, when A. Coffignon published his treatise on corruption in Paris.[3] The term 'lesbian' did not yet exist; *saphisme*, as he called it, was still 'a relatively new word', though the phenomenon was ancient.[4] It was, he insisted, an 'evil which has lain dormant for a long time but which recently has made enormous progress'.[5] Coffignon pursued: 'In certain sections of society, it is not only an acknowledged vice but is flaunted.'[6] His views were damning, but Coffignon had hit upon an uncomfortable truth: by the 1890s, lesbianism had become wildly fashionable.

Coffignon's work unleashed a chain of scientific and sociological studies of lesbianism. Léo Taxil's *Fin-de-siècle Corruption* (1891) pitched lesbianism as yet another outcome of social decadence, while Julien Chevalier's *Sexual Inversion* (1893) pinned the blame on hereditary defects and female emancipation.[7] Meanwhile, medics saw the rise of lesbianism as further confirmation of women's latent mental inferiority.[8] Views on the causes differed, but on one point critics were unanimous: in the threat it posed to the country's demographic situation, lesbianism was unnatural and dangerous.

The Napoleonic Code of 1804 had made no legal provision for penalising private acts of lesbianism: provided they were not seen, women could love each other fully, physically, as much and as often as they desired.[9] The authorities were powerless and the critics enraged. This sordid vice must be stamped out.

As a city, Paris had blossomed with particular vivacity into a hotbed of lesbian activity. 'For several years now,' Chevalier remarked, 'lesbianism, in Paris and in most capital cities, [has] taken on alarming proportions.'[10] The corruptive potential of literature on women readers had always been monitored with suspicion; now, the arts as a whole were vehemently denounced for their hazardous influence on the female population. From painting and literature to the theatre, and including café society, modern Paris, sociologists scorned, had only itself to blame. Its soil provided fertile ground for the roots of lesbianism to take hold.

Few could deny that lesbianism was flourishing with especial vigour in Paris's literary and bohemian circles. When darkness fell, groups of women drew close in low-lit bars and cafés, or else they would gather in intimate soirées, their activities exciting the creative appetites of novelists and artists, while provoking the wrath of the authorities.

The fashion-conscious Valtesse, who had distrusted men since her heart was broken by Richard Fossey and was known for her stoical, even merciless, approach to her work, was immediately cast as a follower of this rising trend. Valtesse had always enjoyed the company of her female friends and publicly expressed her incredulity at men's failure to understand women. Besides, sharing tales of romantic woes and ridiculing men was therapeutic. Valtesse loved to gather her girlfriends together regularly so that they could exchange gossip and advice. Taking tea offered the perfect opportunity.

Tea had been a popular beverage in Europe since the 17th century, but it was not until the 1830s that England's Duchess of Bedford launched the fashion of afternoon tea as a meal.[11] Plagued by hunger pangs between lunch and dinner, the Duchess concluded that a light repast between the two (consisting of sandwiches, pastries and cakes served with tea) would be a pleasant way to stave off her appetite in the company of friends. The English vogue for afternoon tea was set, firmly establishing itself as a social ritual which was replicated throughout Europe.

The wave of Anglomania sweeping the continent at the end of the 19th century carried the fashion of afternoon tea across the Channel, where it found a firm foothold in Parisian society. All over Paris, elegant hostesses hurried to imitate the trend, poring over conduct manuals to familiarise themselves with English menus, style and etiquette. If a person wanted to imitate a true English tea, a certain protocol must be adopted – and everybody knew that the English took their tea at five o'clock.

'The neophyte must be warned against arriving too early,' cautioned one English etiquette manual, 'for "come at four" is only our old friend four to seven, in disguise – a polite euphemism for five o'clock.'[12]

The English were adorable, though why they refused to say what they really meant bewildered French hostesses. A simple solution was found: from the 1880s, Paris's social elite referred to afternoon tea in the English, as a 'five o'clock'.

In 1883, *Gil Blas* explained the fashion for its perplexed readers:

A person does not pay visits anymore; it is all about the five o'clock, that English import recently made fashionable by the Comtesse de Saint-Félix. With our taste for independence, this manner of socialising should prove a great success. People meet up each day at a fixed time, and while tea is taken, reputations are made and destroyed, fashions are set, and nobody chats anymore, everyone gossips. The news of the day is shared between sandwiches, and I can assure you that everything which is said, everything which happens, everything which is done in Paris is repeated during this meeting. [...] While this kind of reception is informal, it does not prevent our elegant ladies appearing in their finest toilettes, since this is where new fashions are launched. These gatherings allow visitors to come in their most elegant attire on their way home from the Bois, and a special kind of dress has already been adopted.[13]

Doctors were soon fretting that the new fashion would wreak havoc with the fairer sex's delicate digestive system. 'A woman should avoid all these snacks, lunches and five o'clocks, formidable enemies to the stomach,' warned *Gil Blas*' Dr Monin.[14]

But if food had catalysed the social ritual, it was no longer the central focus, nor was overeating considered the most perilous by-product. Afternoon visits and invites to tea had long been furnishing upper-class women and artists like Mary Cassatt with an acceptable social context outside the secure environment of home where they could meet without compromising their reputations. Now, the formal rise of the 'five o'clock' breathed new life into the business of taking tea, inferring it with chic prestige. And so while the afternoon tea guest was not exclusively female, women took full advantage of the opportunity to socialise with other members of their sex and demonstrate their awareness of fashion. In a period marked by female emancipation, there could be nothing more dangerous.

While defiantly Parisienne, Valtesse embraced the trend for all things English with as much verve as other ladies in her social circle. English elegance impressed her; the ceremony with which they conducted the simple ritual of taking tea was charming. By the 1890s, Valtesse's all-female 'five o'clocks' had become the talk of Paris. Sometimes she held them on the Boulevard Malesherbes, and occasionally in Ville-d'Avray; but whichever of her luxurious residences she elected as her venue, the Comtesse de la Bigne's afternoon teas were the must-have invitation. Unusually for such gatherings, many of her 'five o'clocks' were reported in the papers, simply because the company Valtesse kept was considered a reliable gauge and checklist of Paris's most fashionable faces.

'There were several beautiful women at Valtesse's last five o'clock,' reported a society page in the 1890s.[15] From the captivating Blanche Duvernet to the exquisitely lovely Angèle de Chartres, the most sought-after socialites in Paris could be seen alighting from carriages at Valtesse's sumptuous abode whenever she was hosting a tea.

The self-styled Ego derived immeasurable pleasure from surrounding herself with women who admired her, whether for her bright mind, her beauty or her astounding success – preferably all three. Conversation was frequently impassioned, particularly where the subjects of love and the opposite sex were concerned.

Is platonic friendship between a man and a woman ever truly possible, one of the ladies enquired one autumn afternoon as the women sat sipping their tea and nibbling cakes in Valtesse's comfortable sitting room in Ville-d'Avray, while gazing absent-mindedly at her verdant, sloping garden?[16]

'Yes, it is possible, and indeed quite common,' nodded Blanche.

The others laughed. How naive; she was being ridiculous.

'No!' objected Suzanne Dalmont, a woman known for her good sense and sound mind.

As always, Valtesse had something to say on the matter. Her eyes sparkled whenever she felt passionately about a subject, as she did now. She believed she recalled a poem. Perhaps she could remember it:

You say friendship, I say love,
but the soul can combine both of the above:
the ideal form of happiness I believe, Madame, might
be that I were your friend in the morning, and your lover come
the night.

There were giggles and gasps, and several of the ladies declared themselves shocked, playfully scolding their hostess for her cheeky recital.

Such amusement was a regular feature of the get-togethers. Valtesse cherished them. At her 'five o'clocks', Valtesse's salon became her stage, her girlfriends, an adoring audience – and she delighted in her role as both director and leading lady.

The props she employed merely increased her subjects' admiration. Guests could be served from her gleaming silver tea and coffee pots, decorated with laurel leaves. Or for bigger parties, she might select the cups and saucers from her 55-piece set of Sèvres porcelain bearing Napoleon III's crest, with its fine chocolate pot – perfect whenever she expected a guest with a sweet tooth.

As the woman's position in society grew more assured, Valtesse found it refreshing and stimulating to exchange ideas on the changing female condition with like-minded companions. In addition to her own parties and her girlfriends' invitations, Valtesse began to attend the women-only gatherings now being organised across Paris.

Certain bars and brasseries were reputed for the warm welcome they extended to their female clientele – and everybody knew that more was exchanged than just gossip. By the 1890s, several bars in the Montmartre district had become notorious.

One of the earliest and most celebrated female haunts was the brasserie Le Hanneton at number 75, Rue Pigalle. It was run by the formidable Mme Armande Brazier, whom all the regulars knew as Amandine.[17] With its dark red curtains, low lighting and small tables – ideal for intimate exchanges – Le Hanneton was unlike other bars. Elsewhere, women went looking for men; here, a contemporary guide explained, 'they come looking for each other'.[18] In the evening, it was rare to see a man at all. Women of different classes drew close around tables, their bodies enlaced, as they exchanged cigarettes, sweets and kisses.

A little further up the street, at number 7, was Le Rat Mort ('The Dead Rat'), so named, popular anecdote held, in memory of the fate which befell a rodent who disturbed a couple's moment of intimacy while they dined there.[19] Known for its *demi-mondaine* clientele, Le Rat Mort's reputation soon extended in response to its increasing numbers of lesbian patrons. It was open all hours, and its convenient second entrance on the Rue Frochot gave visitors the option of leaving discreetly if they wished. Between three and four in the morning, clusters of pretty women could be found savouring the moist sensation of oysters sliding down their throats, or devouring cold meats, while champagne warmed their smiles and numbed their inhibitions. Only when the sun began to rise did the female diners step unsteadily out on to the street and weave their way back through Paris arm in arm.

Valtesse lived conveniently near the Montmartre district. She could even walk to Le Rat Mort if she wished. Casual homosexual experimentation was the norm in Valtesse's circle. It was more unusual not to participate, and Valtesse was often seen out with women known to be lesbians. But she was discreet: she never gave the press solid proof that she herself was of that persuasion. Journalists were more useful when their curiosity was excited. Not that her vigilance made much difference; in the world of journalism, inferences were as good as facts, and just as proliferating to readership.

'A juicy piece of gossip has just reached me,' stirred a journalist in *Gil Blas* one December, 'which might not interest members of the bearded sex, but will be warmly welcomed by the ladies who observe the religion of Saint Sappho. The Villa des Aigles, [...] is going to reopen its doors, which remained closed last year as a mark of respect: now, the beautiful Gabrielle de Guestre has been restored to health, and this happy event warms the heart of the chatelaine of Villa des Aigles, the heraldic Valtesse de la Bigne.'[20] There would be much celebrating, the journalist assured readers provocatively, as Valtesse and her girlfriends spent the long winter nights around her welcoming table – gathered close.

At the heart of the speculation was the certainty that Valtesse had formed close friendships with women known to enjoy same-sex relationships. Émilienne d'Alençon was a full twenty years younger, but like Valtesse, she was blessed with naturally even features, an asset that helped her launch a performing career. At the Cirque d'été in 1890, Émilienne sashayed confidently on to the stage in a costume that bordered on indecent, pursued by a warren of performing rabbits. The creatures had been dyed pink and each fitted with a ruffled collar.[21] At Émilienne's command, the rosy bunnies operated a tiny see-saw, jumped over candles and even took it in turns to fire a miniature pistol. The crowd erupted into peals of laughter and wild applause. The fluffy creatures' beautiful tamer was deluged with bouquets as she left the stage, and the act was found a slot at the Folies Bergère.

But it was less her stage presence than her relationship with a high-profile celebrity, the young Duc Jacques d'Uzès, that propelled Émilienne to fame by the time she was twenty. The Duc was the first in a long line of eminent lovers, which included the Belgian King Leopold II and that unofficial rite of passage of all French courtesans, the future King Edward VII. By the mid-1890s, Émilienne was considered one of Paris's most promising young courtesans.

With her soft blonde curls, her expression of childish innocence (despite firm proof to the contrary) and the pretty dimples which appeared whenever she gave her infectious little chuckle, men and women alike fell under Émilienne's spell. She had 'enormous golden eyes', the courtesan Liane de Pougy reflected, and 'the finest and most brilliant complexion!'[22] Then, with 'a proud little mouth, a tip-tilted nose you could eat' and an oval face, Émilienne epitomised the figure of the silly but adorable blonde.[23] It was a misperception that delighted Émilienne. It carried her far. In fact, she was sly and 'could be beastly', Liane recalled, remembering how Émilienne had once tricked her into shamefully underdressing for a party, on the premise that Émilienne would wear the same outfit; she did not.[24] Liane arrived at the party in her dreary ensemble and looked around awkwardly to locate her friend. Finally, Émilienne wafted in, 'resplendent in sumptuous white and gold brocade, dripping with diamonds, pearls and rubies, her curls full of sparkling jewels.'[25] Incredibly, Liane forgave her; Émilienne 'was really so pretty that one couldn't hold it against her'.[26]

Valtesse prized loyalty, but public displays of confidence always won her admiration, if not her approval. With their ambitious natures and their princely admirers, Valtesse and Émilienne had much in common. While she could be artful, even cruel, Émilienne was acutely sensitive to other women's strengths and vulnerabilities. Besides, a courtesan of Valtesse's standing commanded respect. How much a new recruit could learn from such a woman. And while Valtesse was vocal about her belief that same-sex relationships were a shamefully un-lucrative waste of an evening, her pride was always polished when an admirer, male or female, found her attractive.

From the end of the 1880s, Valtesse and Émilienne were spotted mingling, talking and laughing at the same social functions. Together, they were considered among the cream of Paris's prettiest *horizontales*. At the races, at theatre opening nights, at balls and concerts, the women, one fresh-faced and plucky, the other elegant and self-assured, presented two glorious snapshots of different stages in the life of the Parisienne. People whispered that Valtesse and Émilienne's affection for each other ran deeper than friendship. The speculation amused Valtesse. 'Give a little,' Valtesse always advised her female friends, 'but leave a lot to be desired.'[27] Mystery was a woman's most precious asset. She told the press nothing.

But Valtesse's intimate girlfriends all knew that however much time they spent with her, however close they might believe themselves to the enigmatic redhead, there was one companion with whom they could never compete. Only one occupied the coveted position of Valtesse's favourite. That woman was Liane de Pougy.

Born Anne-Marie Chassaigne in 1869, few could have predicted that the pale-faced, lanky schoolgirl, the butt of all her classmates' jokes, would blossom into one of the fin de siècle's greatest courtesans.[28] On completing her convent education, Mlle Chassaigne married a naval officer, Armand Pourpe, when she was just seventeen. 'Yo' husban' look too husbandish!' hissed Anne-Marie's Creole neighbour, the grandmotherly Maman Lala, before the wedding.[29] How Anne-Marie wished she had heeded the warning; the marriage was a bitter disappointment. Pourpe's character made Anne-Marie desperately miserable, and a traumatic labour with her first child did nothing to alleviate her suffering. Deceived by life, intrigued by the unknown, Anne-Marie sought solace in other men's arms. When M. Pourpe found his wife in bed with a lover, he fired a gunshot in fury. The bullet hit Anne-Marie, puncturing her skin but handing her the passport to freedom that she had only dreamed about. With 400 francs and more hope than belongings, Anne-Marie boarded a train and arrived in Paris in 1890 ready to begin a new life.

Turn-of-the-century Paris was bright and dazzling, as daunting as it was exciting. With no idea what she would do or where she would go, the tall, willowy, chestnut-haired newcomer lodged with a friend in the Rue de Chazelles in the Plaine Monceau quarter of Paris while she considered her next move.

Opposite her friend's apartment was that of the celebrated courtesan Louise Balthy.[30] Then 28 years old, Mme Balthy was elegance itself. She had her own apartment, dressed in expensive silk, velvet and fur, and rode in fine carriages. As a courtesan, she had arrived. Anne-Marie was star-struck. Whenever the jingle of horses' harnesses announced the great woman's departure or arrival, Anne-Marie flew to the window of her friend's living room where she slept to gaze in awe at the magnificent *horizontale* as she passed. The flash of rich clothing and the aura of majesty offered a tantalising glimpse into the luxurious world a courtesan inhabited. A deep longing stirred inside Anne-Marie. Balthy personified all that she hungered for and signposted the means of achieving it. If a girl was young and single and could use her appearance to seduce, all this could be hers. Anne-Marie was decided. Changing her name to the more fashionable 'Liane' and adopting the noble sounding 'de Pougy', with a little help from contacts, Liane began working as a *femme galante*.

With her androgynous appearance, Liane exemplified the chic elegance that was now steering fin-de-siècle trends. Her svelte body, long neck, arms and legs, and elongated, oval face made her look taller than she was. 'Complexion pale and matt,' Liane described herself, 'skin very fine.'[31] She continued:

> I use the merest touch of rouge, it suits me. Rather small mouth, well-shaped, superb teeth. My nose? They say it's a marvel of marvels. Pretty little ears like shells, almost no eyebrows – hence a little pencil line whenever I want. Eyes a green hazel, prettily shaped, not very large – but my look is large. Hair thick and very fine, incredibly fine, a pretty shiny chestnut brown.[32]

Her curious appearance made passers-by stop short and crane their necks for a second look. This power to arrest attention set Liane at an advantage in the sex trade. But she still had much to learn. Every new girl needed a mentor.

Unbeknown to Liane, luck was shining on her in more ways than one when her friend agreed to accommodate her in the Rue de

Chazelles. The Plaine Monceau was a sought-after district where many great courtesans besides Louise Balthy had made their home. And Liane's road was only a few streets away from Boulevard Malesherbes. She had not long been in Paris when she crossed paths with Valtesse.

When Liane and Valtesse met, the pair instantly warmed to each other. Liane was in awe of Valtesse's success, impressed by her strength of character and willpower.[33] And Valtesse, who always felt tenderly towards Parisians less fortunate than herself, softened when she met the spirited but unworldly newcomer to the profession. She admired Liane's independent mind and was endeared by her inexperience.[34] There was no question of competition; Liane's brown-haired androgyny posed no threat to her own untouchable Pre-Raphaelite sexuality. Valtesse had made her career, and now she was nearing the end of it. And she liked Liane. The youngster was grateful for any advice or guidance Valtesse had to offer, and she stood to lose nothing by helping her enthusiastic neighbour.

The pair quickly fell into a student-teacher relationship, with Valtesse coaching the fledgling courtesan in the ways of the profession. She taught her young protégé everything she knew, from how to secure a client, to managing her career and finances, and even techniques to employ in the bedroom.

Visits to each other became a regular and keenly anticipated fixture in both women's social calendars. Barely a week would pass when the pair did not meet at their usual hour of 6.30 to get ready ahead of a night out in Paris.[35] While they perfected their hair and make-up, and sought each other's advice on clothes and accessories, the women joked and laughed like schoolgirls, sharing shocking titbits about mutual acquaintances and lovers. When more serious questions arose, Valtesse resumed her pedagogical role, guiding Liane on any areas of uncertainty. Liane set great store by her mentor's advice.

If Liane were serious about succeeding as a courtesan, Valtesse explained, she must understand that dinners at Maxim's, opening nights at the theatre and carriage rides in the Bois de Boulogne were not merely pleasant diversions to be enjoyed when and if she felt like it: they were essential. A courtesan must be seen. The profession demanded it.

Liane heeded Valtesse's advice. From the early 1890s, the elegant, dark-haired beauty was spotted everywhere. Mlle de Pougy was seen at the horseracing in Ville-d'Avray; in Paris at the theatre, concerts, the opera; in Nice. And just as Valtesse had predicted, the more she was seen, the more the press took interest in her, catapulting her to the enviable realm of Paris's leading courtesans.

But Liane's unworldly, often naive approach to the business would have to change. Valtesse was firm about that. The young courtesan had to accept that she had embarked upon a precarious career.

One day, when Valtesse and Liane were out walking, they were approached by a poor woman who reeked of alcohol.[36] Her dishevelled appearance was startling, her rancid body odour sickening. She drew closer to Liane and Valtesse, her desperate hand outstretched, begging for money. As she lifted her head and her eyes met Valtesse's, recognition flashed across her face. The women had met before. Valtesse realised that she had worked alongside the wretched woman when she first started out as a *lorette*. Where Valtesse had triumphed, the beggar offered a pitiful reminder of the fate which awaited less fortunate girls. Liane should learn from this example, Valtesse advised gravely. Theirs was a profession which left no room for sensitivity.[37]

'What?' Valtesse exclaimed in horror one day when Liane recounted one of her less lucrative tête-à-têtes, 'he saw your legs and he did not pay? He must pay.'[38] Liane would not repeat the mistake.

A courtesan must safeguard her fortune, Valtesse insisted.

And she led by example: when one of her male acquaintances, the wayward son of a powerful businessman, Henri Desgenétais, died unexpectedly, Valtesse publicly announced that the deceased still owed her money, a staggering 25,000 francs (more than half what her bed had cost).[39] She did not hesitate to take the matter to court, where she produced a letter from Desgenétais – a very affectionate letter – ardently promising to pay her the said sum forthwith. The court dismissed her case: the letter proved nothing, it could just as easily have been written in response to a request for money on Valtesse's part. Financial exchanges between courtesans and men fond of pleasure were never straightforward – or clean.

Valtesse let the matter go. An independent woman must reconcile herself to the occasional loss, she taught Liane. But she must always fight to win. It usually paid off. On another occasion, Valtesse had set her heart on an elegant overnight bag containing gold and silver appliances.[40] When her supplier, M. Sormani, delivered the item, it came with a hefty 11,000-franc price tag. It was fine but costly, and Valtesse inspected the bag to ensure that she had invested wisely. She was horrified: the set was missing a thimble, a candle snuffer and a curling iron. What use was a travel bag without a curling iron? Sormani hastily made the necessary amendments, but presented her with a bill for an additional 430 francs. Valtesse was outraged, particularly since the scissors were blunt and the curling iron useless. Valtesse's refusal to pay saw her in court again, and to her delight, the supplement was reduced and the supplier punished with a fine. A woman must not allow herself to be walked over, she told Liane.

Liane watched and learned. With Valtesse's patronage, she started to believe that anything was possible. 'A special mention for Liane de Pougy and Valtesse de la Bigne,' one society page commended; they had 'raised the flag of Cythera and held it with true Parisian flair'.[41]

Valtesse maintained that every courtesan needed a trademark. Liane chose the pearl. Pale yet luxurious, the jewel's smooth simplicity perfectly captured the image she wanted to project. The press rose to the bait: 'The beautiful Liane [...] wears [...] a pearl in her ear – in one ear only. Now, people only refer to her as "the lady with the pearl".'[42]

Valtesse's wisdom and experience helped Liane lay the foundations of a fine career. She appeared briefly at the Folies Bergère, but she hardly needed the exposure now; Liane knew she had no talent, and in any case, everybody was already talking about her.[43] Liane reduced the disbelieving Marquis Charles de Mac-Mahon to tears when, on his request and with perfect composure, she listed her previous amorous conquests, many of whom the horrified Marquis knew personally.[44] There were 43. At the time, it was an outrageous lie, but Liane soon fulfilled the prophecy. She was courted by playwrights, princes and dukes, and people whispered that Offenbach's librettist, the portly Henri Meilhac, had paid 80,000 francs just to gaze greedily at her naked body. 'The greatest beauty ceases to exist beside you,' he had enthused.[45] Valtesse's tutelage had paid off – and Liane knew it.

'In life,' Liane recalled Valtesse saying, 'I ask only beauty and pleasure, and no obstacle shall stand in my way.'[46] Valtesse left Liane in no doubt: a woman was responsible for her own contentment. 'I am happy because I wish to be.'[47]

However, Valtesse's lessons fell short when it came to her student's culture. Despite her best efforts, she failed to instil her own deep appreciation of art in her pupil. Liane liked to read and she cultivated the conversational knowledge of the arts that her profession demanded, but fashion and people interested her far more than paintings. Valtesse reconciled herself to the fact that she would never be able to debate the finer points of a Da Vinci or a Botticelli with Liane. But on one expression of creativity, Valtesse insisted that Liane take note: a courtesan's surroundings were as important as an actress's stage set. The boudoir was an extension of a lady's appearance and personality – and like her, it must ensnare, seduce and vanquish.

As soon as she was able to take her own apartment, Liane obediently decorated it in the utmost of luxury. Impressed by the throne-like 'vessel of Paris' in which her mentor entertained her lovers, Liane had a grand Louis XV bed installed in her home. She too took her holidays on the Riviera in a fabulous villa in Menton, aptly baptised 'La Perle Blanche'.[48] And just like Valtesse, she also began to host 'five o'clocks'. They were soon among the most fashionable gatherings in Paris. Valtesse was proud to attend and admire her pupil's progress. She watched with satisfaction as Liane worked her way around a crowded room with ease and social finesse.

Through dedication and hard work, Liane became a successful courtesan in her own right and a revered fashion icon. She was known for her fabulous hat collection, and her favourite couturier confided that, in a single year, she spent 33,000 francs on dresses, coats and accessories.[49] 'Everyone is copying Liane de Pougy,' the papers declared.[50] Valtesse had nurtured a chrysalis, and now, an elegant social butterfly had emerged. Liane was the first to confess her natural vanity, but she knew she was indebted to Valtesse. Her gratitude was immeasurable. In Liane's eyes, Valtesse was unique and irreplaceable. 'A charming woman,' Liane gushed to anyone who cared to listen, 'very lovely, sensual and intelligent.'[51] In turn, Valtesse's affection and admiration for Liane increased as her career progressed. 'She is a woman,' Valtesse once said of her friend, 'a supreme woman, who understands women better than any man could, and men better than any woman.'[52]

Liane was regularly invited to stay with Valtesse in Ville-d'Avray and in Monte Carlo, and the women would write to each other when apart. A ball or concert would often conclude with the pair returning home together and dissecting the events of the evening late into the night. The next morning, 'it was the custom to take breakfast in "the Golden One's" bed,' Liane fondly recalled. 'An hour often went by in cheerful, affectionate gossip. She gave advice, she drew one out, and she kept her own secrets.'[53]

Liane knew Valtesse to be guarded where her personal fears and anxieties were concerned, but she was taken aback to learn that her friend had concealed two pregnancies from her. And yet Valtesse was closer to Liane than to any other female. Liane brought her much more than just friendship. She offered the more intimate form of affection Valtesse had been denied from men. Valtesse craved that intimacy, but her natural wariness made her guarded. She would happily share her body, and Liane would begin to draw close emotionally too – but the deepest corners of her soul were out of bounds. 'Love is like fear,' Valtesse was once heard to say, 'it makes you believe in everything.'[54] As she saw it, a woman abandoned scepticism at her peril.

But however fond Liane and Valtesse were of each other, there remained a bone of contention between them, one point on which Valtesse regularly scolded her junior. However hard she tried, and despite the demands of her profession, Liane was unable to suppress her insatiable sexual appetite for women.

Valtesse was firm. As she saw it, the occasional dalliance with another woman was one thing; a serious and overt sexual liaison, quite another matter. It could cost Liane her career.

While Valtesse constantly encouraged her towards wealthy male lovers, Liane began a passionate and very public affair with Émilienne d'Alençon. 'She was my leading light in the ways of the theatre and of our pleasures,' Liane later recalled.[55] The pair began to spend more and more time together, until one day, Liane realised that, 'with an impudence as great as her beauty she had moved in on me, had installed herself in my bed, at my table, in my carriages, in my theatre boxes – and all, I must confess, to my great pleasure.'[56] Liane could not resist. Émilienne's 'lips were so soft', she explained, her gestures, 'so coaxing'.[57] The women made no effort to conceal their mutual attraction, to the delight of Paris's gossip columnists. The sensationalist press even published a humorous announcement of the couple's forthcoming marriage and predicted the imminent arrival of their first child.[58]

Valtesse observed the press coverage her protégé was receiving. She too appreciated female intimacy and could recognise a woman's sexual appeal, but she considered Liane's infatuation foolish. It was not jealousy or disgust or even a perverse desire to hamper Liane's enjoyment that spurred her resistance; Liane, Valtesse believed, was wasting herself. Had her pupil not noticed how prematurely lesbians aged, she enquired? At twenty, their wrinkles were already starting to show, Valtesse insisted, lending her support to the cause of lesbianism's adversaries. These women wore the mask of their vice. Liane should take heed; she had set foot on a slippery slope.[59]

But if Liane's relationship with Émilienne made Valtesse uneasy, the threat of the bubbly rabbit tamer paled into insignificance next to another of Liane's great loves. In the 1890s, Liane became infatuated with a young American named Natalie Clifford Barney.

Natalie came to Paris to study Greek in the company of her mother and her fiancé, the young Robert Cassatt, nephew of the Impressionist artist Mary.[60] The marriage had been arranged despite – or because of – Natalie's preference for women, in order to appease her father. Mr Barney was a traditionalist: reputations and opinions mattered. With white-blonde hair, bright blue eyes and heart-shaped face, Natalie was pretty. She was also persuasive, independent, determined, perhaps even a little foolhardy. Certainly, she worried Valtesse – enough to prompt her to do something which compromised all her principles.

Valtesse was party to Liane and Natalie's relationship from the start. The young American first encountered Liane when their carriages passed one spring day in the Allée des Acacias. The women's eyes met and locked magnetically as their vehicles moved away in opposite directions. Natalie was speechless. Liane's ethereal beauty and svelte physique were unique. She did not properly understand what a courtesan was, though reasoned that Liane needed saving. Obtaining Liane's address, Natalie showered the object of her desire with flowers and letters until, finally, Liane agreed to receive her.

With Valtesse sceptical and Liane always ready to have fun, the girlfriends concocted a sly plan. When the American 'Miss' (as Lianne and Valtesse called her) arrived – dressed as a prince – Liane's maid showed her into the dimly lit boudoir, where Natalie could just make out a shadowy figure reclining seductively on a chaise longue.[61] Natalie fell to her knees in respect. But as she lifted her head to behold her idol, she was filled with horror: the woman before her was not Liane – it was Valtesse.

Hiding behind a curtain, Liane could no longer contain herself. She floated out like a vision, dressed in diaphanous white, and extended her equally pale, delicate hand, which gripped Natalie's shoulder with surprising firmness. 'Here I am,' Liane breathed.

Valtesse rose leisurely from the chaise longue. She had marked her territory. Natalie could be in no doubt of the central role she played in Liane's life. Valtesse's work was done. She made to leave, though not before inviting Natalie to come and visit her too. The young American might like to admire her famous stained-glass window – no doubt Natalie knew that she had been intimate with the Emperor? Her point crystal clear, Valtesse made her exit.

One of Liane's greatest and most tempestuous affairs had begun. Valtesse would need to monitor its development closely. She was not about to challenge Liane to end the affair – not yet. But nor would she allow her protégé to jeopardise the career they had toiled to establish. The American upstart had no conception of what Liane risked; and Valtesse, no intention of making things easy for her. She needed little persuasion to collaborate with Liane the next time she wanted to trick Natalie – even if it meant compromising the mystery intrinsic to her success.

One day, Liane brought Natalie (whom she affectionately nick-named 'Flossie') to see Valtesse. When the lovers arrived, Liane recalled, 'I [...] went into a bedroom with Valtesse, locked the door and refused her nothing, highly amused at the thought of Flossie speculating and suffering on the other side of the door.'[62] Afterwards, Liane was full of remorse. 'I was unforgivable,' she conceded, before adding of her relationship with Valtesse, 'We were friends to the limit – both permissible and forbidden.'

The women shared physical closeness, but while Liane wore her Sapphic heart on her sleeve, she was under no illusions: Valtesse had perfected the art of detachment where physical love was concerned; she had spent too long in her profession to do otherwise.

The sun was about to rise on the 20th century, and Valtesse was now in her 50s. At her age, she had two choices. She could continue to expand her empire, or she could simplify.

Valtesse began to plan her next move. But just as she was doing so, a high-profile court case sent shockwaves reverberating through France. Suddenly, a distorted lens was thrust in front of everyday life. In 1898, France was gripped by one of the most radical legal cases the country had ever seen – and it shone the public spotlight on Valtesse as never before, not just in France, but across the globe.

CHAPTER 17

New Beginnings:
The Sale of the House

With hindsight, a whiff of sociopolitical upheaval should have been detected on the air long before the Dreyfus affair made it pungent. The 1890s was a period of dynamic change – for better and worse. Technological advances were radically transforming the face of everyday life. The daily routine of ordinary men and women would have been unrecognisable to their grandparents. Already by the 1880s, the master of an upper-class house could pick up a telephone receiver – often warily – and enter into crackly communication with the ever-expanding world outside. On 28 December 1895, the first moving picture was shown to an audience of disbelieving spectators in the basement of the Grand Café on the Boulevard des Capucines.[1] Even the reassuring contours of Paris's familiar visage were growing strange; the city's old buildings were gradually being demolished, replaced, improved.

Everything smacked of change and progress, and few inventions embraced that ethos more wholeheartedly than the motor car. The automobile burst on to the market in the 1890s, reconfiguring communications and transforming mindsets. The car encompassed fashion and practicality. More than that: it symbolised freedom. Soon, it was the must-have accessory of the new age.

The opportunities and conditions negotiated by young women had altered markedly since Valtesse first stepped on to Offenbach's stage. Women still had to fight, but their war had a different cause. The face of the enemy had changed and so had the weapons. To survive, the Parisienne had to master a new language and perfect the steps of an unfamiliar dance. Though no longer a twenty-year-old *lorette* with stars in her eyes, Valtesse was determined not to fall behind.

By the 1890s, 98, Boulevard Malesherbes had a telephone connected, and Valtesse's friends only had to dial 502-26 to hear her voice speaking as though she were in the next room.[2] To Valtesse, it was as though Paris had presented itself on her doorstep and was awaiting her command. Suddenly, she could find out exactly what was going on anywhere in the city, and at any moment of the day. For the committed socialite, such knowledge was priceless.

Once her telephone was installed, Valtesse bought her first car. It was a classy Charron-Girardot in her trademark blue, with luxurious leather upholstery. 'There can be no car more desirable than a Charron,' commended one motoring review.[3] The vehicle was hailed for its style and ease of handling, and arbiters of taste held that for fashionable chateau stays and elegant seaside jaunts, the 'chic way to travel is in a Charron, the most excellent and gracious car of all'.[4]

Valtesse had to have one. It was a state-of-the-art treat.

The car satisfied multiple aspects of Valtesse's character. It brought independence and freedom, both of which she prized. It also justified a whole new wardrobe, with designers creating specially made furs and gloves for fashion-conscious ladies who travelled by car. Above all, an expensive, gleaming motorcar declared status and commanded respect. Valtesse took to driving. She basked in the attention as curious pedestrians turned their heads and stared in admiration whenever her car roared past. The adrenaline surge was intoxicating. Not content with one car, she also bought herself a Renault.

Yet for all her sensitivity to the ebb and flow of fashion, to Valtesse, fashion was merely a channel through which she could secure her position. It was a means of proving that she was in touch with modernity, that her star was still shining triumphantly. And fashions changed. So Valtesse would embrace a trend and then move on dispassionately when it passed.

Outwardly, Valtesse made herself a mirror to changing fashions. However, underpinning that transient surface was her utter conviction in the importance of tradition and etiquette. They carried far more weight with her than passing trends. Few courtesans allowed themselves the luxury of a footman during the Second Empire; Valtesse insisted on it.[5] Nothing assured respect and admiration so well as processing down the Allée des Acacias in her legendary carriage. As her impeccably groomed, glossy-coated horses trotted proudly along the tree-lined avenue, Valtesse would sit like a queen, her hat ribbon fluttering in the breeze, while her coachman and footman flanked her in their smart livery.[6] Things must be done properly, and the nobility presented the finest model.

Clothing and technology might change, but Valtesse maintained that a woman's conduct should be dictated by tradition. She had perfected an air of natural breeding, superiority and grace. A new acquaintance might never suspect her humble origins. Liane de Pougy observed of her friend, 'She would have suffered from what is called progress, that is to say from the tendency to accept and excuse shoddiness. She would have suffered but she would not have let it show.'[7]

Change is rarely confined to one area alone; technological advances were accompanied by dramatic sociopolitical shifts and outrageous scandals. In 1892, the Panama Scandal hit the headlines, exposing numerous Republican deputies as having accepted bribes to remain silent over corruption in the affairs of the Panama Canal Company.[8] Then in the midst of the drama, anarchists' attacks saw Paris gripped by terror, as bombs were planted in the homes of many public figures as well as significant buildings, not least the Chamber of Deputies and a café in the bustling Gare Saint-Lazare.[9] Finally, in 1894, one of the most sensational legal cases France had ever seen burst on to the front pages of the papers. It divided society, shaking its very foundations – and it directly affected Valtesse.

Alfred Dreyfus seemed an unlikely criminal. The bespectacled, unassuming Jewish army captain had an apparently glowing résumé. The youngest of seven children, Dreyfus had moved to Paris with his family from Alsace after the Franco-Prussian war.[10] Having elected French over German citizenship, the young man consolidated his patriotism to France by joining the army artillery. Dreyfus's conduct impressed his superiors and he was appointed captain in the War Office. By the early 1890s, the Alsatian's star was rising. But then, suddenly, everything changed.

Dreyfus's name first came to public light in October 1894, when a crumpled note was retrieved from the German embassy's waste-paper basket. The French army saw the German–Italian alliance as its active enemy, and as competition for the military secrets of Germany and Italy mounted, a complex web of espionage established itself. The discarded *bordereau* (list or schedule) revealed that someone within the French military was passing secrets to the German attaché in Paris, Max von Schwartzkoppen. The information promised was of minor importance, but that hardly mattered; the army was all-powerful. Criticising or undermining its integrity in any way was considered a form of treason – and treason must be punished.

The condemnatory bin contents were swiftly passed to Colonel Hubert Henry of the French military counter-intelligence service, the Statistical Section.[11] An organisation not unlike MI6, the Statistical Section was dismissed by many as a farcical enterprise. Notwithstanding, its head, the formidable Colonel Sandherr, treated his position with the utmost seriousness. Like Dreyfus, Colonel Sandherr was an Alsatian – but he was also a fierce anti-Semite.

By the 1890s, anti-Semitism was rife in France.[12] After the assassination of Tsar Alexander II of Russia, harsh restrictions had been placed on Russian Jews by the new tsar, while a wave of pogroms had broken out across the country. As a result, floods of Jewish refugees poured into France. They lacked possessions, their clothes were in tatters – and they were denied government assistance. The French eyed them suspiciously. Once accepted in France, Jews now found themselves blamed for every ill and misdemeanour imaginable.

That a French officer should have committed such a heinous crime against the army was deeply humiliating. Panicking, officials realised that the army's fragile reputation depended on the case being resolved quickly. As a Jew, Captain Dreyfus made the perfect scapegoat. Handwriting experts' reports were inconclusive, but the army was decided. Dreyfus was arrested, tried and found guilty at the end of 1894. The prisoner was banished to Devil's Island off the coast of French Guiana, where he was placed in solitary confinement and chained to his bed. Meanwhile, in France, officials sat back in relief as the fierce campaign for the case's review fell on deaf ears.

Then at last, in 1896, there was a breakthrough. The handwriting on the note that had condemned Dreyfus was found to match that of Ferdinand Walsin Esterhazy, a French officer of Hungarian descent. With his shifty eyes and oversized moustache, Esterhazy looked every bit the dastardly villain of storybooks. Evidence against him began to accumulate. Under pressure from the public and notable personalities, not least Émile Zola, in January 1898, the government ordered a court-martial for Esterhazy. But to the despair of Dreyfusards, the trial was rigged in Esterhazy's favour and he was acquitted.

The campaign for Dreyfus's release continued in earnest, until finally in 1899, a change of president made conditions favourable for a review of the case. Dreyfus was sent for, the evidence re-examined and a hearing scheduled to begin in August 1899 in Rennes, where it was hoped that any public protest would be more manageable than in the capital. The whole of Europe was watching. And when the hearing began, Valtesse suddenly found that she had become a key figure in the anti-Dreyfusards' campaign to ensure the Jew never walked free.

It was during the eighth public sitting on 21 August that the court was invited to consider Dreyfus's character.[13] As the principal archivist and keeper of the War Office records, M. Gribelin was called forward. And as he spoke, Dreyfus's character defence started to unravel.

The accused, he explained, was known to keep company with women 'of loose character'.[14] Even Dreyfus's brother, Mathieu, had confessed that he had once been obliged to save his brother 'from the clutches of a woman of this description who lived near the Champs Élysées'.[15] Curiosity mounted. Who might the mysterious femme fatale be, wondered the court?

Then, Major Junck, an engineer who had worked with Dreyfus, was summoned. Anti-Dreyfusards sat poised with anticipation. All hoped for further revelations, spicy snippets regarding the prisoner's private life which would place an indelible stain on his character.

The major conceded that Dreyfus had spoken of large sums that he had lost at the gambling table, and of his fraternising with women of doubtful morals.[16] On one occasion, the two men had been at the Concours Hippique when three women passed them. Dreyfus, the major recalled, tipped his hat in acknowledgement.

'Well,' the major exclaimed, 'for a married man you have nice acquaintances.'

Junck continued his story: 'He said that they were old friends of his bachelor days, and, pointing to one of them, said her name was "la Valtesse", and that she had a house at the Champs Élysées [*sic*], where she gave very nice parties, and where pretty women were to be met and play went on.'

Anti-Dreyfusards were triumphant. This was just the kind of scandalous titbit they had been hoping for: Dreyfus was intimate with one of the most notorious courtesans in Paris, Valtesse de la Bigne.

The major was asked how, knowing such detail, he could possibly affirm that nothing would have given him cause to suspect Dreyfus of misconduct.

'I have recounted the incident involving "la Valtesse",' Junck countered, 'but I never saw Dreyfus undertake a task which would give me cause to suspect him.'[17]

The hearing continued, but the die was cast. Everybody understood the implications of the major's testimony: Dreyfus's friendship with Valtesse left an ugly blemish on his professed reputation as an upstanding citizen with an impeccable moral compass.

Back in Paris, the latest developments in the hearing filled the morning papers. Since the press first got wind of the case, the Dreyfus affair had split French society in two. Polite dinner party conversations broke down into violent dispute. Lifelong friends became sworn enemies. The military's united front was shattered. The 1899 retrial merely intensified emotions.

As newspapers were opened, opponents of Dreyfus and the *demimonde* exchanged satisfied smiles, while fashionable society leaned forward with interest. Of course Dreyfus, a military man, should have been invited to Valtesse's parties. It was clear where her sympathies lay.

But then better-informed socialites began to talk among themselves. Esterhazy had taken up residence at number 49, Rue de Douai, just off Pigalle, with his mistress, a certain Mlle Pays, alias 'Marion Four Fingers' (the unfortunate Mlle Pays had a mutilated hand).[18] The odd-looking couple often took their meals at the concierge's lodge. Sometimes they were joined by guests. People saw Oscar Wilde arriving to dine with them from time to time – and they also saw Valtesse.[19]

Experience had taught Valtesse to stifle her emotions when her name was raised in court. All around her, gossip-mongers burned with curiosity. Did 'la Valtesse' support Dreyfus? Or did she back Esterhazy? Was she the irresistible seductress linking the two?

Valtesse kept her own counsel. She saw qualities – and advantages – in both men, and she spread her loyalties accordingly. But she had a parting retort for the benefit of the press when her renewed media prominence subsequently led a group of military men to presume to greet her too familiarly: 'Everyone who knows me calls me Madame,' Valtesse retorted.[20] She could not abide strangers addressing her without a title.

Dreyfus's court-martial rolled on for five weeks, but this time, when another guilty verdict was returned, justice came to the prisoner's aid: France's new president, Émile Loubet, granted Dreyfus a state pardon that September, and the gossip columns eventually fell silent on Valtesse's involvement in the case.

Putting the Dreyfus affair firmly behind her, Valtesse turned her attention to other matters. A new century was about to dawn. 1899 was like a punctured tyre, declared *Gil Blas*.[21] Nobody would miss it. The death of the 19th century was overshadowed by the birth of the new one. And Paris intended to give it the welcome it deserved.

In the first few weeks of 1900, Liane arrived at Villa les Aigles in a flurry of style and panache. Valtesse was overjoyed. Liane had decided to add writing to her already busy schedule, and, concerned that her friend might be exhausting herself, Valtesse had persuaded her protégé to join her for a dose of carefree fun on the Riviera before they both took off for a short break in Portugal.[22] They would be joined by Gabrielle de Guestre for what promised to be a sparkling winter season, peppered with the usual entertainments and social gatherings, not least Valtesse's famous Monacan 'five o'clocks'.[23]

With her, Liane brought her insatiable appetite for life, as well as the German baron she was courting at the time, trunks of elegant dresses and a selection of marvellous hats crafted by the esteemed milliner, Lewis. Liane had learned well: whatever she wore, she inhabited like a second skin. Her body flowed gracefully draped in white muslin, she walked tall in tight pearl chokers, she glided seductively in soft fur stoles – and at 31, youth was still her ally.

Valtesse would turn 52 that summer. All around her, the shapely figures of younger, fresher-faced women were stealing the hearts – and wealth – of Paris's eminent bachelors.

'Not far from Les Jardies is the property of Mme Valtesse de la Bigne,' announced one travel writer, 'and every year, a size increase is to be observed.' He then quickly clarified: 'A size increase of the property, that is.'[24]

'Her proud pseudonym, Ego, is full of instruction for young debutantes,' commented another journalist.[25] The observation was respectful, it implied her self-confidence and experience, but Valtesse could read between the lines. Conscious that her readers were expecting an autobiography, Valtesse had deliberately made the heroine of *Isola* eight years younger than herself. She was not about to advertise her real age at this point – but before long she would not need to. Her own mother was now dead, a poignant reminder that time was passing, that she too was ageing.[26] Her beauty was still undeniable and her poise invariably won her admiring glances; however, the elegant curves of her body were growing less distinct. Her jowls seemed fuller than they used to be. Her hair was flecked with grey and she looked, as one observer put it, like a beautiful pastel which was starting to fade.[27]

The following year, Liane de Pougy published a scandalous novel, *Idylle saphique* (1901), a semi-autobiographical tale of lesbian romance and intrigue. She based the character Altesse on her beloved mentor, making no attempt to conceal the association. In the novel, Liane told how the young courtesan Annhine (the Liane character) met and befriended Altesse, 'also a courtesan, a bright woman, eminently superior.'[28]

Liane continued her portrait:

Then, Altesse was at the height of her splendour, having reached the age at which the delicate charms of the mature woman so celebrated by Balzac are at their finest. [...] Altesse was young when she reached her elevated position in Parisian gallantry. [...] Paris was fascinated by her, her slightest activities were reported, her witty expressions repeated. [...] Her exceptional position distinguished her from all the rest and placed her above everyone else.

Liane was full of praise and flattery. But Balzac was long dead, and Altesse came across as something of a grand dame of Parisian gallantry.

If ageing made her uncomfortable, Valtesse firmly believed that a woman should retain her dignity. That meant accepting the situation. But she was not prepared to sacrifice pleasure, nor did she see any reason why she should stop receiving male admirers. She had been impressed by the modus operandi of an older courtesan named Antoinette.[29] When Valtesse called on the veteran *femme galante* one day and was invited to view her apartment, she was surprised to see a huge bed positioned in the middle of the bedroom.

'You are still receiving!' Valtesse exclaimed with admiration.

The courtesan's example left its impression. After all, Valtesse reasoned, a woman could never have too much wealth, and, as she told friends with a smile, she did not want to lose her touch. At the Cirque Molier that year, Valtesse's accessories sent her competitors a triumphant message: she had not lost her ability to seduce the opposite sex. The 'sparkle of her jewels and the size of her pearls testify princely affections,' one commentator observed, without speculating which prince that might be.[30]

But even an expert man-pleaser must guard against complacency. One regrettable occasion when Valtesse failed to heed that rule was sufficient reminder that the press were still watching her.

Early one May, Valtesse decided to make one of her forays over to Ville-d'Avray with her latest admirer, a high-ranking military man, for her attraction to men in uniform remained as healthy as ever.[31] The couple boarded the train, the gentleman floating on the happy promise of the romantic interlude which awaited. But his desire burned so intensely that he found himself unable to suppress it until the train reached its destination. The carriage door clanked shut. Conversation ceased. As the train pulled away from the station, the man in the next carriage compartment leaned forwards. He felt certain he could hear noises coming from the neighbouring compartment – breathy noises, the moist sound of lips urgently searching, meeting and parting, searching, meeting and parting. Only when the train pulled into the station at Ville-d'Avray did the rhythmic accompaniment cease. Valtesse should take more care when travelling by rail, advised the journalist who smugly reported the incident in *Gil Blas*. Particularly, the writer continued, when the man in question held an elevated rank and shared his name with a certain town in the Cantal department. With even a hesitant grasp of his country's geography, the average Frenchman would have known that department's prefecture to be located in Aurillac.

The indiscretion was out of character for Valtesse, who usually drew such a clear divide between public dignity and private eroticism. She would be more cautious in future. Vigilance was as crucial as ever. Nobody was in any doubt about her profession, but she was determined people should think of her as an educated romantic, not a common cocotte. Being spotted visiting her favourite bookshop, Floury, on the Boulevard des Capucines, certainly helped advertise her bright mind.[32] But *Gil Blas*'s call for writers, artists and celebrities to share their thoughts on the value of the kiss provided a more direct opportunity to flaunt her poetic side. Valtesse rose to the occasion.

'A kiss is only precious when it is given,' Valtesse affirmed. 'If it is sold, whether by a young girl, a married woman, or a widow, it is worth no more than was paid for it, a kiosk kiss.'[33]

But such opportunities to remind Paris of her wit were growing fewer and farther between. At nearly 55, Valtesse knew herself to be clinging precariously to the life she had built in Paris and the position she had secured. She would always have her friends, her dedicated admirers and the loyalty of the journalists she had befriended. But as a new generation began filling familiar roles with unfamiliar faces, Valtesse's network of contacts was faltering. Once past her prime, a courtesan could still ride on her reputation and her connections – for a time. But when she was no longer pretty, when her story was all but told and there seemed nothing left to know, she simply ceased to be interesting – unless her demise was spectacular.

The still-recent downfall of poor Cora Pearl, with whom Valtesse had often socialised and even shared lovers, continued to be cited as a cautionary tale in fashionable salons. Fellow courtesans shuddered when Cora, the Princess of Paris, was cast out of the society she had once ruled. When a disgruntled lover, Alexandre Duval, accidentally shot himself in an attempt to maim her, a self-centred and heartless woman was publicly exposed; people learned how Cora had shamelessly ruined Duval financially before casting him aside.[34] As her friends disappeared and her fortune dwindled, Cora was once again reduced to common prostitution. Eventually, Cora died of intestinal cancer. But by the time news of her death broke, more than ten years had passed since she was considered part of fashionable society; for Paris's social elite, she had already died.

It was a chilling tale. Valtesse was determined that that should not be her fate. She had always sought perfect control over her public profile, and nothing had changed. She refused to become a victim of chance. Her story would be completed by the most competent author she knew – herself. With foresight and pragmatism, Valtesse began to choreograph her own departure.

In the middle of May 1902, Parisians opened their newspapers to read a shocking announcement, news nobody could have predicted.[35] Comtesse Valtesse de la Bigne was going to auction off all her property: 98, Boulevard Malesherbes, Villa les Aigles and her home in Ville-d'Avray were all to be sold. There would be no more 'five o'clocks' and scintillating conversations in front of great masterpieces on the Boulevard Malesherbes; no more coffees on the sun-drenched balcony overlooking the Mediterranean Sea, no more officers strolling around her personal Eden in Ville-d'Avray on a Sunday afternoon as their cares of the week evaporated in the revitalising country air. Everything Valtesse had worked for, her homes, her precious paintings, furniture and carriages; everything was to go.

The news sent shock waves across Paris. Why would a woman who had attached so much importance to material objects suddenly sell everything? It made no sense. To withdraw from Parisian society was to hasten one's own death – and that was precisely how the newspapers treated the departure.

Under Richard O'Monroy's admiring pen, *Gil Blas* took the lead. The first article on the front page gripped readers' attention with a dramatic headline printed in large letters: 'The Woman Who is Disappearing'.[36]

> Parisians, brothers, pray, show your respects to the woman who is leaving. A fascinating figure is about to disappear, one who is almost a symbol, the last representative – and with what supreme charm – of that special caste which we can rightly call 'the great courtesans'.

O'Monroy's glittering eulogy continued. Valtesse was a true courtesan, he explained, like those who had once ruled ancient Greece: a woman who combined seductive beauty and fierce intellectual capital. Modern-day *demi-mondaines* were pretty, but they lacked taste and refinement, and were seldom educated. Valtesse was different. She was the last of a distinguished breed. With unshakeable self-knowledge, Valtesse never sought a place among the bourgeoisie. She was proud to be a courtesan. A fairy princess with her huge blue eyes, the luminosity of her lily-white skin was startling. Her tiny mouth silently mocked those she considered inferior, while her arched eyebrows gave her face a look of permanent surprise. Unusual, inaccessible, and full of good sense and grace, Valtesse was unique.

But now, lamented O'Monroy, 'all that is over. Madame Valtesse de la Bigne, la Valtesse whom we have known and admired, is disappearing by voluntary abdication, further proof of her coquettish nature […] Some melancholic words by way of farewell: Valtesse is no more,' wrote the journalist, before offering his heartbroken conclusion: 'Oh, my youth! It is you they are burying!'

Valtesse knew that her decision would rouse questions and malicious gossip. She could not rely on her friend's mock obituary to elevate her, and in any case, O'Monroy denied all knowledge of her motivations. People would want answers. If she did not provide them, society's gossips certainly would. So Valtesse took control. Seizing her pen, she began to write her own introduction to the sale catalogue. Referring to herself in the third person, Valtesse opened the piece by laying out her reasons for leaving Paris:

> 'A beautiful woman's capriciousness,' some will say. 'A very sound and carefully thought-out decision,' better-informed people will reply. Life in Paris, hectic life, with its landscape criss-crossed by rails, the air saturated by car fumes and the deafening sound of horns [...] all that seems to lack serene elegance, and it is in Ville-d'Avray [...] that she will seek the asylum of peace, the relaxing spectacle of nature she so cherishes. [...] ceasing contact with outsiders, retaining only her friends, she wishes to live that rare dream of solitude without isolation.[37]

Valtesse had found the perfect property in which to begin her new life. It was the house formerly occupied by Augustine Brohan, the celebrated actress who, like her sister Madeleine, had made a name for herself at the Comédie Francaise and was said to have been the mistress of Louis Napoleon Bonaparte. Besides the contented shiver of prestige at that association, the house offered Valtesse an irresistibly blank canvas to decorate and adapt as she pleased. However, her new home could hardly accommodate a town house and two villas' worth of treasures. That, Valtesse declared, was the true motivation for the sale. But of course, people were understandably curious. And, she conceded slyly, a true artiste would not sell all their possessions if these ripples of interest did not invoke a small frisson of pleasure.

She meticulously detailed all her fabulous works, using powerful rhetoric and glorifying each item's assets, particularly where her bed was concerned. The catalogue was a glorious exercise in self-promotion. Now, Valtesse could only hope that the sale would be a success.

On that front, O'Monroy's forecast proved accurate: the sale became the must-see Parisian event. For weeks before, interest was drummed up by a fervent advertising campaign, with stirring military paintings by Detaille heralded as the key attraction.[38] Huge adverts in the leading newspapers in France and England set amateur collectors salivating greedily over the delicious treasures they would be able to own.[39] But Paris's celebrity-tailing public needed little persuasion to inspect the legendary town house of such a renowned courtesan. Parisians rushed to acquire copies of the sale catalogue, and before long the auctioneers ran out. The interest boded well.

Over two frantic days of private and public viewing, hordes of curious citizens flocked to 98, Boulevard Malesherbes. Men and women jostled through the rooms, inspecting the layout of the apartment and craning their necks to examine the splendid works on view. When the sale officially opened on 2 June, the response was phenomenal. Collectors fought to outbid their competitors and on the first day alone the auctioneers took over 250,000 francs (approximately £2,800,000 in modern currency).[40] At the end of the fourth day, the running total exceeded 470,000 francs (equivalent to just over £5 million today).[41]

As the sale progressed, Valtesse could feel content. She was reducing her encumbrance and increasing her fortune. Besides, she much preferred to oversee the dissemination of her property herself than that it should take place after her death when she would have no control. If she retreated now with her reputation intact, her legend could continue to flourish.

But it also occurred to her that she would remain all the more memorable if she left her public wanting more. So, relishing her power over so many nosy Parisians, Valtesse decided that her bed would have a different fate from the one originally intended: she would take it with her to Ville-d'Avray. The public could read about it, view it, admire it and imagine – but never know – what it might feel like to lie beneath its canopy. Valtesse knew there could be nothing more tantalising.

The sale was an extraordinary success. Detaille's paintings alone earned Valtesse nearly 280,000 francs (just over £3 million in modern currency), even after she had carefully cherry-picked the finest pieces to keep for herself.[42] With takings from the auction totalling more than half a million francs and her properties being sold, Valtesse had ample funds with which to remodel, furnish and decorate her new home to her taste.[43] No expense need be spared. Naturally, she told Jules Claretie with a smile, it would be decorated in 'Valtesstyle'.[44]

Perched high on a hill in Ville-d'Avray, La Chapelle-du-Roy was already a masterpiece of Louis-Philippe-style mock Gothic architecture when Valtesse bought it.[45] With Sèvres just below and the reverberating metropolis of Paris a reassuring distance away, the castle of Valtesse's dreams enjoyed spectacular panoramic views of the landscape she had first discovered through Corot.

No sooner had she become the owner than Valtesse set her team of builders to work. In her mind, she held an image of her ideal home on which she refused to compromise. Her obstinacy brought a spectacular marble palace rising up through the trees.

The old Gothic pavilions were demolished and a brand new structure built. Corinthian columns, each topped with a statue, flanked the majestic, tree-lined driveway leading up to Valtesse's grand chateau. The white, column-fronted building with its magnificent balustrades and balconies overlooking the grounds recalled the Mediterranean elegance of Villa les Aigles. The two main rooms on the ground floor were bathed in light which flooded in through the glass doors opening out on to the terrace.

For the salon and the dining room, Valtesse sought the decorative expertise of Louis Majorelle, the celebrated art nouveau furniture designer and artist.[46] Ornate mahogany furniture, elaborate rugs, potted ferns, and dark wood architraves gave the spaces the same rich intensity Valtesse had appreciated at 98, Boulevard Malesherbes, and barely a wall was left without a mural or decorative pattern. Detaille agreed to paint a number of scenes for the spaces, while a frieze ran along the edge of the ceilings; and throughout the rooms the letter 'V' could be seen embossed, painted or carved. Valtesse's bed took pride of place in her new bedroom, and when she lay down, she could look up and admire the late Pierre-Victor Galland's painting of a dancing bacchant playing a tambourine – a work so exquisite that she insisted it accompany her when she moved from Paris.[47] Adjoining the salon was an enormous library, which Valtesse filled with her favourite volumes. She hardly wanted for furniture and fittings, but her new home provided an irresistible excuse to add some new pieces to her collection. Most treasured among her new additions was a clock with the letters of her name embossed around its face in place of the hours and the two hands fashioned to replicate the branches of the printed letter 'V'.[48]

Valtesse was taken by the idea of turning the salon into a gallery of family portraits, and the ever-biddable Detaille was happy to oblige. Soon, noble faces began to fill the walls. There was the proud-looking Etienne-Michel, Marquis de la Bigne, Louis Antoine-Michel de la Bigne, an 18th-century commander of the National Guards in Caen, Sigismond-Tancrède, Comte de la Bigne, Jean-Baptiste Gabriel François, Marquis de la Bigne, a colonel of the cavalry killed in 1814, and Horace de la Bigne, a member of the General Council of the Seine in the 18th–19th century. Valtesse's ancestral heritage included an enviable line-up of dignitaries and officials, and there, standing defiantly on a barricade, was Cyprien-Georges de la Bigne, a combatant from the 1830 revolution.[49]

'Oh, him,' Valtesse would say dismissively and with feigned disgust as visitors toured her gallery, 'his portrait should be veiled like that of Marino Faliero. He is the black sheep of the family. We call him "the insurgent".'[50]

But as she spoke, she could seldom suppress a giggle: all but one of the painted ancestors were fictitious creations. Only Gacé de la Bigne had really existed. Of Normandy extraction, he had been King John II's chaplain during the 14th century. He had tutored the Dauphin and written poetry and two books. His inclusion had been carefully calculated. So had the appellation Etienne, the name conferred upon all the eldest male children in the true, noble de la Bigne family.[51] Valtesse had done her research. The most implausible fiction could be believed when it contained a grain of truth.

It was now more than 25 years since Isola had declared 'With your fortunes, I will buy myself family, parents, friends, children, the world if it takes my fancy.'[52] At last, the author had honoured her heroine's promise. Finally, Valtesse had a family she could be proud of.

The grounds of La Chapelle-du-Roy were transformed into a magnificent park. It boasted pavilions, greenhouses and the mystical 'Salon Vert', a clearing where overhanging trees met, forming a romantic woodland alcove in the middle of which stood an elegant statue of a couple embracing. The shaded avenues were perfect for summer strolls when guests visited from Paris, and around every corner there was a statue to delight and surprise. Valtesse even had a small studio constructed on the property for Detaille to work in when he visited. Her company was a powerful incentive, and once Valtesse left Paris, the painter could more often be found at La Chapelle-du-Roy than in his studio on the Boulevard Malesherbes.[53]

Valtesse was delighted, and the workmen from the construction company CLEDAT were duly rewarded with the most covetable gift she could conceive of: each man received a copy of her portrait.[54]

Valtesse soon settled into a peaceful daily routine with her two faithful white greyhounds. Close friends would visit, bringing news from the capital. Valtesse listened intently, but felt no urge to return to Paris. The tranquillity in Ville-d'Avray suited her. She could do as she pleased. 'You know, my friend,' Valtesse wrote to Richard O'Monroy, 'our lives now, less noisy, no doubt less youthful, are nevertheless still full of a thousand good things, which we will reveal … in time.'[55]

Valtesse's home in Ville-d'Avray offered all the luxury to which she had grown accustomed in Paris, with none of the inconveniences. It was just the serene existence she had yearned for. She had completed her career and made her fortune; press attention had lost its appeal. In Ville-d'Avray, journalists no longer pursued her and her name seldom appeared in the papers. To Parisians, it was as though she had died.

Some people wondered what had become of the great comtesse, particularly when 98, Boulevard Malesherbes was demolished the following year. 'Valtesse (de la Bigne) is still with us,' *Le Supplément* reassured its readers, 'something I am very pleased about, because I am told she is a charming woman. She has wisely retired to her home in Ville-d'Avray, and leaning on her balcony like a fairytale princess, she daydreams of passing love.'[56]

It was precisely the image Valtesse had wanted to leave. Besides, she could still correspond with the capital from a distance when she desired. In 1906, she sent the satirical publication *Le Rire* an anecdote that had amused her. A dazzling necklace that she had donated to the Musée de l'Armée had been displayed with the inscription 'Gift from Mlle Valtesse de la Bigne'.[57] A visiting general declared the glorification of a *demi-mondaine* an outrage. The necklace was hastily removed from display. A few years later, it reappeared, with a smaller, barely legible inscription: 'Gift from Mme V. de la Bigne'. A curious journalist wrote to the museum seeking a fuller explanation. He received the response: 'Gift from Mme Bigne'. Living outside the capital, Valtesse could now smile at such Parisian hypocrisy and pettiness.

Locals in Ville-d'Avray whispered that she had continued involvement in her former profession, and that unofficially she had become an *entremetteuse*, a kind of madam who would coach young girls to become *femmes galantes* and match them with clients whose payment included her own hefty commission. But nobody could prove the rumour.

Still, for all the visitors, life in Ville-d'Avray was never going to match Paris for diversions and entertainments. And Valtesse's mind had always thrived when it had a project to occupy it. Nowadays, all the fashionable creative types seemed to be dabbling in the theatre, and Valtesse concluded that writing a play would be a marvellous distraction.[58] *Cintho* drew on Valtesse's interest and knowledge of culture in the Far East. It told the tale of a tragic love affair between a Japanese man (to be played by a female) and a Parisian woman. Cultural loyalties spur the besotted Asian to strangle his beloved as they drift in a boat on a lake surrounded by lotus flowers. Eventually, justice is done and the man is made to pay for his crime.

Once satisfied, Valtesse shared her work with friends. 'It stars a woman dressed as a man,' Valtesse told them, 'that is always original, and this one is Japanese, too!'[59] When Sarah Bernhardt expressed a fleeting interest in playing the part of the Japanese man, Valtesse began to wonder whether the Comédie Française might even stage her play. The ever-loyal Jules Claretie assured her that he saw considerable promise in the piece, and tried to persuade the dashing young actor-cum-theatrical impresario Firmin Gémier, as well as Detaille's former mistress, the actress Réjane, to lend their support. But not even Claretie's coaxing tones could win Réjane round, and eventually Sarah Bernhardt also refused to take a role. The play never reached the stage, but Valtesse did not mind. It was too late in life to become unduly attached to any particular project.

Apart from one. The most worthwhile project of all: herself. She had just one more appearance to prepare for. It would be the performance of her life.

CHAPTER 18

The Final Act:
Preparing a Legacy

altesse had long been conscious of her own mortality. She shared Isola's stoical attitude towards death. Pious men and women died with their desperate hands outstretched towards divinity; not Isola. Valtesse's heroine had sworn that whenever the final hour struck, 'I will go to sleep quietly in a bed from which one never rises [...] I will sleep without nightmares, the great slumber of eternal nothingness.'[1]

In 1909, Valtesse fell ill with vascular complications and her doctor advised an operation. At the end of November, she travelled to Paris to undergo surgery. The surgeon emerged from the procedure satisfied, and Valtesse's friends were relieved when she appeared to be making a good recovery.

Her convalescence was lightened by the presence of friends, not to mention some unexpected joys. Valtesse was thrilled to learn that Liane, now 41, was to be married to the Romanian prince Georges Ghika.[2] It gave her indescribable pleasure to know that her protégé had scaled society's hostile walls and reached its summit. Her new position – a princess, no less – would bring her immediate respect. Liane's status and security were now assured.

But Valtesse's joy at her friend's good fortune was short-lived. In the middle of 1910, her health began to deteriorate again – and this time, it did so rapidly.

Valtesse sensed her outlook to be bleak. Her response to her worsening health was unsentimental and practical. Conscious of the need to think ahead, she began to prepare for her final departure.

Valtesse carefully selected an optimum placement high up in the sloping cemetery of Ville-d'Avray. Then, she ordered a beautifully crafted coffin, as well as a set of elegant notecards from the fashionable engraver Appay to be sent to her nearest and dearest when she passed away. The date was left blank.[3]

One night towards the end of July, the staff at La Chapelle-du-Roy were awakened and the household thrown into uproar; Valtesse had had a bad turn.[4] The doctor issued morphine and her pain began to ease. But when he learned of the drama, Detaille could not dismiss a terrible sense of foreboding. On 25 July 1910, the artist noted in his diary:

> Morning in Ville-d'Avray. The illness has got worse – her veins have ruptured. I feel the most terrible grief, and I have to hide it from V who can see, despite being extremely weak. I returned to Paris traumatised, sick to my stomach […] I do not know how I did not succumb to the heart attack I felt sure I would suffer.[5]

Throughout the following week, Detaille travelled mechanically back and forth between Paris and Ville-d'Avray, dazed, numbed by pain and desolation.[6] The doctors Bosviaux and Huguet, as well as Valtesse's faithful lawyer, 63-year-old Jullemier, and three of her close female friends including Gabrielle Dupuy, hovered close to the patient, united by their common concern. At times, Valtesse's condition appeared to worsen, and the household were alerted that the end was surely close. Then she would pick up, to the delight and disbelief of the anxious faces around her bedside, not least those of the doctors. Her resilience was astounding. The moments of respite were encouraging, but Detaille knew that they could not last.

On 29 July 1910, Valtesse's doctor came to her, his expression grave. He explained that it was now certain: she had only a few hours to live. Weak and vague, weary from her fight, Valtesse struggled to focus on the words being spoken. Slowly, she began to digest the prognosis. Once she understood, she accepted the news calmly. Summoning all her energy, Valtesse called for the announcement cards she had had printed to be brought to her. Taking her pen and steadying her hand, she proceeded to write the date of her own death on each and every single card.[7] Then, she carefully inscribed the names and addresses of all her friends and associates on the envelopes she wished to be sent. And she lay back and waited.

Just before 10.45 that evening, Comtesse Valtesse de la Bigne closed her bright blue eyes for the last time.[8] As she lay in her grand bed, her face wore the expression of one at peace, and she appeared not to be suffering.[9] Then, like the guttering flame of a dying candle, Valtesse slipped away. She was 62 years old (though her death certificate declared her to be 48).[10]

The notecards she had so painstakingly addressed were swiftly dispatched. All across Paris, doors were opened, post was received, and maids and footmen came to their mistresses and their masters with a small envelope. In their respective homes, Liane de Pougy, Richard O'Monroy, Jules Claretie and other recipients opened the envelope in their hands to find a crisp white card framed by a black border. The card was stamped with a crown, a logo people had come to associate with Valtesse. In Gothic lettering, the message read:

Madame
Valtesse de la Bigne
Died on the 29 July 1910.
Remember.

Valtesse's friends were aghast. Liane was inconsolable. Claretie, stunned, thought it a joke: no doubt the card was a coded message sent only to close friends to inform them that the writer had resolved to disappear, to start again, to assume a new identity, like the heroine of a novel. That was Valtesse's style after all.

But the card was no hoax. That familiar, confident, cursive handwriting from beyond the grave was the last communication the addressee would receive from Valtesse.

On 31 July 1910, Valtesse left La Chapelle-du-Roy for the very last time. She was setting out for her final home: the cemetery of her beloved Ville-d'Avray.

The residents of Ville-d'Avray awoke that morning to find the sky heavy, grey and oppressive.[11] Shopkeepers were obliged to light their premises, and a persistent rain matched the overriding sense of gloom. Everything seemed eerie and unnatural. For the height of summer, it felt like a winter's day.

Outside La Chapelle-du-Roy, Valtesse's four white horses assumed a sinister, ghostly appearance as they stood in their ornate funeral tack. At the driver's command, they lifted their hooves and the stately funeral hearse began its solemn journey. Slowly, the carriage wound its way down the steady slope leaving La Chapelle-du-Roy, its wheels crunching over the gravel. Once outside the gates, the sombre procession attracted reverent stares as it passed through the streets.

The coffin transported was crafted from highly polished wood, and locals whispered that it had a cost a fortune. It was chilling in its austerity. There were no elaborate flower arrangements to adorn it, no brightly coloured bouquets; instead, merely a handful of violets in an effort to soften the uncompromising lines of the coffin's dark-veneered surface. It was just as Valtesse had wanted. 'No flowers, no garlands,' she had firmly instructed those with her at the end.[12] Only violets. As usual, her request was granted.

Valtesse had insisted that she did not want a great commotion when she died.[13] Nonetheless, friends were welcome, and a glittering cortège of mourners dotted with celebrity faces walked soberly behind the funeral procession, their heads bowed respectfully. But Jullemier had been charged with a special responsibility: family were to be kept at a distance. Valtesse may have maintained contact with Pâquerette, but so many of her family had brought her shame, not least her sister Emilie (or Marquesse). And who knew what scandalous scene a disgruntled relative might cause, or which shady individuals might try to use the funeral as an opportunity to claim a connection with the late courtesan – and her fortune? To Valtesse, her reputation was her most precious bequest. Exercising a veto on all blood relatives had seemed the safest policy. Jullemier saw to it that Valtesse's stipulation was respected.

For all the funerals they had witnessed in recent years, few townspeople could recall a tomb so awe-inspiring as the one the mourners now stood before. On a square-based plinth, a tiered circular mounting supported an enormous marble structure which resembled an inverted tripod. The three legs were mounted on clawed feet, and they rose up to the sky at steep angles, the space between them growing progressively wider. On top of each leg, a golden eagle spread its wings and hovered imposingly like a triumphant gargoyle, well above the height of an average man's head. At the eagles' backs was a vast, acorn-shaped urn. The urn was gripped firmly in the tripod's centre and topped with a bronze flame, which gave it the appearance of an Olympic torch. The whole structure was finished with intricate floral decoration and a bold letter 'V'. At over 3.5m tall, proudly overlooking the more modest gravestones below, the tomb that would soon receive Valtesse's remains was impossible to ignore.[14]

As midday struck, Valtesse's friends and loved ones stood contemplating the awesome structure, each lost in private reflection.

'With this wonderful woman, a whole era has disappeared,' Claretie philosophised, 'a fleeting moment in the history of Paris.'[15]

Liane was devastated. 'That charming woman's death has left a hole in my life which no one else has yet filled,' she would write in her diaries, years after the event, while Detaille would change his will, an indication that Valtesse had been a key beneficiary.[16]

Suddenly, as mourners stood around the tomb, they noticed that the rain had eased. Then all at once, the clouds parted and the sun appeared. It was as though nature had been choreographed just to Valtesse's taste.

When the secular funeral ceremony was over and people began to filter away, Jules Claretie moved closer to examine the collection of wreaths and floral tributes which had been left at the base of the tomb. He was struck by one particular offering. To a simple wreath, a note had been pinned. The uncertain handwriting betrayed the concerted efforts of a child: 'To Mme de la Bigne, in memory from her family.'[17] Moved, Claretie realised that the tribute had been offered by the poor schoolchildren whom he had seen peppered incongruously among the well-dressed celebrities in the funeral procession. Their unassuming little faces showed no awareness of Valtesse's past. They knew only that she was very beautiful. They knew too that she had shown them great charity since she moved to the town.

But on closer inspection, there was something else about the tomb which was peculiar. Claretie was not the only one to spot it. Carved into the marble on either side of Valtesse's name, there were two others: 'L.M. Auriac' and 'E. Una'. The names bore no date, and there was no further explanation. The enigmatic Ego had triumphed: she had left one final mystery. It would keep her audience guessing. This was her greatest riddle yet.

Epilogue: The Legacy

Valtesse's tombstone left her friends perplexed and her public enthralled. Who were E. Una and L.M. Auriac? A triumphant society gossip claimed to have the answer.

'A woman has recently died in Ville-d'Avray, whose name used to be well known,' began an anonymous article in *Paris-Journal*, just a few days after her funeral.[1]

E. Una and L.M. Auriac were two of Valtesse's lovers who had killed each other fighting over her, the author insisted. Valtesse was so moved that she arranged for them to be buried with her in her tomb. 'Between them, she will sleep her last sleep, having spent twenty years [*sic*] forgotten in her splendid villa with its immense park and which one of her admirers gave her,' gushed the writer.

Within days, Jules Claretie reprimanded the author for his romanticised, yet erroneous account: 'How much truth is there in this legend? Absolutely none, as in most legends.'[2] E. Una and L.M. Auriac, Claretie insisted, were merely men to whom Valtesse had extended the hand of friendship. One had no family, the other passed away in a monastery. She was goodness itself.

But the public were not convinced. A little research shed more light on the riddle.

Commander Louis Marius Auriac was an esteemed figure in the military and an excellent musician besides. Knight of the Legion of Honour, Auriac served as leader of a division of the French cavalry and spent the final part of his career in Tonkin. When he died in 1903 at the age of 48, he was buried in a plot held in perpetuity.[3] The full cost of the 1,050-franc plot was met by Valtesse. Was Auriac the concupiscent lover in the train to Ville-d'Avray, people wondered; the man whose name the journalist from *Gil Blas* had hinted at back in 1900 after Valtesse was overheard canoodling in public? And was he more than just a lover? One woman certainly thought so. A Mme P. confided to *Au Pays Virois* that she had been at boarding school with Pâquerette and that Auriac had been a regular visitor.[4] It was widely suspected at the school that the commander was Pâquerette's biological father. However, Auriac was only twelve years older than Pâquerette, and few readers subscribed to the notion of Valtesse falling pregnant to a child. The story was soon forgotten, but Valtesse's particular attachment to the commander was never uncovered.

Yet more perplexing was E. Una. This man was not yet dead when Valtesse was laid to rest. Some swore that he was originally from the Far East, others maintained that he was Austrian.[5] Either way, his corpse joined Valtesse in the tomb just a few years later, with no further explanation as to his identity or their relationship.

No one could solve the puzzle of Valtesse's mysterious funereal bedfellows.

Meanwhile, behind the closed doors of Paris's fashionable salons, another wave of gossip was gathering momentum. It centred on Valtesse's connections with prominent men. Gaggles of women chattered in shrill voices, while in corners, well-dressed men leaned in close and muttered shiftily. Valtesse's involvement in the Dreyfus affair was verbally dissected, her relationship with Gambetta re-examined. Her catalogue of artist lovers was now said to have included the eminent – and much older – painters Gustave Courbet and Eugène Boudin. Meanwhile, her supposed affairs with Napoleon III and Edward VII became the subject of passionate debate. Some people claimed that she was the last of Napoleon's mistresses; others held that her friendship with Detaille, an intimate acquaintance of the Prince of Wales, was irrefutable proof that she had entertained the future King of England.[6]

But the true nature of Valtesse's relationship with all these men would never be firmly clarified. She had built her career on teasing public curiosity, always hinting at the path she had walked while making certain that she covered her tracks. The lasting speculation ensured that Valtesse was talked about and remembered – exactly as she had wished.

In the weeks following her death, another question burned on many lips: what of Valtesse's last will and testament? Detaille feared that her sudden decline might have prevented her from making one. He was mistaken. Valtesse had given it considerable thought.

The 40-page document had long been in the trusted hands of her *notaires*, Girardin and Ch. Champetier de Ribes, in Paris.[7] Soon, the suspense was broken as the document's contents were revealed.

Nobody Valtesse judged important was forgotten. Her friends and staff were generously accounted for and their loyalty rewarded. Besides monetary gifts, there was a house full of costly furniture and objets d'art to share. Nothing could alleviate Liane's grief, but an exquisite tea service and Valtesse's cherished desk brought some comfort and made her feel closer to her late mentor.[8]

A sale was organised at the Hôtel Drouot in December to disperse what remained of the house contents. The auction room was transformed into a shimmering treasure trove. There were extraordinary wonders and collectors' items to be fought for and won, and their association with a great, now deceased courtesan made every lot even more covetable. Highlights included the autograph of Napoleon Bonaparte, Chinese and Japanese bronzes, countless works by Detaille, porcelain, jewels, sculptures (notably a copy of a work by Canova, the sculptor so favoured by Empress Josephine), Valtesse's two cars, and a magnificent array of antique furniture and fine objets d'art. Like the 1902 auction, the four-day sale drew swarms of people, and by the final day the auctioneers had taken 94,000 francs (over £1 million in modern currency).[9]

The following February, an announcement of a forthcoming property auction appeared in Paris's leading papers:

> Succession of Mme Valtesse de la Bigne, 'La Chapelle-du-Roy' in Ville-d'Avray, with two large paintings by Ed. Detaille, ceiling by Galland, approximately 16,638m (park with beautiful trees).[10]

The material remnants of Valtesse's life were gradually being disbanded.

English administrative sources reported Valtesse's remaining personal effects to be worth in the region of £11,600 (over £1 million in today's money).[11] To most, such wealth was inconceivable. The money must go somewhere. But if Valtesse was unmarried, people wondered, who was her next of kin? Who were the descendants through whom she would continue to live? What was her human legacy?

Some people remembered Pâquerette. If the mother and daughter had seen little of each other in later years, Valtesse had nevertheless maintained a healthy communication with Pâquerette. With just a little research, the curious Parisian would have discovered that by the time Valtesse died, the awkward teenager who had been fought over so publicly had become a woman and a wife. But that was not all: there was another family secret, one which Valtesse had been sure to keep quiet. When *Le Figaro* confirmed that the lion's share of Valtesse's fortune would be passed to Pâquerette, the paper had an additional scoop to surprise its readers: Paris's most aloof and beautiful late courtesan was not only a mother – she was a grandmother.[12]

Paul, Margot and Andrée were the fruit of Pâquerette's 20-year marriage to Paul Jules Auguste Godard. The girls in particular proved strength of character and the ability to charm to be enduring family traits.

While the children only met their grandmother a few times, relations were amicable enough for Margot to become Liane de Pougy's goddaughter. 'What a lovely girl,' Liane enthused when Margot visited her some years after Valtesse's death, 'fresh, stylish, dazzling rosy complexion, the look of an archangel at the gates of heaven! Her skirt was very short, and revealed her right leg, imperious and agile.'[13] Liane adored her goddaughter – until Margot grossly betrayed her. When Pâquerette died within a few years of her mother, Margot came across a bundle of Liane's most personal letters to Valtesse – and sold them. 'She put them in an auction!' Liane exclaimed, 'My twenty-four letters fetched sixty francs. Indecent treachery! Nothing on earth would surprise me now.'[14]

But Margot's pluck was far surpassed by that of her sister, Andrée. Born in 1903 while Valtesse was busily setting up home at La Chapelle-du-Roy, as a child Andrée fell passionately in love with the theatre. Having inherited her grandmother's hunger for public recognition, Andrée became entranced by the cinema and all things American. She thought of herself as a star. Even Liane was impressed at the entrance the youngster made when she arrived at her house for tea one summer day in 1920. 'Last but not least we opened the gates to a ravishing grey motorcar from which Andrée de la Bigne emerged, all golden in a dress of blue Japanese silk – really stunning, that girl – and loaded with chocolate caramels.'[15]

In the early 1920s, Andrée set out for America, and her dream of stardom began to take tangible form. Assuming a stage name that flaunted her French heritage, Andrée Lafayette arrived in New York fixed on becoming a star of the big screen, and in 1923 her determination was rewarded when she won her first major role in the film version of George du Maurier's *Trilby*. The spectacular professional break also triggered a personal one, since the film caused Andrée's path to cross that of American actor Max Constant, who would become her husband.

In the age of silent films there were no linguistic hurdles to overcome, and with her beauty and the exotic appeal of her French heritage, public and directors alike adored her. Hollywood stills show a beautiful blonde with hypnotic, sultry eyes who shared the even features and smooth, porcelain-white complexion which secured Valtesse's fortune. 'A delight,' commended one American reviewer, 'a girl of a type unusual to the American theatregoer, she adds to the charm of a vivid personality a particular talent.'[16] Andrée soon discovered that parading her ancestry, and even on occasion selling information to the papers, worked to her advantage. Another critique in America described her as 'a dazzling blonde with hair of finely spun gold, and limpid blue eyes, characteristics of her Normandy ancestry. She comes by her beauty naturally enough, for her grandmother was the beautiful and noble Valtesse de la Bigne, whose portrait now hangs in the Luxembourg museum.'[17] Du Maurier was said to have admired Valtesse, so it was 'fitting that her granddaughter should play the title role in the picturization'.[18]

Trilby launched a 30-year film career which saw Andrée travelling the world and taking roles in films including *The Three Musketeers* (1932) and, even more aptly, *The Lady of the Camellias* (1934).[19] For a time, Andrée and Constant were the ultimate Hollywood couple. Wherever they went, they were photographed, while their relationship – and rows – were closely monitored by the press. When Constant called for a divorce, it instantly became public knowledge.[20] Still, Andrée persevered in her career. She effortlessly made the perilous transition from silent to audible films, her French accent and Parisian mystique merely expanding her fan base. But if she boasted Valtesse's pretty face and allure, Andrée had also acquired her grandmother's fierce self-preservation instinct. She rejected any contract she deemed unreasonably demanding. As a result, her film appearances were not numerous, and during the 1940s she disappeared from cinema screens entirely.

But by the time the Second World War broke out, the de la Bigne name was back in the public domain, and once again connected with royalty. A rich widow and former actress, the self-styled Comtesse Andrée de la Bigne, had taken up residence aboard the 176-ton yacht *Davida* on the Riviera and begun a very public affair with one of the most prominent men in Europe: the Greek Prince Andrea, father of Prince Philip of Greece and Denmark, later the Duke of Edinburgh.[21] Some held that the bewitching beauty denounced in the royal household as 'an adventuress feathering her own nest' was the very same Andrée Lafayette attempting to start anew; others insisted that this Andrée was actually Margot's daughter (Valtesse's great-granddaughter).[22] If she remained elusive about the precise nature of her relationship to Valtesse, Comtesse Andrée de la Bigne openly flaunted her gallant heritage.

She was nothing if not committed: Andrée was with Andrea when he died of heart failure in Monte Carlo's Hôtel Métropole in 1944. Hence it was Andrée that Prince Philip and his private secretary, Michael Parker, went to meet in the Café de Paris in Monte Carlo to collect the late Andrea's possessions. The royal mistress strode into the café with all the confidence of a film star. The men found her to be elegant, beguiling and disarmingly self-assured.[23] But as the full extent of Andrea's debts were revealed, it became clear that, along with her grace and charm, the current Comtesse de la Bigne had also inherited Valtesse's magnetic command of a male admirer's assets.

❧

Valtesse had always known that she could not control her family, merely do her utmost to conceal their connection to her. But there was one last thing she could control, even after her death: her paintings and her objets d'art. It was in the arts that she had made her reputation, and it was through the arts that it could best endure.

Valtesse had been fluent in the intricate language of the art world. She knew all the leading museums and galleries. She understood how they worked, which were the most eminent, the subtle distinctions in nuance that each would inflect on a donor's reputation. Crucially, she recognised the power the art world exerted. She had tasted it, and she was not prepared to give it up.

To the Louvre, Valtesse bequeathed two fans painted by Detaille. The Musée de Versailles received the artist's painting *The Tsarevitch Reviewing the Troops*, while the Musée de Cluny was offered a costly Indian gold bracelet.[24] To all the donations, Valtesse attached two conditions: each museum should display the pieces fittingly and, more importantly, they must ensure that Valtesse's name be indicated on a plaque next to each exhibit. She decided that the Musée de Luxembourg would be the choicest venue for Gervex's 1879 portrait of her, on the understanding that the museum display a notice next to the work with the wording: 'Portrait of Mme Valtesse de la Bigne, displayed in the exhibition of portraits of the century, donated by herself.' The Mairie in Ville-d'Avray was offered four portraits, and the church, a decorative panel.[25] Her bed was bequeathed to the Musée des arts décoratifs where it could be seen and admired – though no doubt the donor's primary motivation was to justify having purchased such a luxury, reasoned one journalist generously.[26] Meanwhile, Valtesse's other paintings and portraits were distributed to galleries across the world. Her conquest was now complete.

But there were also the two paintings of her fictitious relatives, the pair of portraits that the journalist saw when he visited the museum in Caen in May 1933. The two pieces were donated along with a portrait by Pezzela of Valtesse's friend Gabrielle Dupuy (who had been with her when she died), and a plaster medallion by Deloye, with similar stipulations concerning their exhibition. There they hung on the museum walls until 1944. Then, when the museum was bombed during the Second World War, the paintings of the de la Bigne ancestors were reported missing, presumed destroyed.

However, as they passed the heap of devastation left in the aftermath, several locals swore that they had seen stooped figures sifting frantically through the rubble. Somewhere in Europe, those paintings may sit tucked away, gathering dust. Perhaps one day those last traces of Valtesse will be found.

Acknowledgements

My first chance encounter with Valtesse occurred one spring afternoon in the peaceful sanctuary of a university library. I was researching Henri Gervex's painting *The Civil Marriage* (1880–81) in the final stages of my PhD. As I scanned the painting, my eyes met those of a single figure looking back at me. I was startled. In a crowd of celebrities and royalty, in a still male-orientated society, this woman appeared confident and self-assured. I became fascinated by the figure before me. Little did I know that at that moment, a journey had begun. *The Mistress of Paris* is the culmination of that journey, and it would not have been possible without the assistance of some remarkable individuals and organisations.

First and foremost, I am grateful to the Biographers' Club for awarding the proposal for *The Mistress of Paris* the runner-up prize in the 2012 Tony Lothian Competition for best proposal by an uncommissioned, first-time biographer. The society has continued to provide support since the book was commissioned, for which I am deeply appreciative. I am also indebted to The Society of Authors' Authors' Foundation for the grant which assisted me in the final stages of writing this book.

Sincere thanks are due to Duncan Heath, Kate Hewson, Andrew Furlow, Robert Sharman and the publishing team at Icon Books. I am profoundly grateful to my agent, Andrew Lownie, for his unwavering commitment, dedication and hard work.

This book would not have been the same without the assiduity of Anna Swan and Sarah Sears. Thanks are also due to Kate Williams for the support and advice throughout this project, and to Gillian Tindall for her encouragement in the early stages of my non-fiction writing.

Valtesse's story has taken me on a voyage of discovery across France. I have followed her down passages and side streets in Paris's 10th arrondissement; she has led me to forgotten archives in Normandy and guided me to a fairytale palace in Ville-d'Avray. Along the way, we have stopped off at museums and galleries, libraries and theatres, where I have encountered many knowledgeable individuals. All these people have come together to help me tell Valtesse's tale.

I am indebted to Christophe Marcheteau de Quinçay at the Musée des Beaux-Arts de Caen for sacrificing a sunny afternoon to go through archives with me, and to his staff for their assistance in my research on Detaille and Valtesse's donation to the museum. I am grateful to Jean-Marie Levesque at the Musée de Normandie for his detailed knowledge on the migration of peasants to Paris in the 19th century. Jean-Christophe Pralong-Gourvennec's insights into Gervex's personal life and his relationship with Valtesse have been invaluable. Information supplied by the Musée Carnavelet documentation centre and the wisdom of Gérard Leyris informed my understanding of Valtesse's childhood and the squalid living conditions in the 10th arrondissement. The Musée de l'Armée were helpful in assisting me in my research of Detaille's paintings, while thanks are also due to the Musée d'Orsay, the préfecture de police, and the Mairie of the 19th arrondissement in Paris for permitting me to view the *The Civil Marriage* while a wedding was under way. Immeasurable thanks are due to Damien and Florence Bachelot for their hospitality on an unforgettable Sunday in Ville-d'Avray, and for their assistance in my research of Valtesse's property. I am also indebted to Sophie Huet at the Service Communication et Culture at the Mairie de Ville-d'Avray for her help with my research. Dominique Cécile Claudius-Petit has been a fount of knowledge on the history of Ville-d'Avray. I am grateful to Audrey Gay-Mazuel and the staff at the Musée des Arts décoratifs in Paris for allowing me access to the archives on Valtesse's bed. I am equally indebted to the Mairie de Monaco and the Palais Princier de Monaco for their assistance with my research of Valtesse's time in Monte Carlo.

Finally, my deepest thanks go to those who equipped me with the tools needed to undertake this journey. I am fortunate to have benefited from the wisdom and guidance of the late Professor John House at the Courtauld Institute of Art, to whom I owe my introduction to Gervex. Professor Colin Davis at Royal Holloway, University of London has also been a consistent source of support and knowledge.

I am ever thankful to my grandparents, John and Muriel Maskell, Jenifer Wayne and the inspirational C.H. Rolph, whose absence is keenly felt, but whose wisdom happily lives on.

Last but not least, I should like to thank my family, John, Elaine and Sam Hewitt: the greatest support team, the most tireless of proofreaders and the best of friends.

Picture acknowledgements

Selected bibliography

Alis, Harry, *Reine Soleil, une fille de la glèbe* (Paris, 1884)

Allnutt, Sidney, *Corot* (London: T.C. & E.C. Jack, 1911)

L'Ami du lettré: année littéraire et artistique, ed. by L'Association des courrieristes littéraires des journaux quotidiens (Paris: Bernard Grasset, 1927)

Anon, *What's What in Paris* (London, 1867)

Anon, *Les Courtisanes du Second Empire: Marguerite Bellanger*, 10th edn (Brussels: Office de Publicité, 1871)

Antonini, Paul, *L'Annam, Le Tonkin et l'intervention de la France en Extrême Orient* (Paris, 1889)

Ariès, Philippe, and George Duby, eds, *A History of Private Life*, trans. by Arthur Goldhammer, 5 vols (Cambridge, MA and London: Belknap Press of Harvard University Press, 1987–1991)

Mrs Armstrong, *Good Form: A Book of Every Day Etiquette* (London, 1895)

Auriant, *Les Lionnes du Second Empire* (Paris: Gallimard, 1935)

—— *La Véritable histoire de Nana* (Brussels: Mercure de France, 1942)

Barielle, Jean-François, and others, *Champs-Elysées, Faubourg St Honoré, Plaine Monceau* (Paris: Henri Veyrier, 1982)

Barrès, Maurice, *Le Quartier Latin; ces messieurs, ces dames* (Paris, 1888)

Comtesse de Bassanville, *Code du cérémonial. Guide des gens du monde dans toutes les circonstances de la vie* (Paris, 1867)

Bazire, Edmond, *Manet* (Paris, 1884)

Beaumont-Maillet, Laure, *Vie et histoire du Xe arrondissement* (Paris: Éditions Hervas, 1991)

Bédoyère, Charles Angélique François Huchet la, *Memoirs of the Public and Private Life of Napoleon Bonaparte*, 2 vols (London: G. Virtue, 1827), vol. 2.

Bergerat, Émile, *Les Chroniques de l'homme masqué* (Paris: C. Marpon et E. Flammarion, 1882)

Bernheimer, Charles, *Figures of Ill Repute: Representing Prostitution in Nineteenth-Century France* (Cambridge, MA and London: Harvard University Press, 1989)

Bertaut, Jules, *Paris 1870–1935*, trans. by R. Millar, ed. by John Bell (London: Eyre and Spottiswoode, 1936)

Besançon, Dr Julien, *Le Visage de la femme* (Paris: Éditions Terres Latines, 1940)

Bigne, Yolaine de la, *Valtesse de la Bigne ou Le pouvoir de la volupté* (Paris: Perrin, 1999)

Blanchard, Claude, *Dames de coeur* (Paris: Éditions du Pré aux Clercs, 1946)

Blavet, Émile, *La Vie parisienne – la ville et le théâtre* (Paris, 1884)

Booth, Michael R., 'Nineteenth-Century Theatre', in *The Oxford Illustrated History of Theatre*, ed. by John Russell Brown (Oxford and New York: Oxford University Press, 1997), pp. 299–340.

Bouvier, Jeanne, 'My Memoirs', in *The French Worker: Autobiographies from the Early Industrial Era*, ed. and trans. by Mark Traugott (Berkeley: University of California Press, 1993), pp. 336–380.

Briais, Bernard, *Au Temps des frou-frous – Les Femmes célèbres de la Belle Époque* (Paris: Éditions France-Empire, 1985)

Brilliant, Richard, *Portraiture* (London: Reaktion Books Ltd., 1991)

Brown, Frederick, *Zola: A Life* (London: Papermac, 1997)

Bury, J.P.T., *Gambetta and the Making of the Third Republic* (London: Longman Group Limited, 1973)

C., E., *Le Livre* (Paris, 1884), p. 756.

Caccia, Joseph, *Nouveau guide général du voyageur en Italie* (Paris, 1875)

Camp, Maxime du, *Paris: ses organes, ses fonctions et sa vie dans la seconde moitié du XIXième siècle*, 6 vols (Paris, 1869–75), vol. 3.

Camp Davis, Bradley, 'States of Banditry: The Nguyen Government, Bandit Rule and the Culture of Power in the Post-Taiping China-Vietnam Borderlands' (doctoral thesis, University of Washington, 2008)

Casselaer, Catherine van, *Lot's Wife: Lesbian Paris 1890–1914* (Liverpool: The Janus Press, 1986)

Catalogue de tableaux modernes, pastels, aquarelles, dessins etc de Mme Valtesse de la Bigne (Paris: Imprimerie de la Gazette des Beaux-Arts, June 1902)

Chaix, N., ed., *Nouveau guide en Italie – Guide-Chaix* (Paris, 1864)

Chalon, Jean, *Liane de Pougy: courtisane, princesse et sainte* (Paris: Flammarion, 1994)

Champsaur, Félicien, *Les Parisiennes* (Paris, 1877)

—— *Paris, le massacre* (Paris, 1885)

Charleston, Robert J., ed., *World Ceramics: An illustrated history from earliest times* (New York: Crescent Books, 1990)

Chevalier, Julien, *Inversion sexuelle* (Paris, 1893)

Claretie, Jules, *L'Art et les artistes français contemporains* (Paris, 1876)

—— *La Vie à Paris* (Paris: Charpentier, 1911)

Clark, T.J., *The Painting of Modern Life: Paris in the Art of Manet and His Contemporaries* (New York: Knopf, 1984 and London: Thames and Hudson, 1985)

Claudius-Petit, Dominique Cécile, *Ville-d'Avray: mémoire en images* (Saint-Avertin: Éditions Sutton, 2013)

—— 'Histoire de la maison Rostand' (unpublished article, 2014)

Clayson, Hollis, *Paris in Despair: Art and Everyday Life under Siege (1870–71)* (Chicago and London: University of Chicago Press, 2002)

—— *Painted Love: Prostitution in French Art of the Impressionist Era* (Los Angeles, California: The Getty Research Institute, 2003)

Clément, Félix and Pierre Larousse, *Dictionnaire des opéras* (Paris, 1881)

Clifford Barney, Natalie, *Souvenirs indiscrets* (Paris: Flammarion, 1960)

Coffignon, A., *Paris vivant: La Corruption à Paris* (Paris: Kolb, 1889)

Cole, Charles Augustus, *The Imperial Paris Guide* (London, 1867)

Conty, H.A. de, *Paris en poche – Guide pratique Conty*, 6th edn (Paris, 1875)

Cope, Susan, and others, eds, *Larousse Gastronomique* (London: Mandarin, 1990)

Cope Devereux, W., *Fair Italy: The Riviera and Monte Carlo* (London, 1884)

Corbin, Alain, 'The Secret of the Individual' in *A History of Private Life*, ed. by Philippe Ariès and George Duby, trans. by Arthur Goldhammer, 5 vols (Cambridge, MA and London: Belknap Press of Harvard University Press, 1987–1991), vol. 4: *From the Fires of Revolution to the Great War*, ed. by Michelle Perrot (1990), pp. 457–547.

—— *Women for Hire: Prostitution and Sexuality in France after 1850*, trans. by Alan Sheridan (Cambridge, MA and London: Harvard University Press, 1990)

Cosse, Victor, 'Gambetta', in *Plutarque populaire contemporain illustré* (Paris, 1870), pp. 48–54.

Comtesse Dash, *Comment on fait son chemin dans le monde, code du savoir-vivre* (Paris, 1868)

Decaux, Alain, *L'Empire, l'amour et l'argent* (Paris: Librairie Académique Perrin, 1982)

Delvau, Alfred, *Les Cynthères parisiennes* (Paris, 1864)

Désert, Gabriel, *Les Paysans du Calvados 1815–1895: Une société rurale au XIXe siècle* (Caen: Centre de recherche d'histoire quantitative de Caen, 2007)

Dumas, Alexandre, *Filles, lorettes et courtisanes* (Paris, 1874)

Eade, Philip, *Young Prince Philip: His Turbulent Early Life* (London: Harper Press, 2012)

Ego, *Isola* (Paris: Dentu, 1876)

England and Wales, National Probate Calendar (Index of Wills and Administrations), 1858–1966 for Louise Emilie Valtesse de la Bigne

Esquiros, Alphonse, *Les Vierges folles* (Paris, 1840)

Faderman, Lillian, *Surpassing the Love of Men: Romantic Friendship and Love between Women from the Renaissance to the Present* (London: The Women's Press Ltd, 1997)

Fare, A. la (ed.), *Annuaire des châteaux 1900–1901* (Paris, 1901)

Faris, Alexander, *Jacques Offenbach* (London: Faber and Faber Ltd., 1980)

Flaubert, Gustave, *Madame Bovary*, trans. by Geoffrey Wall (London: Penguin Books, 1992)

Foley, Susan K. and Charles Sowerwine, *A Political Romance; Léon Gambetta, Léonie Léon and the Making of the French Republic, 1872–1882* (London: Palgrave MacMillan, 2012)

Fouquières, André de, *Mon Paris et ses parisiens*, 5 vols (Paris: Éditions Pierre Horay, 1953–1955)

Frascina, Francis, and others, *Modernity and Modernism: French Painting in the Nineteenth Century* (New Haven and London: Yale University Press, 1993)

Fuchs, Rachel, *Abandoned Children: Foundlings and Child Welfare in 19th-Century France* (Albany: State University of New York Press, 1984)

Gammond, Peter, *Offenbach: His Life and Times* (Kent: Midas Books, 1980)

Garb, Tamar, 'Gender and Representation' in Francis Frascina and others, *Modernity and Modernism: French Painting in the Nineteenth Century* (New Haven and London: Yale University Press, 1993), pp. 219–89.

—— *Sisters of the Brush: Women and Artistic Culture in Late 19th-Century Paris* (New Haven and London: Yale University Press, 1994)

Gasquet, Martine, *Impératrices, artistes et cocottes: Les femmes sur la Riviera à la Belle Époque* (Nice: Gilletta nice-matin, 2013)

Gildea, Robert, *Children of the Revolution: The French 1799–1914* (London: Allen Lane, 2008)

Goncourt, Edmond de, *Paris under Siege, 1870–1871: From the Goncourt Journal*, ed. and trans. by George J. Becker (Ithaca and London: Cornell University Press, 1969)

Grafe, Etienne, *Portraitistes Lyonnais 1800–1914* (Lyon: Musée des Beaux-Arts, 1986)

Griffin, Susan, *The Book of the Courtesans* (London: Pan Macmillan, 2003)

Groom, Gloria, and others, *L'Impressionisme et la mode*, exhib. cat. Musée d'Orsay (Paris: Skira/Flammarion, 2013)

Guerrand, Roger-Henri, 'Private Spaces' in *A History of Private Life*, ed. by Philippe Ariès and George Duby, trans. by Arthur Goldhammer, 5 vols (Cambridge, MA and London: Belknap Press of Harvard University Press, 1987–1991), vol. 4: *From the Fires of Revolution to the Great War*, ed. by Michelle Perrot (1990), pp. 359–449.

Guide des plaisirs à Paris (Paris: Éditions photographiques, 1899)

Guides Joanne – Nice, Monaco (Paris, 1887)

Halévy, Ludovic, *La Famille Cardinal* (Paris: Calmann-Lévy, 1946)

Harding, James, *Jacques Offenbach: A Biography* (London: John Calder & New York: Riverrun Press, 1980)

Havard, Oscar, *Guide de Rome, Turin, Milan, Venise, Padoue, Florence, Assise, Ancône, Lorette, Naples, etc.* (Paris, 1877)

Hayhurst, J.D., *The Pigeon Post into Paris 1870–1871* (1970)

Henri Gervex 1852–1929, exhib. cat. (Paris: Paris-Musées, 1992)

Herbert, Robert L., *Impressionism: Art, Leisure, and Parisian Society* (New Haven and London: Yale University Press, 1988)

Higonnet, Anne, *Berthe Morisot* (California: University of California Press, 1995)

Hillairet, Jacques, *Dictionnaire historique des rues de Paris*, 2 vols (Paris: Les Éditions de minuit, 1957–1961), vol. 2

Horne, Alistair, *Seven Ages of Paris* (London: Pan Macmillan, 2003)

Houbre, Gabrielle, *Le Livre des courtisanes: archives secrètes de la police des moeurs, 1861–1876* (Paris: Tallandier, 2006)

House, John, *Impressionism: Paint and Politics* (New Haven and London: Yale University Press, 2004)

—— *Impressionists by the Sea*, exhib. cat. (London: Royal Academy of Arts, 2007)

Humbert, Jean-Marcel, *Édouard Detaille: L'héroisme d'un siècle* (Paris: Éditions Copernic, 1979)

Hunt, Lynn, 'The Unstable Boundaries of the French Revolution' in *A History of Private Life*, ed. by Philippe Ariès and George Duby, trans. by Arthur Goldhammer, 5 vols (Cambridge, MA and London: Belknap Press of Harvard University Press, 1987–1991), vol. 4: *From the Fires of Revolution to the Great War*, ed. by Michelle Perrot (1990), pp. 13–45.

Inventaire de Chaville, IA000 51459

Janet, Paul, *La Famille*, 17th edn (Paris, 1900)

Jill, Duchess of Hamilton, *Napoleon, the Empress & the Artist: the Story of Napoleon, Josephine's Garden at Malmaison, Redouté and the Australian Plants*, ed. by Anne Savage (East Roseville, NSW: Kangaroo Press, 1999)

Jones, Colin, *Cambridge Illustrated History of France* (Cambridge: Cambridge University Press, 1994)

Kavanagh, Julie, *The Girl Who Loved Camellias: The Life and Legend of Marie Duplessis* (New York: Alfred A. Knopf, 2013)

Kenyon, Olga, ed., *Women's Voices through two thousand years of letters* (London: Constable, 1997)

Kiefer, Carol Solomon, *The Empress Josephine: Art and Royal Identity* (Mead Art Museum: Amherst, Massachusetts, 2005)

King, Graham, *Garden of Zola: Émile Zola and His Novels for English Readers* (London: Barry and Jenkins Ltd, 1978)

Kinsman, Jane, 'Henri Gervex – Madame Valtesse de la Bigne' in Sylvie Patry and others, *Van Gogh, Gauguin, Cézanne & Beyond – Post-Impressionism from the Musée d'Orsay*, exhib. cat. (London: Prestel, 2011)

Koning, Victor, *Tout Paris* (Paris, 1872)

Kracauer, Siegfried, *Jacques Offenbach and the Paris of His Time*, trans. by Gwenda David and Eric Mosbacher (New York: Zone Books, 2002)

Lamber, Juliette, *Le Siége de Paris – journal d'une parisienne* (Paris, 1873)

Lasalle, Albert de, *Histoire des Bouffes-Parisiens* (Paris, 1860)

Latouche, Robert, *Histoire de Nice de 1860 à 1914*, 2 vols (Nice: Ville de Nice, 1954)

Lefebvre, Christiane, *Alfred Stevens – 1823–1906* (Paris: Brame & Lorenceau, 2006)

Lehmbeck, Leah Rosenblatt, 'Édouard Manet's Portraits of Women' (doctoral thesis, Institute of Fine Arts, New York, May 2007)

—— '"L'Esprit de l'atelier": Manet's Late Portraits of Women, 1878–1883' in Maryanne Stevens and others, *Manet: Portraying Life*, exhib. cat. (Toledo: Toledo Museum of Art; London: Royal Academy of Arts; New York: Distributed in the United States and Canada by Harry N. Abrams, Inc., 2012), pp. 50–57.

Lepelletier, Edmond, *Émile Zola: sa vie, son oeuvre* (Paris: Mercure de France, 1908)

Limouzin, Charles, *Almanach illustré de Monaco et de Monte-Carlo* (Nice, 1894)

Loliée, Frédéric, *La Fête impériale* (Paris: Tallandier, 1926)

Mainardi, Patricia, *Husbands, Wives, and Lovers: Marriage and Its Discontents in Nineteenth-Century France* (New Haven and London: Yale University Press, 2003)

Mardoche and Desgenais, *Les Parisiennes* (Paris, 1882)

Martin-Fugier, Anne, 'Bourgeois Rituals' in *A History of Private Life*, ed. by Philippe Ariès and George Duby, trans. by Arthur Goldhammer, 5 vols (Cambridge, MA and London: Belknap Press of Harvard University Press, 1987–1991), vol. 4: *From the Fires of Revolution to the Great War*, ed. by Michelle Perrot (1990), pp. 261–337.

Marx, Adrien, *Les Petits mémoires de Paris* (Paris, 1888)

Matlock, Jan, *Scenes of Seduction: Prostitution, Hysteria and Reading Difference in 19th-Century France* (New York: Columbia University Press, 1994)

Mazon, A., *Nice en 1861 – Guide de l'étranger* (Paris and Nice, 1861)

McMillan, James F., *France and Women, 1789–1914: Gender, Society and Politics* (London: Routledge, 2000)

McPherson, Heather, *The Modern Portrait in 19th-Century France* (Cambridge: Cambridge University Press, 2001)

Michel, Pierre and Jean-François Nivet, eds, *Octave Mirbeau – Correspondance générale*, 3 vols (Lausanne: Âge d'homme, 2002–2009), vol. 1 (2002)

Milne, Anna-Louise, ed., *The Cambridge Companion to the Literature of Paris* (Cambridge: Cambridge University Press, 2013)

Mitchell, Peter, *Jean Baptiste Antoine Guillemet, 1841–1918* (London: John Mitchell & Son, 1981)

Mogador, Céleste, *Memoirs of a Courtesan in 19th-Century Paris*, trans. by Monique Fleury Nagem (Lincoln and London: University of Nebraska Press, 2001)

Naugrette-Christophe, Catherine, *Paris sous le Second Empire: le théâtre et la ville* (Paris: Librairie théâtrale, 1998), annexe 4

Nouvel-Kammerer, Odile, 'La création de la chambre conjugale', in *Rêves d'Alcôves: la chambre au cours des siècles*, exhib. cat. (Paris: Musée des Arts décoratifs, 1995), pp. 104–127.

—— 'Le lit d'une lionne: Valtesse de la Bigne', in *Rêves d'Alcôves: la chambre au cours des siècles*, exhib. cat. (Paris: Musée des Arts décoratifs, 1995), pp. 211–13.

Olivier-Martin, Yves, *Histoire du roman populaire en France* (Paris: Albin Michel, 1980)

Parent-Duchâtelet, Alexandre, *De la Prostitution dans la ville de Paris, considérée sous le rapport de l'hygiène publique, de la morale et de l'administration*, 3rd edn (Paris, 1857)

Parisis (Émile Blavet), *La Vie parisienne, la ville et le théâtre* (Paris, 1887)

Patry, Sylvie, and others, *Van Gogh, Gauguin, Cézanne & Beyond – Post-Impressionism from the Musée d'Orsay*, exhib. cat. (London: Prestel, 2011)

Père, Henry de, *Paris Guide, par les principaux écrivains et artistes de la France* (Paris, 1867)

Perthes, Justus, ed., *Almanach de Gotha – Annuaire généalogique, diplomatique et statistique* (Paris, 1872)

Perrot, Michelle, 'The Curtain Rises – Introduction', in *A History of Private Life*, ed. by Philippe Ariès and George Duby, trans. by Arthur Goldhammer, 5 vols (Cambridge, MA and London: Belknap Press of Harvard University Press, 1987–1991), vol. 4: *From the Fires of Revolution to the Great War*, ed. by Michelle Perrot (1990), pp. 9–11.

Pougetoux, Alain, 'Josephine as Patron and Her Collection of Paintings' in Carol Solomon Kiefer, *The Empress Josephine: Art and Royal Identity* (Mead Art Museum: Amherst, Massachusetts, 2005), pp. 93–5.

Pougy, Liane de, *Idylle saphique* (Paris: Éditions des Femmes, 1987)

—— *My Blue Notebooks*, trans. by Diane Athill (New York: Tarcher Putnam, 2002)

Price, Roger, *A Social History of Nineteenth-Century France* (London: Hutchinson, 1987)

Privat d'Anglemont, Alexandre, *Paris inconnu* (Paris, 1861)

Recueil des dépêches télégraphiques reproduites par la photographie et adressées à Paris au moyen de pigeons-voyageurs pendant l'investissement de la capitale, 6 vols, vol. 1 (Bordeaux)

Reid, Joyce M.H., ed., *The Concise Oxford Dictionary of French Literature* (Oxford and New York: Oxford University Press, 1976)

Rêves d'Alcôves: la chambre au cours des siècles, exhib. cat. (Paris: Musée des Arts décoratifs, 1995)

Rewald, John, *The History of Impressionism*, 4th edn (New York: Museum of Modern Art and London: Secker & Warburg, 1973)

Richardson, Joanna, *La Vie Parisienne 1852–1870* (London: Hamish Hamilton Ltd., 1971)

—— *The Courtesans: The Demi-Monde in 19th-Century France* (London: Phoenix, 2000)

Robichon, François, *Édouard Detaille: un siècle de gloire militaire* (Paris: Bernard Giovanangeli, 2007)

Mme Romieu, Marie-Sincère, *La Femme au XIXe siècle* (Paris, 1858)

—— *Des Paysans et de l'agriculture en France au XIXe siècle* (Paris, 1865)

Ronzeville, Edmond, *Paris Xe* (Amiens: Martelle Editions, 1996)

Roqueplan, Nestor, 'Les Théâtres', in de Père, Henry, *Paris Guide* (Paris, 1867)

Rounding, Virginia, *Grandes Horizontales: The Lives and Legends of Four 19th-Century Courtesans* (London: Bloomsbury, 2003)

Sanchez, Jean-Pierre, 'Un mariage réaliste: Gervex et la critique du Salon de 1881', in *Henri Gervex 1852–1929* (Paris: Paris-Musées, 1992), pp. 152–61.

Simond & Poinsot, *La Vie galante aux Tuileries sous le Second Empire* (Paris: Albert Méricant, 1912)

Souhami, Diana, *Wild Girls – Paris, Sappho and Art: The Lives and Loves of Natalie Barney and Romaine Brooks* (London: Weidenfeld and Nicolson, 2004)

Sterling, Charles, and Margaretta Salinger, *French Paintings: A Catalogue of the Collection of the Metropolitan Museum of Art*, vol. 2: *Nineteenth and Twentieth Centuries* (New York: The Metropolitan Museum of Art, 1966); vol. 3: *Nineteenth and Twentieth Centuries* (New York: The Metropolitan Museum of Art, 1967)

Stevens, Maryanne, and others, *Manet: Portraying Life*, exhib. cat. (Toledo: Toledo Museum of Art; London: Royal Academy of Arts; New York: Distributed in the United States and Canada by Harry N. Abrams, Inc., 2012)

Sulzberger, Max, *Une Visite chez Alfred Stevens* (Brussels, 1876)

Tabarant, A., *Manet, histoire catalographique* (Paris: F. Aubier, 1931)

Taxil, Léo, *La Corruption fin-de-siècle* (Paris: Henri Noirot, 1891)

Tétart-Vittu, Françoise, 'Édouard Manet, *La Parisienne*' in Gloria Groom and others, *L'Impressionisme et la mode*, exhib. cat. (Paris: Skira-Flammarion, 2013), pp. 125–8.

Traugott, Mark, ed. and trans., *The French Worker: Autobiographies from the Early Industrial Era* (Berkeley: University Of California Press, 1993)

MM Tréfeu et Prével, *La Romance de la Rose – opéra bouffe, partition chant et piano* (Paris, 1870)

Vizetelly, Ernest Alfred, *With Zola in England: A Story of Exile* (Middlesex: The Echo Library, 2007)

Voilquin, Suzanne, 'Recollections of a Daughter of the People' in Traugott, Mark (ed. and trans.), *The French Worker: Autobiographies from the Early Industrial Era* (Berkeley: University of California Press, 1993), pp. 92–115.

Willemin, Véronique, *La Mondaine: Histoire et archives de la police des moeurs* (Paris: Hoëbeke, 2009)

Wolff, Albert, *La Haute-Noce* (Paris: Victor-Havard, 1885)

Zeldin, Theodore, *France 1848–1945: Taste and Corruption* (Oxford, New York, Toronto and Melbourne: Oxford University Press, 1980)

Zola, Émile, *L'Assommoir* (Paris: Fasquelle, 1977)

—— *Correspondence*, ed. by B.H. Bakker and Colette Becker, 10 vols (Montréal: Les Presses de l'Université de Montréal, Paris: Édition du centre national de la recherche scientifique, 1978–1995), vol. 3.

—— *Nana*, trans. Douglas Parmée (Oxford: Oxford University Press, 1992)

—— *Nana*, preface Henri Mitterand (Paris: Gallimard, 2002)

——*The Drinking Den*, trans. Robin Buss (London: Penguin Books, 2003)

ARTICLES

'Les Arts incohérents', *L'Europe Artiste*, 21 October 1883, p. 34.

'Chronique', *Le Droit populaire*, 26 November 1881, p. 402.

'Chronique de l'audience', *Gil Blas*, 16 November 1881, p. 3.

'Court and Fashion', *Belfast News-Letter*, 29 August 1862

'Court and Fashion – Foreign Courts', *Era*, 26 May 1867

'L'Enfant de Mme Valtesse', *Le Rappel*, 16 November 1881, pp. 2–3.

'Essais de psychologie politique', *La Nouvelle Revue*, 55 (November–December 1888), p. 295.

'Fatal Gas Explosions', *Oamaru Mail*, Volume IV, Issue 1322, 19 September 1882, p. 4.

'French Actress Quits Hubby and Goes Home', *Reading Eagle*, 26 November 1924, p. 1.

'France', *The Morning Post*, 1 October 1880

'Gazette des tribunaux', *Le Figaro*, 9 November 1881, p. 5.

'Gazette des tribunaux', *Le Figaro*, 15 November 1881, p. 2.

'The Italian Opera in Paris', *The Morning Post*, 13 June 1883, p. 5.

'M. Gambetta et Mlle Valtesse', *Le Gaulois*, 11 June 1883, p. 1.

'Nécrologie', *Gil Blas*, 21 December 1903, p. 2.

'Nécrologie', *Le Matin*, 21 December 1903, p. 5.

'Obituary', *Standard*, 22 March 1898, p. 5.

'Obsèques d'Offenbach', *Le Gaulois*, 8 October 1880, p. 2.

'Parisian Actresses', *Hampshire Telegraph and Sussex Chronicle etc.*, 17 November 1880

'Petits bruits', *Le Gaulois*, 12 November 1881, p. 1.

'Les Premières', *Le Figaro*, 5 March 1872, p. 1.

'Les Premières', *Le Figaro*, 11 April 1872, p. 1.

'The Queen's Visit to the Riviera', *The Morning Post*, 28 February 1895, p. 5.

'Sporting', *Belfast News-Letter*, 26 April 1860

Auriant, 'Quelques sources ignorées de "Nana"', *Mercure de France*, 252 (1934), pp. 180–8.

B., V. de la, 'Courrier d'Indo-Chine', *Le Figaro*, 22 September 1880, p. 4.

Bataille, Albert, *Le Figaro*, 2 August 1896, p. 4.

Blavet, Émile, 'La Princesse de Trébizonde', *Le Figaro*, 3 August 1869, p. 3.

Blum, Ernest, *Le Rappel*, 30 January 1870, p. 4.

Bory, A. de, 'Théâtre des bouffes-parisiens – soirée de réouverture', *La France musicale*, 4 October 1868, p. 311.

Boudan, Gaston, 'Madame Valtesse de la Bigne', *Au Pays Virois* (October–December 1933), pp. 164–70.

Chambourcy, 'Hommes et Choses – L'Union des Artistes', *Le Radical*, 13 June 1883, p. 1.

Chapelou, *Le Tintamarre*, 11 June 1876, p. 3.

Chincholle, C., 'Les Arts incohérents', *Le Figaro*, 10 October 1883, p. 2.

Dandeau, 'Un Collaborateur inattendu', *Le Gaulois*, 6 January 1883, p. 2.

Desprez, Adrian, 'Petites scènes', *Gazette littéraire, artistique et scientifique*, 32 (10 December 1864), p. 324.

Le Diable Boiteux, *Gil Blas*, 8 November 1884, p. 1.

Fénéon, Félix, 'Les Arts incohérents', *La Libre Revue*, November 1883

Froufrou, 'Les Premières', *Le Gaulois*, 9 December 1869, p. 1.

Houssaye, Arsène, 'Les Parisiennes d'Amour – Valtesse', *Panurge*, 22 October 1882

Jouve, André, *Le Courrier de Lyon*, 17 January 1844, cited in Grafe, Etienne, *Portraitistes Lyonnais 1800–1914* (Lyon: Musée des Beaux-Arts, 1986), p. 25.

Jouy, Jules, *Le Tintamarre*, 25 November 1877, p. 6.

Lafargue, Gustave, *Le Figaro*, 28 February 1870, p. 4.

Lasalle, Albert de, in *Le Monde illustré*, 10 February 1866, p. 95.

Lauwick, Béatrice, and Odile Nouvel Kammerer, 'Le Lit de Valtesse de La Bigne', *Histoire de l'art*, 32 (December 1995), pp. 71–7.

Lévêque, Jean-Jacques, 'Trois intérieurs du début de la IIIe République', *Gazette des Beaux-Arts*, (March 1976), pp. 92–4.

Loudun, Eugène, 'Le Salon de 1881', *La Revue du monde catholique*, 31 May 1881

Mareuil, 'L'Accident de Ville-d'Avray', *Le Gaulois*, 29 November 1882, p. 1.

Marx, Adrien, 'La Plaine Monceau', *Le Figaro*, 21 June 1880, p. 1.

Monin, Dr E.,'Propos du docteur – La responsibilité en matière criminelle', *Gil Blas*, 3 January 1888, p. 2.

Monin, Dr E., 'Propos du Docteur – Hygiène et éducation féminines', *Gil Blas*, 18 March 1890, p. 2.

Morand, Eugène, 'Nouvelles diverses', *Le Figaro*, 24 January 1870, p. 3.

Morgan, O.R., 'Zola et Valtesse de la Bigne', *Les Cahiers naturalistes*, 39 (1970), pp. 70–1.

O'Monroy, Richard, 'Celle qui disparaît', *Gil Blas*, 24 May 1902, p. 1.

Oswald, François 'Bruits de coulisses', *Le Gaulois*, 15 December 1869, p. 3.

Parisis, 'Bal Incohérent', *Le Figaro*, 13 March 1885, p. 1.

Un passant, *Le Rappel*, 9 December 1869, p. 1.

Picard, René, conclusion to Gaston Boudan, 'Madame Valtesse de la Bigne', *Au Pays Virois* (October–December 1933), p. 170.

Picard, René, and Gaston Boudan, 'Deux Tableaux d'Édouard Detaille au Musée de Caen et Valtesse de la Bigne', in *Au Pays Virois* (October–December 1933), pp. 161–3.

Polo, Roberto, 'Édouard Lièvre, un créateur des arts décoratifs au XIXe', *L'Estampille – L'Objet d'art*, 394 (September 2004), pp. 102–113.

E.R., 'Le Salon de 1879', *La Presse*, 27 May 1879, p. 2.

Richet, Etienne, 'La vie parisienne', *Revue nouvelle: Le Feu follet* (May 1900), p. 307.

Rigaud, M. l'abbé, 'La dépopulation des campagnes', *Annuaire des cinq départements de la Normandie*, 34 (1868)

Robaut, Alfred, 'L'Atelier de Corot', *L'Illustration*, 6 March 1875, p. 158.

Sussman, George, 'The Wet-Nursing Business in Nineteenth-Century France', *French Historical Studies*, 9 (1975), pp. 304–328.

V., L. de, 'Hôtel privé, boulevard Malesherbes à Paris, par M.J. Février, architecte', *Le Moniteur des architectes*, (1877), pp. 35–6.

Villemot, Émile, 'A qui la fille?', *Gil Blas*, 19 November 1881, p. 1.

Ward-Jackson, Philip, 'A sculptor-mayor and his family: Le mariage civil by Henri Gervex', *Sculpture Journal*, 14 (2005), pp. 41–50.

Wolff, Albert, *Le Figaro*, 20 March 1876, p. 1.

Maître X., *Le Gaulois*, 1 March 1882, p. 3.

Xau, Fernand, 'Valtesse de la Bigne', *Gil Blas*, 13 June 1883, p. 2.

Y., Z. and C., 'Au Jour le jour – Les Merveilleuses', *Le Gaulois*, 18 December 1873, p. 1.

Zola, Émile, *L'Événement*, 29 March 1866

Zola, Émile 'Gambetta', *Le Figaro*, 13 November 1880, p. 1.

Zola, Émile, 'Revue dramatique et littéraire', *Le Voltaire*, 28 October 1879, p. 1.

Newspapers and periodicals consulted

Aberdeen Weekly Journal

Au Pays Virois

Belfast News-Letter

Les Cahiers naturalistes

Chronique des arts et de la curiosité

Le Courrier de Cannes

Le Courrier de Lyon

Le Droit populaire

Dundee Courier & Argus

L'Estampille – L'Objet d'art

L'Europe Artiste

L'Événement

Le Figaro

La France musicale

French Historical Studies

Le Gaulois

Gazette des Beaux-Arts

Gil Blas

Hampshire Telegraph and Sussex Chronicle etc.

Histoire de l'art

L'Illustration

Le Journal de Nice

Lehigh Brown and White

Le Matin

Mercure de France

Le Monde Illustré

Le Moniteur des architectes

The Morning Post

Niagara Falls Gazette

L'Orchestre

Panurge

Paris–Plaisir
Le Petit Journal
La Presse
Le Rappel
Reading Eagle
La Revue du monde catholique
Revue nouvelle: Le Feu follet
Le Rire
Sculpture Journal
The Standard
Le Supplément
Le Temps
The Times
Le Tintamarre, Critique de la réclame, satire des puffistes
Le Voltaire

Websites consulted

http://www.ancestry.co.uk

All currency equivalents calculated according to http://www.measuringworth.com/ukcompare/relativevalue.php

http://www.gallica.fr

http://www.mediatheque.mc/home/patrimoniaux/fonds-regional.dot

http://www.cix.co.uk/~mhayhurst/jdhayhurst/pigeon/pigeon.html (accessed 4 April 2014)

http://www.osenat.fr/html/fiche.jsp?id=3408505&np=14&lng=fr&npp=20&ordre=1&aff=1&r (accessed 9 June 2014)

http://ecole.nav.traditions.free.fr/officiers_dekergaradec_alexandre.htm (accessed 10 October 2014)

http://www.brittanica.com/EBchecked/topic/224764/Leon-Gambetta (accessed 20 August 2014)

Orr, Lyndon, 'Famous Affinities of History – Léon Gambetta and Léonie Léon', pp. 1–9, http://www.authorama.com/famous-affinities-of-history-iii-3.html (accessed 29 August 2014)

Celine Colassin, '663 – Andrée Lafayette', http://cinevedette4.unblog.fr/663-andree-lafayette/ (accessed 18 February 2015)

Galleries, museums, libraries and archives

Les archives de la préfecture de police, Paris

Bibliothèque Nationale de France

The British Library

The Courtauld Institute of Art Book Library

Farnham Library, Surrey

Mairie du 19e arrondissement, Paris

Mairie de Monaco

Mairie de Ville-d'Avray

Musée des arts décoratifs

Musée des Beaux-Arts de Bordeaux

Musée des Beaux-Arts de Caen

Musée Carnavalet

Musée de Normandie

Musée d'Orsay

Palais Princier de Monaco

Royal Holloway, University of London Library

Senate House Library

University for the Creative Arts Library, Farnham

The Witt Library

Notes

PROLOGUE

1. The following is drawn from an article in the journal *Au Pays Virois* in 1933. René Picard, 'Deux Tableaux d'Édouard Detaille au Musée de Caen et Valtesse de la Bigne', *Au Pays Virois* (October–December 1933), 161–3. I am indebted to Christophe Marcheteau de Quinçay and the staff at the Musée des Beaux-Arts de Caen for their kind assistance with my research on Detaille and Valtesse's donation to the museum.

CHAPTER 1

1. I am indebted to Jean-Marie Levesque at the Musée de Normandie for his detailed knowledge of the migration of peasants to Paris in the 19th century.

2. Roads in Normandy were notoriously poor, and even after governmental investment in roads during the 1830s they remained wanting. Robert Gildea, *Children of the Revolution: The French 1799–1914* (London: Allen Lane, 2008), pp. 75–6.

3. Roger Price, *A Social History of Nineteenth-Century France* (London: Hutchinson, 1987), p. 87.

4. Mme Romieu (Marie-Sincère), *Des Paysans et de l'agriculture en France au XIXe siècle* (Paris, 1865), p. 440.

5. Abbé Rigaud, 'La Dépopulation des campagnes', *Annuaire des cinq départements de la Normandie*, 34 (1868), 41–8 (p. 44).

6. The trousseau consisted of clothing, linen and jewellery that the bride-to-be would accumulate in preparation for her change of status. A family's wealth and social standing could be gauged by the content of the trousseau.

7. Words used to describe Emilie's family in 'Chronique de l'audience', *Gil Blas*, 16 November 1881, p. 3.

8. The number of schools in the Calvados department increased under the Restoration, and Emilie's literacy could have been the result of this. Price, p. 337.

9. Price, p. 334.

10. Alistair Horne, *Seven Ages of Paris* (London: Pan Macmillan, 2003), p. 243.

11. Gabriel Désert, *Les Paysans du Calvados 1815–1895: Une société rurale au XIXe siècle* (Caen: Centre de Recherche d'Histoire Quantitative de Caen, 2007), p. 73.

12. Information supplied by the Musée de Normandie.

13. When Emilie later appeared in court in 1881, her partner's name was given only as 'T'. 'L'Enfant de Mme Valtesse', *Le Rappel*, 16 November 1881, pp. 2–3.

14. Rachel Fuchs, *Abandoned Children: Foundlings and Child Welfare in 19th-Century France* (Albany: State University of New York Press, 1984), p. 92.

15. Colin Jones, *Cambridge Illustrated History of France* (Cambridge: Cambridge University Press, 1994), pp. 210–11.

16. Fuchs, p. 88.

17. Now known as the Rue de Paradis. Edmond Ronzeville, *Paris Xe* (Amiens: Martelle Editions, 1996); Laure Beaumont-Maillet, *Vie et histoire du Xe arrondissement* (Paris: Éditions Hervas, 1991).

18. Information supplied by the Musée Carnavelet documentation centre. I am indebted to Gérard Leyris for his assistance in my research.

19. Gildea, p. 156.

20. Gildea, pp. 80–1.

21. Fuchs, p. 88. The sou was a unit of currency created at the time of the Revolution. It was equal to 5 centimes, or approximately a halfpenny in English currency. See Émile Zola, *The Drinking Den*, trans. by Robin Buss (London: Penguin Books, 2003), p. 433, n. 5.

22. Gildea, p. 156.

23. Félicien Champsaur, *Paris, le massacre* (Paris, 1885), p. 268.

24. Jules Claretie, *La Vie à Paris* (Paris, 1911), p. 234.

25. Alfred Robaut vividly described Corot's studio in 1875. Alfred Robaut, 'L'Atelier de Corot', *L'Illustration*, 6 March 1875, p. 158.

26. Sidney Allnutt, *Corot* (London: T.C. & E.C. Jack, 1911), p. 38.

CHAPTER 2

1. Roger Price, *A Social History of Nineteenth-Century France* (London: Hutchinson, 1987), p. 342.

2. Jeanne Bouvier, 'My Memoirs', in *The French Worker: Autobiographies from the Early Industrial Era*, ed. and trans. by Mark Traugott (Berkeley: University of California Press, 1993), pp. 336–80 (p. 348).

3. Price, p. 158.

4. Cited in Joanna Richardson, *La Vie Parisienne 1852–1870* (London: Hamish Hamilton, 1971), p. 78.

5. Gloria Groom and others, *L'Impressionisme et la mode*, exhib. cat. (Paris: Musée d'Orsay, 2013), p. 96.

6. Comtesse Dash, *Comment on fait son chemin dans le monde, code du savoir-vivre* (Paris, 1868), p. 76. Cited in Groom and others, p. 258.

7. Jeanne Bouvier, 'My Memoirs', in *The French Worker: Autobiographies from the Early Industrial Era*, ed. and trans. by Mark Traugott (Berkeley: University of California Press, 1993), pp. 336–80 (p. 346).

8. Catherine Naugrette-Christophe, *Paris sous le Second Empire: Le Théâtre et la ville* (Paris: Librairie Théâtrale, 1998), annexe 4. Other sources set the average wage a little higher, between 3 and 5 francs. See Émile Zola, *The Drinking Den*, trans. by Robin Buss (London: Penguin Books, 2003), p. 433, n. 5. Auriant, *Les Lionnes du Second Empire* (Paris: Gallimard, 1935), p. 199.

9. Jeanne Bouvier in Traugott, p. 380.

10. Jeanne Bouvier in Traugott, p. 380.

11. Zola, Émile Zola, *L'Assommoir* (Paris: Fasquelle, 1977), p. 400.

12. Ego, *Isola* (Paris, 1876), p. 164.

13. Suzanne Voilquin, 'Recollections of a Daughter of the People' in *The French Worker: Autobiographies from the Early Industrial Era*, ed. and trans. by Mark Traugott (Berkeley: University of California Press, 1993), pp. 92–115 (p. 112).

14. Anon, *What's What in Paris* (London, 1867), p. 58. Cited in Richardson, *La Vie Parisienne*, p. 72.

15. Maxime du Camp, *Paris: ses organes, ses fonctions et sa vie dans la seconde moitié du XIXième siècle*, 6 vols (Paris, 1869–75), III, 458.

16. 'L'Enfant de Mme Valtesse', *Le Rappel*, 16 November 1881, p. 2.

17. Ego, p. 165.

18. Ego, pp. 163–5.

19. Jeanne Bouvier in Traugott, p. 374.

20. A. Coffignon, *Paris Vivant, La Corruption à Paris* (Paris, 1889), p. 21.

21. Gildea, pp. 80–1.

22. On the authorities' attempts to control prostitution, see: Gildea, pp. 80–1; Gabrielle Houbre, *Le Livre des courtisanes: archives secrètes de la police des moeurs, 1861–1876* (Paris: Tallandier, 2006); Alain Corbin, *Women for Hire: Prostitution and Sexuality in France after 1850*, trans. by Alan Sheridan (Cambridge, Mass and London: Harvard University Press, 1990), pp. 3–7 and pp. 128–55; Virginia Rounding, *Grandes Horizontales: The Lives and Legends of Four 19th-Century Courtesans* (London: Bloomsbury, 2003), pp. 1–29.

23. On the hierarchy that existed and the differences between the categories of prostitute, see: Virginia Rounding, *Grandes Horizontales: The Lives and Legends of Four 19th-Century Courtesans* (London: Bloomsbury, 2003), pp. 1–29; Joanna Richardson, *The Courtesans: The Demi-Monde in 19th-Century France* (London: Phoenix Press, 2000), pp. 1–4; Susan Griffin, *The Book of the Courtesans* (London: Pan Macmillan, 2003), pp. 1–17; Julie Kavanagh, *The Girl Who Loved Camellias: The Life and Legend of Marie Duplessis* (New York: Alfred A. Knopf, 2013), pp. 49–59; Alexandre Dumas, *Filles, lorettes et courtisanes* (Paris, 1874); Alphonse Esquiros, *Les Vierges folles* (Paris, 1840).

24. Alexandre Privat d'Anglemont, *Paris inconnu* (Paris, 1861). Cited in Richardson, *La Vie Parisienne*, p. 102.

25. Maurice Barrès, *Le Quartier Latin; ces messieurs, ces dames* (Paris, 1888).

26. Henry de Père, *Paris Guide, par les principaux écrivains et artistes de la France* (Paris, 1867), p. 1,000.

27. Theodore Zeldin, *France 1848–1945: Taste and Corruption* (Oxford, New York, Toronto and Melbourne: Oxford University Press, 1980), pp. 312–15.

28. Charles Augustus Cole, *The Imperial Paris Guide* (London, 1867), p. 13. Cited in Richardson, *La Vie Parisienne*, p. 157.

29. Alfred Delvau, *Les Cynthères parisiennes* (Paris, 1864), pp. 59–68.

30. H.A. de Conty, *Paris en poche – Guide pratique Conty*, 6th edn (Paris, 1875), p. 264.

31. Félicien Champsaur, *Paris, le massacre* (Paris, 1885), p. 268.

32. Maurice Barrès, *Le Quartier Latin; ces messieurs, ces dames* (Paris, 1888), pp. 27–9.

33. Barrès, p. 27.

34. A. Coffignon, *Paris Vivant, La Corruption à Paris* (Paris, 1889), p. 99.

CHAPTER 3

1. Valtesse would have known that people would interpret the character of Leys as Fossey when she wrote *Isola*. The meeting she describes in the novel was undoubtedly designed to shape people's opinion. Ego, *Isola* (Paris, 1876)

2. Ego, p. 174.

3. A letter written by Emilie describing the couple's first meeting was quoted in the papers. 'L'Enfant de Mme Valtesse', *Le Rappel*, 16 November 1881, p. 3.

4. Ego, p. 173.

5. Ego, p. 175.

6. The Théâtre de Cluny finally closed its doors in 1989.

7. Theodore Zeldin, *France 1848–1945: Taste and Corruption* (Oxford, New York, Toronto, Melbourne: Oxford University Press, 1980), p. 361.

8. Zeldin, p. 361.

9. Robert Gildea, *Children of the Revolution: The French 1799–1914* (London: Allen Lane, 2008), pp. 177–8.

10. Catherine Naugrette-Christophe, *Paris sous le Second Empire: Le Théâtre et la ville* (Paris: Librairie Théâtrale, 1998), annexe 4.

11. Naugrette-Christophe, annexe 4.

12. Gildea, pp. 178–9.

13. 'Parisian Actresses', *Hampshire Telegraph and Sussex Chronicle etc.*, 17 November 1880.

14. Adrien Desprez, 'Petites scènes', *Gazette Littéraire, Artistique et Scientifique*, 32 (10 December 1864), 324.

15. Naugrette-Christophe, pp. 90, 120.

16. Joanna Richardson, *La Vie Parisienne 1852–1870* (London: Hamish Hamilton, 1971), pp. 264–73.

17. Richardson, *La Vie Parisienne*, p. 264.

18. Richardson, *La Vie Parisienne*, p. 266.

19. Albert de Lasalle, *Histoire des Bouffes-Parisiens* (Paris, 1860), p. 116.

20. Peter Gammond, *Offenbach: His Life and Times* (Kent: Midas Books, 1980), pp. 37–8.

21. Nestor Roqueplan, 'Les Théâtres', in *Paris-Guide* (Paris, 1867), pp. 829–30.

22. H.A. de Conty, *Paris en poche – Guide pratique Conty*, 6th edn (Paris, 1875), p. 254.

23. Gammond, p. 47.

24. Gammond, pp. 47–8.

25. Siegfried Kracauer, *Jacques Offenbach and the Paris of His Time*, trans. by Gwenda David and Eric Mosbacher (New York: Zone Books, 2002), p. 190.

26. Kracauer, p. 241.

27. *L'Orchestre*, 2 February 1866, p. 1.

28. *Le Monde Illustré*, 10 February 1866, p. 83.

29. Albert de Lasalle, *Le Monde Illustré*, 10 February 1866, p. 95.

30. Michael R. Booth, 'Nineteenth-Century Theatre', in *The Oxford Illustrated History of Theatre*, ed. by John Russell Brown (Oxford and New York: Oxford University Press, 1997), pp. 299–340 (p. 331).

31. *Le Tintamarre*, 8 April 1866, p. 2.

32. Booth, 'Nineteenth-Century Theatre', p. 302.

33. Ego, p. 2.

34. Émile Zola, *Nana*, trans. by Douglas Parmée (Oxford: Oxford University Press, 1992), p. 121.

35. Ludovic Halévy, *La Famille Cardinal* (Paris: Calmann-Lévy, 1946), p. 36.

36. Kracauer, pp. 190–1.

CHAPTER 4

1. Céleste Mogador, *Memoirs of a Courtesan in 19th-Century Paris*, trans. by Monique Fleury Nagem (Lincoln and London: University of Nebraska Press, 2001), pp. 74–5.

2. George Sussman, 'The Wet-Nursing Business in Nineteenth-Century France', *French Historical Studies*, 9 (1975), 304–28.

3. 'Gazette des tribunaux', *Le Figaro*, 9 November 1881, p. 5.

4. Ego, *Isola* (Paris: Dentu, 1876), p. 172.

5. Ego, pp. 160–1.

6. Ego, p. 176.

7. Gustave Flaubert, *Madame Bovary*, trans. by Geoffrey Wall (London: Penguin Books, 1992), p. 70.

8. Michelle Perrot, 'The Curtain Rises – Introduction', in *A History of Private Life*, ed. by Philippe Ariès and George Duby, trans. by Arthur Goldhammer, 5 vols (Cambridge, MA and London: Belknap Press of Harvard University Press, 1987–1991), vol. 4: *From the Fires of Revolution to the Great War*, ed. by Michelle Perrot (1990), pp. 9–11 (p. 9).

9. On prevailing views of the family and the legal changes which influenced it from the ancien régime to the early 19th century, see Patricia Mainardi, *Husbands, Wives, and Lovers: Marriage and Its Discontents in Nineteenth-Century France* (New Haven and London: Yale University Press, 2003), pp. 4–18.

10. Mme Romieu (Marie-Sincère), *La Femme au XIXe siècle* (Paris, 1858), p. 239.

11. 'Gazette des tribunaux', *Le Figaro*, 15 November 1881, p. 2. *Le Temps*, 16 November 1881, p. 3.

12. *Le Figaro*, 21 September 1868, p. 3.

13. A. de Bory, 'Théâtre des Bouffes-Parisiens – Soirée de Réouverture', *La France Musicale*, 4 October 1868, p. 311.

14. *Le Figaro*, 10 October 1868, p. 3; *Le Figaro*, 1 November 1868, p. 3.

15. *Le Figaro*, 25 March 1869, p. 3.

16. Émile Blavet, 'La Princesse de Trébizonde'. *Le Figaro*, 3 August 1869, p. 3.

17. Un passant, *Le Rappel*, 9 December 1869, p. 1.

18. Félix Clément and Pierre Larousse, *Dictionnaire des opéras* (Paris, 1881), p. 808.

19. Un passant, *Le Rappel*, 9 December 1869, p. 1. *Cocodès* was the name the Duc de Gramont-Caderousse gave to his intimate friends. These were society men who were attached to courtesans. Their mistresses were known as *cocodettes*. Siegfried Kracauer, *Jacques Offenbach and the Paris of His Time*, trans. by Gwenda David and Eric Mosbacher (New York: Zone Books, 2002), p. 252.

20. Froufrou, 'Les Premières', *Le Gaulois*, 9 December 1869, p. 1.

21. Ibid.

22. Ibid.

23. Ibid.

24. François Oswald, 'Bruits de coulisses', *Le Gaulois*, 15 December 1869, p. 3.

25. Kracauer, p. 177.

26.   Oh very good!

           Oh very well!

           Pretty, charming, spiritual.

           Oh, sire, it was very good, very chic!

           Oh! What is sweet love in music.

           [...]

           Sir, I am a rich widow!

           Will you marry me, my dear?

    M.M. Tréfeu et Prével, *La Romance de la Rose – opéra bouffe, partition chant et piano* (Paris, 1870).

27. Félix Clément and Pierre Larousse, *Dictionnaire des opéras* (Paris, 1881), p. 813.

28. *Le Petit Journal*, 20 December 1869, p. 2.

CHAPTER 5

1. Siegfried Kracauer, *Jacques Offenbach and the Paris of His Time*, trans. by Gwenda David and Eric Mosbacher (New York: Zone Books, 2002), p. 142.

2. On Zulma, see Kracauer, pp. 262–5. See also Alexander Faris, *Jacques Offenbach* (London: Faber and Faber, 1980), pp. 102–3.

3. James Harding, *Jacques Offenbach: A Biography* (London: John Calder & New York: Riverrun Press, 1980), p. 139.

4. Gabrielle Houbre, *Le Livre de Courtisanes: Archives secrètes de la police des moeurs* (Paris: Tallandier, 2006), p. 253.

5. Kracauer, p. 331.

6. Ego, *Isola* (Paris, 1876), p. 146.

7. Ego, pp. 4–5.

8. Offenbach's grandson insisted that his grandfather's weight never exceeded 50kg. Harding, p. 129.

9. Victor Koning gave a detailed report of the event and its guests. Victor Koning, *Tout Paris* (Paris, 1872), p. 52–5.

10. Gustave Lafargue, *Le Figaro*, 28 February 1870, p. 4.

11. Faris, p. 128.

12. *Nouveau guide en Italie – Guide-Chaix*, (Paris, 1864), p. 17.

13. Ibid.

14. Joseph Caccia, *Nouveau guide général du voyageur en Italie* (Paris, 1875), p. III.

15. Ernest Blum, *Le Rappel*, 30 January 1870, p. 4.

16. Oscar Havard, *Guide de Rome, Turin, Milan, Venise, Padoue, Florence, Assise, Ancône, Lorette, Naples, etc.* (Paris, 1877), p. 7.

17. Caccia, p. 253.

18. Ego, p. 47. The items listed in the sale catalogue when Valtesse auctioned many of her belongings in the early 20th century confirm her attraction to Italian lace and earthenware.

19. Houbre, p. 253.

20. Kracauer, p. 118.

21. Kracauer, pp. 118, 269.

22. Joanna Richardson, *The Courtesans: The Demi-Monde in 19th-Century France* (London: Phoenix Press, 2000), p. 33.

23. Richardson, *The Courtesans*, pp. 9–11.

24. Faris, p. 149.

25. Valtesse's relationship with Millaud was recorded in her police file. Houbre, p. 253.

26. On Paris in 1870, see Alistair Horne, *Seven Ages of Paris* (London: Pan Macmillan, 2003), pp. 282–313.

27. Edmond de Goncourt, cited in Horne, p. 294.

28. Edmond de Goncourt, *Paris under Siege, 1870–1871: From the Goncourt Journal*, ed. and trans. by George J. Becker (Ithaca and London: Cornell University Press, 1969), p. 190.

29. Théophile Gautier, cited in Horne, p. 295.

30. Hollis Clayson, *Paris in Despair: Art and Everyday Life under Siege (1870–71)* (Chicago and London: University of Chicago Press, 2002), p. 83.

31. Clayson, p. 83.

32. Horne, p. 288.

33. Eugène Morand, 'Nouvelles Diverses', *Le Figaro*, 24 January 1870, p. 3.

34. A. Mazon, *Nice en 1861 – Guide de l'étranger* (Paris and Nice, 1861), pp. 127–9. Robert Latouche, *Histoire de Nice de 1860 à 1914*, 2 vols (Nice: Ville de Nice, 1954), vol. II, p. 86.

35. Horne, p. 290.

36. J.D. Hayhurst, *The Pigeon Post into Paris 1870–1871* (1970) http://www.cix.co.uk/~mhayhurst/jdhayhurst/pigeon/pigeon.html (accessed 4 April 2014)

37. *Recueil des dépêches télégraphiques reproduites par la photographie et adressées à Paris au moyen de pigeons-voyageurs pendant l'investissement de la capitale*, 6 vols, I (Bordeaux), 29 December 1870, message written 9 December 1870.

38. *Recueil des dépêches télégraphiques reproduites par la photographie et adressées à Paris au moyen de pigeons-voyageurs pendant l'investissement de la capitale*, 6 vols, I (Bordeaux), 3 January 1871, message written 31 December 1870.

39. *Recueil des dépêches télégraphiques reproduites par la photographie et adressées à Paris au moyen de pigeons-voyageurs pendant l'investissement de la capitale*, 6 vols, I (Bordeaux), 29 December 1870, message written 9 December 1870.

40. *Recueil des dépêches télégraphiques reproduites par la photographie et adressées à Paris au moyen de pigeons-voyageurs pendant l'investissement de la capitale*, 6 vols, I (Bordeaux), 3 January 1871, message written 31 December 1870.

41. J.D. Hayhurst, *The Pigeon Post into Paris 1870–1871*, (1970) http://www.cix.co.uk/~mhayhurst/jdhayhurst/pigeon/pigeon.html (accessed 4 April 2014)

42. Juliette Lamber, *Le Siége de Paris – Journal d'une Parisienne* (Paris, 1873), p. 371.

43. *Le Journal de Nice*, 1 January 1871, p. 1.

44. Edmond de Goncourt, *Paris under Siege, 1870–1871: From the Goncourt Journal*, ed. and trans. by George J. Becker (Ithaca and London: Cornell University Press, 1969), p. 187.

45. Ibid.

46. Valtesse's confidences interpreted in Liane de Pougy, *Idylle saphique* (Paris: Éditions des Femmes, 1987), p. 15.

CHAPTER 6

1. On Paris during the siege and the Commune, see Alistair Horne, *Seven Ages of Paris* (London: Pan Macmillan, 2003), pp. 282–313.

2. Edmond de Goncourt, *Paris under Siege, 1870–1871: From the Goncourt Journal*, ed. and trans. by George J. Becker (Ithaca and London: Cornell University Press, 1969), p. 311–2.

3. Goncourt, p. 312.

4. Goncourt, p. 315.

5. Valtesse's confidences interpreted in Liane de Pougy, *Idylle saphique* (Paris: Éditions des Femmes, 1987), p. 15.

6. 'Les Premières', *Le Figaro*, 5 March 1872, p. 1.

7. 'Les Premières', *Le Figaro*, 11 April 1872, p. 1.

8. *Le Figaro*, 25 November 1872, p. 3.

9. Richard O'Monroy, cited in Claude Blanchard, *Dames de coeur* (Paris: Éditions du Pré aux Clercs, 1946), p. 132.

10. *Almanach de Gotha – Annuaire généalogique, diplomatique et statistique* (Paris, 1872), pp. 164–6.

11. Frédéric Loliée, *La Fête impériale* (Paris: Tallandier, 1926), p. 73.

12. Cited in Auriant, *Les Lionnes du Second Empire* (Paris: Gallimard, 1935), p. 183.

13. Valtesse's taste in clothing and jewellery can be gauged from the items in the sale of her house in 1902. See *Catalogue de tableaux modernes, pastels, aquarelles, dessins etc. de Mme Valtesse de la Bigne* (Paris: Imprimerie de la Gazette des Beaux-Arts, June 1902).

14. Gabrielle Houbre, *Le Livre de Courtisanes: Archives secrètes de la police des moeurs* (Paris: Tallandier, 2006), p. 253.

15. H.A. de Conty, *Paris en poche – Guide pratique Conty*, 6th edn (Paris, 1875), p. 287.

16. H.A. de Conty, *Paris en poche – Guide pratique Conty*, 6th edn (Paris, 1875), pp. 24–5.

17. Houbre, p. 253. All currency equivalents calculated according to http://www.measuringworth.com

18. Houbre, pp. 252–3.

19. Houbre, p. 252. Rue Blanche is situated on the right bank in Paris, where upper apartments did not receive running water until 1865. See Roger-Henri Guerrand, 'Private Spaces' in *A History of Private Life*, vol. 4, ed. by Michelle Perrot, trans. by Arthur Goldhammer (Cambridge, MA: Harvard University Press, 1990), pp. 359–449 (pp. 370–2).

20. Valtesse's confidences interpreted in Liane de Pougy, *Idylle saphique* (Paris: Éditions des Femmes, 1987), p. 15.

21. Auriant, *Les Lionnes du Second Empire* (Paris: Gallimard, 1935), p. 208.

22. Auriant, *Les Lionnes du Second Empire*, p. 193.

23. This fact and Valtesse's manner of greeting lovers have been recorded by Claude Blanchard. See Claude Blanchard, *Dames de coeur* (Paris: Éditions du Pré aux Clercs, 1946), pp. 129–34.

24. Auriant, *La Véritable histoire de Nana* (Brussels: Mercure de France, 1942), p. 44.

25. Houbre, p. 528.

26. Blanchard, p. 140.

27. Valtesse's confidences interpreted in Liane de Pougy, *Idylle saphique* (Paris: Éditions des Femmes, 1987), p. 15.

28. Houbre, p. 252.

29. This complaint is recorded in Houbre, p. 575.

30. Liane de Pougy, *My Blue Notebooks*, trans. by Diane Athill (New York: Tarcher Putnam, 2002), p. 44.

31. Houbre, p. 254.

32. H.A. de Conty, *Paris en poche – Guide pratique Conty*, 6th edn (Paris, 1875), p. 129.

33. 'Obituary', *The Standard*, 22 March 1898, p. 5; 'The Italian Opera in Paris', *The Morning Post*, 13 June 1883, p. 5.

34. 'Court and Fashion', *The Belfast News-Letter*, 29 August 1862.

35. 'Court and Fashion – Foreign Courts', *The Era*, 26 May 1867.

36. 'Sporting', *The Belfast News-Letter*, 26 April 1860.

CHAPTER 7

1. All currency equivalents calculated according to: http://www.measuringworth. com/uk

2. Adrien Marx, *Les Petits mémoires de Paris* (Paris, 1888), p. 1.

3. Françoise Tétart-Vittu, 'Édouard Manet, *La Parisienne*' in Gloria Groom and others, *L'Impressionisme et la mode*, exhib. cat. (Paris: Skira-Flammarion, 2013), pp. 125–8.

4. Jules Claretie, *La Vie à Paris* (Paris, 1910), p. 239.

5. Marx, p. 169.

6. Unpublished text cited in Claude Blanchard, *Dames de coeur* (Paris: Éditions du Pré aux Clercs, 1946), p. 133.

7. Y. Z. and C., 'Au Jour le jour – Les Merveilleuses', *Le Gaulois*, 18 December 1873, p. 1.

8. Joanna Richardson, *The Courtesans: The Demi-Monde in 19th-Century France* (London: Phoenix Press, 2000), pp. 11, 35.

9. Jill, Duchess of Hamilton, *Napoleon, the Empress and the Artist: the Story of Napoleon, Josephine's Garden at Malmaison, Redouté and the Australian Plants*, ed. by Anne Savage (East Roseville, NSW: Kangaroo Press, 1999), p. 95. Charles Angélique François Huchet La Bédoyère, *Memoirs of the Public and Private Life of Napoleon Bonaparte*, 2 vols (London, 1827), vol. II, p. 747.

10. Fernand Xau, 'Valtesse de la Bigne', *Gil Blas*, 13 June 1883, p. 2.

11. 'Gazette des tribunaux', *Le Figaro*, 15 November 1881, p. 2. 'Tribunaux', *Le Temps*, 16 November 1881, p. 3.

12. Joanna Richardson, *La Vie Parisienne 1852–1870* (London: Hamish Hamilton Ltd., 1971), pp. 110–12; Julie Kavanagh, *The Girl Who Loved Camellias: The Life and Legend of Marie Duplessis* (New York: Alfred K. Knopf, 2013), pp. 108–9.

13. Siegfried Kracauer, *Jacques Offenbach and the Paris of His Time*, trans. by Gwenda David and Eric Mosbacher (New York: Zone Books, 2002), p. 97.

14. Richardson, *The Courtesans*, p. 21.

15. H.A. de Conty, *Paris en poche – Guide pratique Conty*, 6th edn (Paris, 1875), p. 272.

16. Ibid.

17. Émile Blavet, *La Vie Parisienne – La Ville et Le Théâtre* (Paris, 1884), p. 177.

18. H.A. de Conty, *Paris en poche – Guide pratique Conty*, 6th edn (Paris, 1875), p. 272.

19. P. Juillerat, cited in Robert L. Herbert, *Impressionism: Art, Leisure, and Parisian Society* (New Haven and London: Yale University Press, 1988), p. 195.

20. Anne Martin-Fugier, 'Bourgeois Rituals' in *A History of Private Life*, ed. by Philippe Ariès and George Duby, trans. by Arthur Goldhammer, 5 vols (Cambridge, MA and London: Belknap Press of Harvard University Press, 1987–1991), vol. 4: *From the Fires of Revolution to the Great War*, ed. by Michelle Perrot (1990), pp. 261–337 (pp. 299–304).

21. Martin-Fugier, p. 299.

22. I am indebted to Damien and Florence Bachelot for their kind assistance in my research of Valtesse's property in Ville-d'Avray; I am also grateful to Sophie Huet at the Service Communication et Culture at the Mairie de Ville-d'Avray for her assistance in my research.

23. Dominique Claudius-Petit, 'Histoire de la maison Rostand', (unpublished article, 2014), p. 3.

24. Félicien Champsaur, *Paris, le massacre* (Paris, 1885), p. 268.

25. Gabrielle Houbre, *Le Livre des courtisanes: Archives secrètes de la police des moeurs, 1861–1876* (Paris: Tallandier, 2006), p. 252.

26. Jean-François Barielle and others. *Champs-Elysées, Faubourg St Honoré, Plaine Monceau* (Paris: Henri Veyrier, 1982), pp. 283–6.

27. Jacques Hillairet, *Dictionnaire historique des rues de Paris*, 2 vols (Paris: Les Éditions de minuit, 1957–1961), vol. II, pp. 92–3.

28. L. de V., 'Hôtel privé, boulevard Malesherbes à Paris, par M. J. Février, architecte', *Le Moniteur des architectes*, (1877), pp. 35–6.

29. A description of the property can be found in L. de V., 'Hôtel privé, boulevard Malesherbes à Paris, par M. J. Février, architecte', *Le Moniteur des architectes*, (1877), pp. 35–6; On the property's contents and impact, see Fernand Xau, 'Valtesse de la Bigne', *Gil Blas*, 13 June 1883, p. 2.

30. L. de V., 'Hôtel privé, boulevard Malesherbes à Paris, par M. J. Février, architecte', *Le Moniteur des architectes*, (1877), pp. 35–6.

31. H.A. de Conty, *Paris en poche – Guide pratique Conty*, 6th edn (Paris, 1875), p. 295.

32. Fernand Xau, 'Valtesse de la Bigne', *Gil Blas*, 13 June 1883, p. 2.

33. Maître X, *Le Gaulois*, 1 March 1882, p. 3.

34. I am indebted to Audrey Gay-Mazuel and the staff at the Musée des Arts décoratifs in Paris for allowing me access to the archives on Valtesse's bed and assisting me in my research. On Valtesse's bed, see Roberto Polo, 'Édouard Lièvre, un créateur des arts décoratifs au XIXe', *L'Estampille – L'Objet d'art*, 394 (September 2004), pp. 102–113; Odile Nouvel-Kammerer, 'Le lit d'une lionne: Valtesse de la Bigne', in *Rêves d'Alcôves: la chambre au cours des siècles*, exhib. cat. (Paris: Musée des Arts décoratifs, 1995), pp. 211–13; Odile Nouvel-Kammerer, 'La création de la chambre conjugale', in *Rêves d'Alcôves: la chambre au cours des siècles*, exhib. cat. (Paris: Musée des Arts décoratifs, 1995), pp. 104–127; *Catalogue de tableaux modernes, pastels, aquarelles, dessins etc. de Mme Valtesse de la Bigne* (Paris: Imprimerie de la Gazette des Beaux-Arts, June 1902), p. 106; Jean-Jacques Lévêque, 'Trois intérieurs du début de la IIIe République', *Gazette des Beaux-Arts*, (March 1976), pp. 92–4; Béatrice Lauwick and Odile Nouvel-Kammerer, 'Le Lit de Valtesse de La Bigne', *Histoire de l'art*, 32 (December 1995), 71–7.

35. *Catalogue de tableaux modernes, pastels, aquarelles, dessins etc. de Mme Valtesse de la Bigne* (Paris: Imprimerie de la Gazette des Beaux-Arts, June 1902), pp. II–III.

36. Liane de Pougy, *My Blue Notebooks*, trans. by Diane Athill (New York: Tarcher Putnam, 2002), p. 108.

CHAPTER 8

1. Émile Zola, cited in John Rewald, *The History of Impressionism*, 4th edn (New York: Museum of Modern Art and London: Secker & Warburg, 1973), p. 198.

2. Edmond Duranty, cited in Rewald, pp. 197–8.

3. T.J. Clark, *The Painting of Modern Life: Paris in the Art of Manet and His Contemporaries* (New York: Knopf, 1984 and London: Thames and Hudson, 1985), p. 92.

4. Jules Claretie, cited in T.J. Clark, *The Painting of Modern Life*, p. 86.

5. Conversation recorded in Auriant, *Les Lionnes du Second Empire* (Paris: Gallimard, 1935), pp. 187–8.
   Leah Rosenblatt Lehmbeck, 'Édouard Manet's Portraits of Women' (doctoral thesis, Institute of Fine Arts, New York, May 2007).

6. Tamar Garb, 'Gender and Representation' in Francis Frascina and others, *Modernity and Modernism: French Painting in the Nineteenth Century* (New Haven and London: Yale University Press, 1993), pp. 219–89 (p. 231).

7. Edmond de Goncourt, cited in Garb, 'Gender and Representation', p. 231.

8. Garb, 'Gender and Representation', p. 235.

9. Alain Pougetoux, 'Josephine as Patron and Her Collection of Paintings' in Carol Solomon Kiefer, *The Empress Josephine: Art and Royal Identity* (Mead Art Museum: Amherst, Massachusetts, 2005), pp. 93–5.

10. Edmond Bazire, *Manet* (Paris, 1884), p. 30.

11. Rewald, p. 197

12. Rewald, p. 197.

13. Christiane Lefebvre, *Alfred Stevens – 1823–1906* (Paris: Brame & Lorenceau, 2006), pp. 126–33; Max Sulzberger, *Une Visite chez Alfred Stevens* (Brussels, 1876), pp. 3–11.

14. Comte Robert de Montesquiou-Fezensac, cited in Lefebvre, p. 131.

15. Anne Higonnet, *Berthe Morisot* (California: University of California Press, 1995), p. 23.

16. Jules Claretie, *La Vie à Paris* (Paris: Charpentier, 1911), p. 240.

17. Peter Mitchell, *Jean Baptiste Antoine Guillemet, 1841–1918* (London: John Mitchell & Son, 1981).

18. Jean-Marcel Humbert, *Édouard Detaille: L'héroisme d'un siècle* (Paris: Éditions Copernic, 1979), p. 20.

19. Goncourt journals, May 1887, cited in Yolaine de la Bigne, *Valtesse de la Bigne ou Le pouvoir de la volupté* (Paris: Perrin, 1999), p. 174.

20. The female figure in another of the artist's paintings of civilian subjects, *Two Elegant Figures on Horseback* (1873), bears a striking resemblance to Valtesse, suggesting that the couple were already intimate by this date.

21. *Henri Gervex 1852–1929*, exhib. cat. (Paris: Paris-Musées, 1992). I am indebted to Jean-Christophe Pralong-Gourvennec for his detailed knowledge of Gervex's personal life.

22. *Gil Blas*, 2 December 1894, p. 1.

23. http://www.osenat.fr/html/fiche.jsp?id=3408505&np=14&lng=fr&npp= 20&ordre=1&aff=1&r (accessed 9 June 2014).

24. *World Ceramics: An illustrated history from earliest times*, ed. by Robert J. Charleston (New York: Crescent Books, 1990). I am indebted to the expert knowledge of ceramicist Elaine Hewitt for the information on the history of porcelain.

25. She was also sometimes referred to as *'l'Union des peintres'*.

26. André de Fouquières, *Mon Paris et ses Parisiens*, 5 vols (Paris: Éditions Pierre Horay, 1953–1955), vol. II, (1954), p. 124.

CHAPTER 9

1. Jules Claretie, *La Vie à Paris* (Paris, 1911), p. 234.

2. Félicien Champsaur, *Paris, le massacre* (Paris, 1885), p. 269.

3. Claretie, p. 234.

4. Yves Olivier-Martin, *Histoire du roman populaire en France* (Paris: Albin Michel, 1980), p. 128.

5. Tamar Garb, 'Gender and Representation', in Francis Frascina and others, *Modernity and Modernism: French Painting in the Nineteenth Century* (New Haven and London: Yale University Press, 1993), pp. 219–90 (p. 280).

6. Tamar Garb, 'Gender and Representation', in Frascina and others, p. 231.

7. *Women's Voices through two thousand years of letters*, ed. by Olga Kenyon (London: Constable, 1997), p. 157.

8. Ego, pp. 84–5.

9. Céleste Mogador, *Memoirs of a Courtesan in 19th-Century Paris*, trans. by Monique Fleury Nagem (Lincoln and London: University of Nebraska Press, 2001), p. 106.

10. Mogador, p. 108.

11. Liane de Pougy, *My Blue Notebooks*, trans. by Diane Athill (New York: Tarcher Putnam, 2002), p. 44.

12. Gabrielle Houbre, *Le Livre des Courtisanes: Archives secrètes de la police des moeurs* (Paris: Tallandier, 2006), pp. 230–2.

13. *Octave Mirbeau – Correspondance générale*, ed. by Pierre Michel and Jean-François Nivet, 3 vols (Lausanne: Âge d'homme, 2002–2009), vol. I (2002), p. 186–7.

14. *Octave Mirbeau – Correspondance générale*, vol. I, p. 186.

15. Ibid.

16. Event recounted in Claretie, p. 237.

17. Theodore Zeldin, *France 1848–1945: Taste and Corruption* (Oxford, New York, Toronto and Melbourne: Oxford University Press, 1980), pp. 144–225.

18. Auriant, *Les Lionnes du Second Empire* (Paris: Gallimard, 1935), p. 214.

19. Félicien Champsaur, *Les Parisiennes* (Paris, 1877), p. 62.

20. Félicien Champsaur, *Les Parisiennes* (Paris, 1877), p. 64.

21. The Académie was limited to strictly 40 seats.

22. Arsène Houssaye, 'Les Parisiennes d'Amour – Valtesse', *Panurge*, 22 October 1882.

23. Dr Besançon, *Le Visage de la femme* (Paris: Éditions Terres Latines, 1940) cited in Yolaine de la Bigne, *Valtesse de la Bigne ou Le pouvoir de la volupté* (Paris: Perrin, 1999), p. 132.

24. Auriant, *Les Lionnes du Second Empire*, p. 213.

25. Liane de Pougy, *My Blue Notebooks*, trans. by Diane Athill (New York: Tarcher Putnam, 2002), p. 44.

26. André de Fouquières, *Mon Paris et ses Parisiens*, 5 vols (Paris: Éditions Pierre Horay, 1953-1955), vol. II, (1954), p. 126.

27. Ego, *Isola* (Paris, 1876).

28. Ego, pp. 10–11.

29. Ego, pp. 2–3.

30. Ego, p. 61.

31. Ego, p. 13.

32. Ego, p. 59.

33. Ego, p. 61.

34. *Le Figaro*, 12 February 1876, p. 3.

35. *Le Figaro*, 13 February 1876, p. 3.

36. Claretie, p. 234.

37. Albert Wolff, *Le Figaro*, 20 March 1876, p. 1.

38. Mardoche and Desgenais, *Les Parisiennes* (Paris, 1882), p. 362.

39. Albert Wolff, *Le Figaro*, 20 March 1876, p. 1.

40. Ibid.

41. Ego, p. 144.

42. Mardoche and Desgenais, p. 360.

CHAPTER 10

1. *Le Gaulois*, 24 March 1878, p. 1.

2. *Paris–Plaisir*, 14 April 1878, p. 7.

3. Manuscrits nouv. acq. fr., 24520, f. 184, cited in O.R. Morgan, 'Zola et Valtesse de la Bigne', *Les Cahiers Naturalistes*, 39 (1970), 70–1.

4. Of Offenbach's operetta *La Belle Hélène*, Zola wrote: '[it] amounts to nothing more than a grimace of convulsive gaiety, a display of gutter wit and gestures.' Frederick Brown, *Zola: A Life* (London: Papermac, 1997), p. 117.

5. O.R. Morgan, 'Zola et Valtesse de la Bigne', *Les Cahiers Naturalistes*, 39 (1970), pp. 70–1.

6. Émile Zola, *L'Événement*, 29 March 1866, cited in Henri Mitterand, preface to Émile Zola, *Nana* (Paris: Gallimard, 2002), pp. 9–17 (p. 11).

7. Paul Alexis, cited in Graham King, *Garden of Zola: Émile Zola and His Novels for English Readers* (London: Barry and Jenkins Ltd, 1978), p. 125.

8. Adrien Marx, *Les Petits mémoires de Paris* (Paris, 1888), pp. 163–5.

9. Émile Zola, *Correspondence*, ed. by B.H. Bakker and Colette Becker, 10 vols (Montréal: Les Presses de l'Université de Montréal, Paris: Édition du Centre National de la Recherche Scientifique, 1978–1995), vol. III, p. 174.

10. Adrien Marx, 'La Plaine Monceau', *Le Figaro*, 21 June 1880, p. 1.

11. Albert Wolff, *La Haute-Noce* (Paris, 1885), p. 52.

12. Anecdote recounted in Yolaine de la Bigne, *Valtesse de la Bigne ou Le pouvoir de la volupté* (Paris: Perrin, 1999), p. 114.

13. Some people insisted that it was Guillemet and not Hennique who made the introduction, though the correspondence between Hennique and Zola suggests otherwise. Edmond Lepelletier, *Émile Zola: sa vie, son oeuvre* (Paris: Mercure de France, 1908), p. 250.

14. Ernest Alfred Vizetelly, *With Zola in England: A Story of Exile* (Middlesex: The Echo Library, 2007), p. 177.

15. King, p. 272.

16. Jules Bertaut, *Paris 1870–1935*, trans. by R. Millar, ed. by John Bell (London: Eyre and Spottiswoode, 1936), pp. 69–70.

17. Émile Zola, *Nana*, trans. by Douglas Parmée (Oxford: Oxford University Press, 1992), p. 294; Zola, *Nana*, p. 275–6.

18. Zola, *Nana*, p. 294.

19. Auriant, *La Véritable histoire de Nana* (Brussels: Mercure de France, 1942), p. 44.

20. Liane de Pougy, *My Blue Notebooks*, trans. by Diane Athill (New York: Tarcher Putnam, 2002), p. 44.

21. Félicien Champsaur, *Paris, le massacre* (Paris, 1885), p. 271.

22. Pougy, p. 44.

23. Ego, *Isola* (Paris, 1876), pp. 28, 47.

24. Auriant, *La Véritable histoire de Nana*, p. 45.

25. Champsaur, p. 269.

26. Alexis, cited in Auriant, 'Quelques sources ignorées de "Nana"', *Mercure de France*, 252 (1934), 180–8 (p. 183).

27. Zola, *Nana*, p. 274.

28. Zola, *Nana*, p. 274.

29. Zola, *Nana*, p. 275.

30. Zola, *Nana*, p. 374.

31. When the bed lately underwent restoration, the dates '1880' and '1881' and the name of the fitter were found written in pencil on the bedhead under Valtesse's circular crest. It was assumed that the bed was not yet in place when Zola visited Valtesse's home in 1878. If the dates are accurate, and judging by Zola's description of Nana's excitement at the plans and the work that went into preparing it, it is possible that even if the bed were not in place, Valtesse proudly showed the plans to Zola after dinner; Zola, *Nana*, p. 375.

32. Champsaur, p. 267.

33. Liane de Pougy acknowledges that her friend's bed was widely understood 'to be the model Zola used when describing his Nana's luxury'. Pougy, *My Blue Notebooks*, p. 108.

34. Zola, *Nana*, p. 369.

35. Céard in a letter to Zola on 15 October 1879, cited in Brown, p. 431.

36. *Le Gaulois*, 14 October 1879, p. 4.

37. Parmée quotes Henry James's review. Émile Zola, *Nana* (Oxford: Oxford University Press, 1992), p. xx.

38. Brown, p. 434.

39. Auriant, *La Véritable histoire de Nana*, p. 99.

40. Auriant, *La Véritable histoire de Nana*, p.121.

41. *Le Gaulois*, 14 October 1879, p. 1.

42. Auriant even cites an article in which Valtesse's pseudonym was used: '*Ego nominor Nana*'. Auriant, *La Véritable histoire de Nana*, p. 114.

43. Émile Zola, *L'Assommoir* (Paris: Fasquelle, 1977), p. 360.

44. Jules Claretie, *La Vie à Paris* (Paris, 1911), p. 234.

45. Ego, *Isola* (Paris, 1876), p. 166.

46. Auriant, *Les Lionnes du Second Empire* (Paris: Gallimard, 1935), p. 172.

47. Auriant, *La Véritable histoire de Nana*, p. 76.

48. Émile Zola, 'Revue dramatique et littéraire', *Le Voltaire*, 28 October 1879, p. 1.

49. Zola, *Nana*, p. 275.

50. See Yolaine de la Bigne, *Valtesse de la Bigne ou Le pouvoir de la volupté* (Paris: Perrin, 1999), p. 121.

51. Georges Ohnet, cited in Auriant, *La Véritable histoire de Nana*, p. 121.

52. Auriant, *Les Lionnes du Second Empire*, p. 198.

53. 'France', *The Morning Post*, 1 October 1880.

54. Auriant, *Les Lionnes du Second Empire*, p. 198.

CHAPTER 11

1. Detaille's diary, held at the Bibliothèque de l'Institut, Paris, extracts held by the Musée des arts décoratifs, Paris, MS 5506, February 1880.

2. Detaille's diary, MS 5506, March 1880.

3. Both women were present at Offenbach's funeral. 'Obsèques d'Offenbach', *Le Gaulois*, 8 October 1880, p. 2.

4. Detaille's diary, MS 5506, 17 July 1880.

5. Detaille's diary cited in François Robichon, *Édouard Detaille: Un siècle de gloire militaire* (Paris: Bernard Giovanangeli, 2007), p. 65.

6. Robichon, p. 65.

7. Jean-Marcel Humbert, *Édouard Detaille: L'héroisme d'un siècle* (Paris: Éditions Copernic, 1979), p. 7.

8. Jules Claretie, *L'Art et les artistes français contemporains* (Paris, 1876), p. 65.

9. Alain Corbin, 'The Secret of the Individual' in *A History of Private Life*, ed. by Philippe Ariès and George Duby, trans. by Arthur Goldhammer, 5 vols (Cambridge, MA and London: Belknap Press of Harvard University Press, 1987–1991), vol. 4: *From the Fires of Revolution to the Great War*, ed. by Michelle Perrot (1990), pp. 457–547 (p. 460).

10. André Jouve, *Le Courrier de Lyon*, 17 January 1844, cited in Etienne Grafe, *Portraitistes Lyonnais 1800–1914* (Lyon: Musée des Beaux-Arts, 1986), p. 25.

11. On this, see Heather McPherson, *The Modern Portrait in 19th-Century France* (Cambridge: Cambridge University Press, 2001), pp. 1–13.

12. Richard Brilliant, *Portraiture* (London: Reaktion Books Ltd, 1991), p. 90.

13. Jean-Jacques Lévèque, 'Trois intérieurs du début de la IIIe République', *Gazette des Beaux-Arts*, (March 1976), 92–4.

14. E.R., 'Le Salon de 1879, *La Presse*, 27 May 1879, p. 2.

15. *Catalogue de tableaux modernes, pastels, aquarelles, dessins etc. de Mme Valtesse de la Bigne* (Paris: Imprimerie de la Gazette des Beaux-Arts, June 1902), p. III.

16. I am indebted to the Musée d'Orsay for allowing me access to their archives when researching this painting.

17. *Henri Gervex 1852–1929*, exhib. cat. (Paris: Paris-Musées, 1992), p. 107.

18. E.R., 'Le Salon de 1879', *La Presse*, 27 May 1879, p. 2.

19. E.R., 'Le Salon de 1879', *La Presse*, 27 May 1879, p. 2.

20. Jane Kinsman, 'Henri Gervex – Madame Valtesse de la Bigne' in Sylvie Patry and others, *Van Gogh, Gauguin, Cezanne & Beyond – Post-Impressionism from the Musee d'Orsay*, exhib. cat. (London: Prestel, 2011).

21. Jules Claretie, *La Vie à Paris* (Paris, 1883), pp. 206–8.

22. Leah Lehmbeck, '"L'Esprit de l'atelier": Manet's Late Portraits of Women, 1878–1883' in Maryanne Stevens and others, *Manet: Portraying Life* (Toledo: Toledo Museum of Art; London: Royal Academy of Arts; New York: Distributed in the United States and Canada by Harry N. Abrams, Inc., 2012), p. 50.

23. Lehmbeck, p. 54.

24. It is generally agreed that the portrait was Manet's idea and that he approached Valtesse. Charles Sterling and Margaretta M. Salinger, *French Paintings: A Catalogue of the Collection of the Metropolitan Museum of Art, 19th and 20th Centuries* (New York: Metropolitan Museum of Art, 1967), vol. III, p. 51.

25. A. Tabarant, *Manet, histoire catalographique* (Paris: F. Aubier, 1931), pp. 462–3.

26. Lehmbeck, p. 55.

27. Tabarant, p. 463.

28. *The Concise Oxford Dictionary of French Literature*, ed. by Joyce M.H. Reid (Oxford and New York: Oxford University Press, 1976), p. 108.

29. Yolaine de la Bigne, *Valtesse de la Bigne ou Le pouvoir de la volupté* (Paris: Perrin, 1999), p. 172.

30. Tabarant, p. 463.

31. I am indebted to the Mairie of the 19th arrondissement in Paris for assisting in my research of this painting; Philip Ward-Jackson, 'A sculptor-mayor and his family: Le Mariage civil by Henri Gervex', *Sculpture Journal*, 14 (2005), pp. 41–50 (p. 43).

32. Lynn Hunt, 'The Unstable Boundaries of the French Revolution' in *A History of Private Life*, ed. by Philippe Ariès and George Duby, trans. by Arthur Goldhammer, 5 vols (Cambridge, MA and London: Belknap Press of

Harvard University Press, 1987–1991), vol. 4: *From the Fires of Revolution to the Great War*, ed. by Michelle Perrot (1990), pp. 13–45 (p. 29); Martin-Fugier, 'Bourgeois Rituals ', in *A History of Private Life*, vol. 4, ed. by Michelle Perrot, p. 316.

33. Cited in Ward-Jackson, p. 44.

34. Ward-Jackson, pp. 44–5.

35. Ward-Jackson, p. 44.

36. The traditional white dress was usually worn to the religious ceremony. On this, see Comtesse de Bassanville, *Code du cérémonial. Guide des gens du monde dans toutes les circonstances de la vie* (Paris, 1867), pp. 25–35.

37. On this, see Ward-Jackson, p. 44.

38. Eugène Loudun, 'Le Salon de 1881', *La Revue du monde catholique*, 31 May 1881. Cited in Jean-Pierre Sanchez, 'Un mariage réaliste: Gervex et la critique du Salon de 1881', in *Henri Gervex 1852–1929* (Paris: Paris-Musées, 1992), pp. 152–161 (p. 159).

39. Cited in Ward-Jackson, p. 44.

CHAPTER 12

1. Chapelou, *Le Tintamarre*, 11 June 1876, p. 3.

2. Jules Jouy, *Le Tintamarre*, 25 November 1877, p. 6.

3. http://ecole.nav.traditions.free.fr/officiers_dekergaradec_alexandre.htm (accessed 10 October 2014)

4. Bradley Camp Davis, 'States of Banditry: The Nguyen Government, Bandit Rule and the Culture of Power in the Post-Taiping China-Vietnam Borderlands' (doctoral thesis, University of Washington, 2008), p. 187.

5. Paul Antonini, *L'Annam, Le Tonkin et l'intervention de la France en Extrême Orient* (Paris, 1889), p. 32.

6. Antonini, p. 34.

7. Antonini, pp. 96–7.

8. 'Léon Gambetta', *Encyclopaedia Brittanica*, http://www.brittanica.com/EBchecked/topic/224764/Leon-Gambetta (accessed 20 August 2014)

9. Lyndon Orr, 'Famous Affinities of History – Léon Gambetta and Léonie Léon', pp. 1–9, http://www.authorama.com/famous-affinities-of-history-iii-3.html (accessed 29 August 2014)

10. Susan K. Foley and Charles Sowerwine, *A Political Romance; Léon Gambetta, Léonie Léon and the Making of the French Republic, 1872–1882* (London: Palgrave MacMillan, 2012), p. 57.

11. Foley and Sowerwine, pp. 113–14.

12. Foley and Sowerwine, p. 115.

13. Foley and Sowerwine, p. 191.

14. Victor Cosse, 'Gambetta', *Plutarque populaire contemporain illustré* (Paris, 1870), p. 53.

15. The incident was written by Valtesse herself, and reported by Félicien Champsaur in *Paris, le massacre* (Paris, 1885), pp. 269–71.

16. 'M. Gambetta et Mlle Valtesse', *Le Gaulois*, 11 June 1883, p. 1.

17. 'M. Gambetta et Mlle Valtesse', *Le Gaulois*, 11 June 1883, p. 1.

18. 'M. Gambetta et Mlle Valtesse', *Le Gaulois*, 11 June 1883, p. 1.

19. 'M. Gambetta et Mlle Valtesse', *Le Gaulois*, 11 June 1883, p. 1.

20. Valtesse's report was reprinted in *Le Gaulois*, 6 January 1883, p. 2.

21. In her report, Valtesse refers to the Emperor as 'King'.

22. 'Essais de psychologie politique', *La Nouvelle Revue*, 55 (November–December, 1888), 295.

23. V. de la B., 'Courrier d'Indo-Chine', *Le Figaro*, 22 September 1880, p. 4.

24. Émile Bergerat, *Les Chroniques de l'homme masqué* (Paris, 1882), p. 297.

25. Émile Zola, 'Gambetta', *Le Figaro*, 13 November 1880, p. 1.

26. Jules Claretie, *La Vie à Paris* (Paris, 1911), pp. 237–8.

27. *Badinguiste* was a pejorative term for a Bonapartist in the 19th century.

28. Yolaine de la Bigne, *Valtesse de la Bigne ou Le pouvoir de la volupté* (Paris: Perrin, 1999), p. 226.

CHAPTER 13

1. Félicien Champsaur, *Paris, le massacre* (Paris, 1885), p. 271.

2. 'Gazette des tribunaux', *Le Figaro*, 9 November 1881, p. 5.

3. Albert Wolff, *La Haute-Noce* (Paris, 1885), p. 47.

4. 'Petits bruits', *Le Gaulois*, 12 November 1881, p. 1.

5. 'Gazette des tribunaux', *Le Figaro*, 9 November 1881, p. 5.

6. 'Petits bruits', *Le Gaulois*, 12 November 1881, p. 1.

7. Ego, *Isola* (Paris, 1876), pp. 59–60.

8. Ego, p. 158.

9. Ego, p. 159.

10. 'L'Enfant de Mme Valtesse', *Le Rappel*, 16 November 1881, p. 2.

11. 'L'Enfant de Mme Valtesse', p. 3.

12. *Le Temps*, 16 November 1881, p. 3.

13. 'L'Enfant de Mme Valtesse', p. 3.

14. 'Chronique', *Le Droit populaire*, 26 November 1881, p. 402.

15. 'Chronique', p. 402.

16. Paul Janet, *La Famille*, 17th edn (Paris, 1900), p. 110.

17. 'Gazette des tribunaux', *Le Figaro*, 15 November 1881, p. 2.

18. Letter reprinted in 'Chronique de l'audience', *Gil Blas*, 16 November 1881, p. 3. Valtesse claimed her daughter to be two years younger than she actually was.

19. 'Chronique de l'audience', p. 3.

20. Mardoche and Desgenais, *Les Parisiennes* (Paris, 1882), p. 360.

21. Émile Villemot, 'A qui la fille?', *Gil Blas*, 19 November 1881, p. 1.

22. 'L'Enfant de Mme Valtesse', *Le Rappel*, 16 November 1881, p. 3.

23. 'Chronique', p. 402.

24. 'Petits bruits', *Le Gaulois*, 12 November 1881, p. 1.

25. Villemot, p. 1.

26. Wolff, p. 47.

CHAPTER 14

1. *Gil Blas*, 12 September 1883, p. 1.

2. Arsène Houssaye, 'Les Parisiennes d'Amour – Valtesse', *Panurge*, 22 October 1882.

3. *Le Rappel*, 26 March 1882, p. 2.

4. *Le Rappel*, 26 March 1882, p. 2.

5. *Le Rappel*, 26 March 1882, p. 2.

6. *Le Rappel*, 26 March 1882, p. 2.

7. *Gil Blas*, 26 March 1882, p. 3.

8. *Le Rappel*, 26 March 1882, p. 2.

9. *Le Gaulois*, 27 June 1882, p. 3.

10. *Octave Mirbeau – Correspondance générale*, ed. by Pierre Michel and Jean-François Nivet, 3 vols (Lausanne: Âge d'homme, 2002–2009), vol. I (2002), p. 186.

11. Mareuil, 'L'Accident de Ville-d'Avray', *Le Gaulois*, 29 November 1882, p. 1.

12. Mareuil, 'L'Accident de Ville-d'Avray', *Le Gaulois*, 29 November 1882, p. 1.

13. Mareuil, 'L'Accident de Ville-d'Avray', *Le Gaulois*, 29 November 1882, p. 1.

14. *Le Gaulois*, 23 December 1882, p. 1.

15. Dandeau, 'Un Collaborateur inattendu', *Le Gaulois*, 6 January 1883, p. 2.

16. *The Morning Post*, 13 June 1883, p. 5.

17. Chambourcy, 'Hommes et Choses – L'Union des Artistes', *Le Radical*, 13 June 1883, p. 1.

18. *Aberdeen Weekly Journal*, 13 January 1883.

19. *Le Gaulois*, 13 June 1883, p. 1.

20. Ferdinand Xau, 'Valtesse de la Bigne', *Gil Blas*, 13 June 1883, p. 2.

21. Chambourcy, 'Hommes et Choses – L'Union des Artistes', *Le Radical*, 13 June 1883, p. 1.

22. *Gil Blas*, May 3 1883, p. 1; *Gil Blas*, 12 May 1883, p. 1; Ferdinand Xau, 'Valtesse de la Bigne', *Gil Blas*, 13 June 1883, p. 2.

23. Colin Jones, *Cambridge Illustrated History of France* (Cambridge: Cambridge University Press, 1994), pp. 226–31.

24. Alistair Horne, *Seven Ages of Paris* (London: Pan Macmillan, 2003), p. 331.

25. 'Fatal Gas Explosions', *Oamaru Mail*, Volume IV, Issue 1322, 19 September 1882, p. 4.

26. *L'Europe Artiste*, 2 September 1883, p. 3.

27. *L'Europe Artiste*, 7 October 1883, p. 3.

28. C. Chincholle, 'Les Arts incohérents', *Le Figaro*, 10 October 1883, p. 2.

29. C. Chincholle, 'Les Arts incohérents', *Le Figaro*, 10 October 1883, p. 2.

30. Félix Fénéon 'Les Arts incohérents', *La Libre Revue*, November 1883, article held by the Musée des arts décoratifs, also cited in Yolaine de la Bigne, *Valtesse de la Bigne ou Le pouvoir de la volupté* (Paris: Perrin, 1999), p. 182.

31. *Gil Blas*, 14 October 1883, p. 1.

32. C. Chincholle, 'Les Arts incohérents', *Le Figaro*, 10 October 1883, p. 2.

33. 'Les Arts incohérents', *L'Europe Artiste*, 21 October 1883, p. 34.

34. Parisis, 'Bal Incohérent', *Le Figaro*, 13 March 1885, p. 1.

35. Parisis, 'Bal Incohérent', *Le Figaro*, 13 March 1885, p. 1.

36. *Gil Blas*, 12 June 1883, p. 1.

37. Harry Alis, *Reine Soleil, une fille de la glèbe* (Paris, 1884), pp. 283–4.

38. Alis, pp. 283–4.

39. Alis, p. 284.

40. Le Diable Boiteux, *Gil Blas*, 8 November 1884, p. 1.

41. Alis, p. 285.

42. E.C., *Le Livre* (Paris, 1884), p. 756.

43. E.C., *Le Livre* (Paris, 1884), p. 756.

CHAPTER 15

1. H.A. de Conty, *Paris en poche – Guide pratique Conty*, 6th edn (Paris, 1875), pp. 132–3.

2. *Gil Blas*, 10 June 1884, p. 2.

3. *Le Figaro*, 21 March 1884, p. 1.

4. *Le Figaro*, 28 March 1885, p. 2.

5. *Gil Blas*, 30 March 1885, p. 1.

6. *Le Figaro*, 28 March 1885, p. 2.

7. *Le Figaro*, 28 March 1885, p. 2.

8. *Le Figaro*, 28 March 1885, p. 2.

9. Anne Martin-Fugier, 'Bourgeois Rituals' in *A History of Private Life*, ed. by Philippe Ariès and George Duby, trans. by Arthur Goldhammer, 5 vols (Cambridge, MA and London: Belknap Press of Harvard University Press, 1987–1991), vol. 4: *From the Fires of Revolution to the Great War*, ed. by Michelle Perrot (1990), pp. 261–337 (p. 304).

10. W. Cope Devereux, *Fair Italy: The Riviera and Monte Carlo* (London, 1884), p. viii.

11. *Le Figaro*, 21 March 1884, p. 1.

12. *Le Gaulois*, 12 January 1890, p. 4.

13. *Le Courrier de Cannes*, 24 January 1886, p. 1.

14. *Henri Gervex 1852–1929*, exhib. cat. (Paris: Paris-Musées, 1992), p. 134.

15. Yolaine de la Bigne, *Valtesse de la Bigne ou Le pouvoir de la volupté* (Paris: Perrin, 1999), p. 212.

16. Advertisement in classifieds section in *Guides Joanne – Nice, Monaco* (Paris, 1887), p. 72.

17. John House, *Impressionists by the Sea*, exhib. cat. (London: Royal Academy of Arts, 2007) p. 16.

18. W. Cope Devereux, p. viii.

19. W. Cope Devereux, p. 63.

20. W. Cope Devereux, p. 63.

21. W. Cope Devereux, p. 63.

22. *Guides Joanne – Nice, Monaco* (Paris, 1887), p. 38.

23. *Le Gaulois*, 12 January 1890, p. 4.

24. All currency equivalents calculated according to: http://www.measuringworth.com/ukcompare/relativevalue.php

25. Charles Limouzin, *Almanach illustré de Monaco et de Monte-Carlo* (Nice, 1894)

26. *Le Gaulois*, 22 July 1888, p. 4.

27. *Gil Blas*, 10 April 1889, p. 3.

28. Pâquerette's marriage banns were published on 22 December 1889; *Le Figaro*, 31 August 1910, p. 4.

29. *Gil Blas*, 30 July 1889, p. 1.

30. *Gil Blas*, 17 January 1892, p. 1.

31. I am indebted to the Palais Princier de Monaco for their assistance with my research of Valtesse's time in Monte Carlo.

32. *Le Gaulois*, 7 February 1894, p. 1. Journalists refer to Valtesse's villa in Monte Carlo variously as 'Villa des Aigles' or 'Villa les Aigles'.

33. *Gil Blas*, 14 June 1894, p. 1.

34. *Gil Blas*, 13 December 1899, p. 1.

35. Martine Gasquet, *Impératrices, artistes et cocottes: Les femmes sur la Riviera à la Belle Époque* (Nice: Gilletta nice-matin, 2013), pp. 40–1.

36. 'The Queen's Visit to the Riviera', *The Morning Post*, 28 February 1895, p. 5.

37. *Gil Blas*, 13 September 1889, p. 1.

CHAPTER 16

1. James F. McMillan, *France and Women, 1789–1914: Gender, Society and Politics* (London: Routledge, 2000), pp. 141–92.

2. Catherine Van Casselaer, *Lot's Wife: Lesbian Paris 1890–1914* (Liverpool: The Janus Press, 1986), p. 10.

3. A. Coffignon, *Paris Vivant, La Corruption à Paris* (Paris, 1889)

4. Casselaer, p. 10.

5. Casselaer, p. 11.

6. Casselaer, p. 11.

7. Léo Taxil, *La Corruption fin-de-siècle* (Paris, 1891); Julien Chevalier, *Inversion sexuelle* (Paris, 1893); Van Casselaer, pp. 11–12.

8. Dr E. Monin, 'Propos du Docteur – La Responsibilité en matière criminelle', *Gil Blas*, 3 January 1888, p. 2.

9. Casselaer, p. 13.

10. Casselaer, p. 13.

11. *Larousse Gastronomique*, ed. by Susan Cope and others (London: Mandarin, 1990), p. 1290.

12. Mrs Armstrong, *Good Form: A Book of Every Day Etiquette* (London, 1895), p. 123.

13. *Gil Blas*, 3 April 1883, p. 1.

14. Dr E. Monin, 'Propos du Docteur – Hygiène et éducation féminines', *Gil Blas*, 18 March 1890, p. 2.

15. *Gil Blas*, 27 June 1889, p. 1.

16. *Gil Blas*, 13 September 1894, p. 1.

17. *The Cambridge Companion to the Literature of Paris*, ed. by Anna-Louise Milne (Cambridge: Cambridge University Press, 2013).

18. *Guide des Plaisirs à Paris* (Paris, 1899), pp. 115–16.

19. *Guide des Plaisirs à Paris* (Paris, 1899), p. 118.

20. *Gil Blas*, 13 December 1899, p. 1.

21. *Gil Blas*, 13 June 1890, p. 3.

22. Liane de Pougy, *My Blue Notebooks*, trans. by Diane Athill (New York: Tarcher Putnam, 2002), pp. 50–1.

23. Pougy, *My Blue Notebooks*, pp. 50–1.

24. Pougy, *My Blue Notebooks*, pp. 50–1.

25. Pougy, *My Blue Notebooks*, p. 50.

26. Pougy, *My Blue Notebooks*, p. 50.

27. *Gil Blas*, 22 November 1892, p. 1.

28. Jean Chalon, *Liane de Pougy: Courtisane, princesse et sainte* (Paris: Flammarion, 1994), pp. 15–43.

29. Pougy, *My Blue Notebooks*, p. 24.

30. Pougy, *My Blue Notebooks*, p. 73.

31. Pougy, *My Blue Notebooks*, p. 49.

32. Pougy, *My Blue Notebooks*, p. 49.

33. Liane de Pougy, *Idylle saphique* (Paris: Éditions des femmes, 1987), p. 22.

34. Pougy, *Idylle saphique*, p. 22.

35. Pougy, *Idylle saphique*, p. 23.

36. Chalon, p. 111.

37. Pougy, *Idylle saphique*, p. 15.

38. Chalon, p. 42.

39. *Le Temps*, 7 January 1894, p. 3.

40. *Le Temps*, 28 December 1895, p. 3; *Le Temps*, 23 January 1896, p. 4.

41. *Gil Blas*, 19 January 1892, p. 2. Cythera was the Greek island heralded in ancient times as the centre of worship of Aphrodite. The term was often evoked in reference to courtesans and *femmes galantes* in the 19th century.

42. *Gil Blas*, 24 September 1893, p. 1.

43. Pougy, *My Blue Notebooks*, p. 13.

44. Pougy, *My Blue Notebooks*, p. 106.

45. Pougy, *My Blue Notebooks*, p. 101.

46. Pougy, *Idylle saphique*, p. 15.

47. Pougy, *Idylle saphique*, p. 15.

48. Martine Gasquet, *Impératrices, artistes et cocottes: Les femmes sur la Riviera à la Belle Époque* (Nice: Gilletta nice-matin, 2013), p. 190.

49. Albert Bataille, *Le Figaro*, 2 August 1896, p. 4.

50. *Gil Blas*, 24 September 1893, p. 1.

51. Pougy, *My Blue Notebooks*, p. 3.

52. Undated back issue of *La Grande Vie*, held by the Musée des arts décoratifs, Paris.

53. Pougy, *My Blue Notebooks*, p. 108.

54. *Gil Blas*, 21 October 1894, p. 1.

55. Pougy, *My Blue Notebooks*, p. 50.

56. Pougy, *My Blue Notebooks*, p. 50.

57. Pougy, *My Blue Notebooks*, p. 51.

58. Chalon, p. 57.

59. Pougy, *Idylle saphique*, p. 99.

60. Diana Souhami, *Wild Girls – Paris, Sappho and Art: The Lives and Loves of Natalie Barney and Romaine Brooks* (London: Weidenfeld and Nicolson, 2004), pp. 12–15.

61. For Natalie's account, see Natalie Clifford Barney, *Souvenirs indiscrets* (Paris: Flammarion, 1960), p. 37.

62. Pougy, *My Blue Notebooks*, p. 44.

CHAPTER 17

1. Theodore Zeldin, *France 1848–1945: Taste and Corruption* (Oxford: Oxford University Press, 1980), p. 40.

2. *Annuaire des Châteaux 1900–1901*, ed. by Armand La Fare (Paris, 1901).

3. *Le Figaro*, 17 December 1910, p. 7.

4. *Le Figaro*, 26 August 1910, p. 5.

5. *Gil Blas*, 23 May 1899, p. 1.

6. Richard O'Monroy, 'Celle qui disparaît', *Gil Blas*, 24 May 1902, p. 1.

7. Liane de Pougy, *My Blue Notebooks*, trans. by Diane Athill (New York: Tarcher Putnam, 2002), p. 44.

8. Colin Jones, *Cambridge Illustrated History of France* (Cambridge: Cambridge University Press, 1994), p. 233.

9. Alistair Horne, *Seven Ages of Paris* (London: Pan Macmillan, 2003), p. 323.

10. Graham King, *Garden of Zola: Émile Zola and his novels for English readers* (London: Barrie and Jenkins Ltd, 1978), p. 332.

11. King, p. 331.

12. King, p. 332.

13. *The Dundee Courier & Argus*, 22 August 1899, p. 5.

14. *The Dundee Courier & Argus*, 22 August 1899, p. 5.

15. *The Dundee Courier & Argus*, 22 August 1899, p. 5.

16. *Aberdeen Weekly Journal*, 22 August 1899.

17. *Le Temps*, 22 August 1899, p. 4.

18. André de Fouquières, *Mon Paris et ses Parisiens*, 5 vols (Paris: Éditions Pierre Horay, 1953–1955), vol. III, (1955), p. 112.

19. Fouquières, *Mon Paris*, vol. III, p. 112.

20. *Gil Blas*, 7 May 1899, p. 1.

21. *Gil Blas*, 1 January 1900, p. 1.

22. Jean Chalon, *Liane de Pougy: Courtisane, princesse et sainte* (Paris: Flammarion, 1994), p. 87.

23. *Gil Blas*, 26 January 1900, p. 1; *Gil Blas*, 17 December 1899, p. 1.

24. Parisis (Émile Blavet), *La Vie Parisienne, La Ville et le théâtre* (Paris, 1887), p. 167.

25. *Gil Blas*, 17 January 1892, p. 1.

26. Gaston Boudan, 'Madame Valtesse de la Bigne', *Au Pays Virois*, (October–December 1933), pp. 164–9 (p. 168).

27. Simond & Poinsot, *La Vie galante aux Tuileries sous le Second Empire* (Paris: Albert Méricant, 1912), p. 294.

28. Liane de Pougy, *Idylle saphique* (Paris: Éditions des femmes, 1987) p. 22.

29. *Gil Blas*, 12 December 1891, p. 1.

30. Etienne Richet, 'La Vie Parisienne', *Revue Nouvelle: Le Feu Follet*, (May 1900), 307.

31. *Gil Blas*, 9 May 1900, p. 1.

32. *L'Ami du lettré: Année littéraire et artistique*, ed. by L'Association des courrieristes littéraires des journaux quotidiens (Paris: Bernard Grasset, 1927), p. 244.

33. *Gil Blas*, 11 July 1899, p. 2.

34. Joanna Richardson, *The Courtesans: The Demi-Monde in 19th-Century France* (London: Phoenix Press, 2000), pp. 36–9.

35. *Le Figaro*, 15 May 1902, p. 6.

36. Richard O'Monroy, 'Celle qui disparaît', *Gil Blas*, 24 May 1902, p. 1.

37. *Catalogue de tableaux modernes, pastels, aquarelles, dessins etc de Mme Valtesse de la Bigne* (Paris: Imprimerie de la Gazette des Beaux-Arts, June 1902), pp. I–II.

38. *Le Figaro*, 15 May 1902, p. 6.

39. *The Times*, 22 May 1902, p. 1.

40. *Le Figaro*, 3 June 1902, p. 1. All currency equivalents calculated according to: http://www.measuringworth.com/ukcompare/relativevalue.php

41. *Le Figaro*, 6 June 1902, p. 1.

42. *Gil Blas*, 10 June 1902, p. 1.

43. *Le Matin*, 8 June 1902, p. 4.

44. Jules Claretie, *La Vie à Paris* (Paris, 1911), p. 240.

45. Claretie, pp. 239–40. I am indebted to Dominique Cécile Claudius-Petit for her kind assistance in my research of Valtesse's property in Ville-d'Avray.

46. Dominique Cécile Claudius-Petit, *Ville-d'Avray: mémoire en images* (Saint-Avertin: Éditions Sutton, 2013), p. 94.

47. Odile Nouvel-Kammerer, 'Le lit d'une lionne: Valtesse de la Bigne', in *Rêves d'Alcôves: la chambre au cours des siècles*, exhib. cat. (Paris: Musée des Arts décoratifs, 1995), pp. 211–13 (p. 212).

48. Claretie, p. 240.

49. *Chronique des arts et de la curiosité*, 31 December 1910, p. 321.

50. The 55th doge of Venice lived between the 13th and 14th centuries, and was beheaded for attempting to stage a coup d'état. He was condemned to death and his portrait in the Doge's Palace was removed and the space covered with a black veil.

51. René Picard, conclusion to Gaston Boudan, 'Madame Valtesse de la Bigne', *Au Pays Virois*, (October–December 1933), p. 170.

52. Ego, *Isola* (Paris, 1876), pp. 160–1.

53. Jean-Marcel Humbert, *Édouard Detaille: L'héroisme d'un siècle* (Paris: Éditions Copernic, 1979), p. 29.

54. Letter dated 16 June 1994 from the Commune de Ville-d'Avray held by the Musée des Arts décoratifs.

55. Auriant, *Les Lionnes du Second Empire* (Paris: Gallimard, 1935), pp. 223–4.

56. *Le Supplément*, 16 July 1903, p. 1.

57. *Le Rire*, 21 September 1906, p. 5.

58. Claretie, p. 242.

59. Claretie, p. 242.

CHAPTER 18

1. Jules Claretie, *La Vie à Paris* (Paris, 1911), p. 244.

2. Jean Chalon, *Liane de Pougy: Courtisane, princesse et sainte* (Paris: Flammarion, 1994), pp. 147–51; *Gil Blas*, 9 June 1910, p. 1.

3. Claretie, p. 245.

4. Detaille's diary, held at the Bibliothèque de l'Institut, Paris, extracts held by the Musée des arts décoratifs, Paris, MS 5525 and MS 5526.

5. Detaille's diary, MS 5525 and MS 5526.

6. Detaille's diary, MS 5525 and MS 5526.

7. Jules Claretie noted how the handwriting on Valtesse's notecards was 'large' but 'resolute'. Claretie, p. 245.

8. Gaston Boudan, 'Madame Valtesse de la Bigne', *Au Pays Virois*, (October–December 1933), 164–9 (p. 168).

9. Detaille's diary, MS 5525 and MS 5526.

10. Boudan, p. 168.

11. *Le Figaro*, 1 August 1910, p. 1.

12. Claretie, p. 245.

13. *Le Temps*, 3 August 1910, p. 3.

14. *Inventaire de Chaville*, IA000 51459. Valtesse's tomb was recently dismantled. All that remains is the square plinth and a circular base where it once stood.

15. Claretie, p. 238.

16. Liane de Pougy, *My Blue Notebooks*, trans. by Diane Athill (New York: Tarcher Putnam, 2002), p. 44; Jean-Marcel Humbert, *Édouard Detaille: L'héroisme d'un siècle* (Paris: Éditions Copernic, 1979), p. 30.

17. Claretie, p. 246.

EPILOGUE

1. Auriant, *Les Lionnes du Second Empire* (Paris: Gallimard, 1935), p. 226.

2. Jules Claretie, *La Vie à Paris* (Paris, 1911), p. 245.

3. 'Nécrologie', *Le Matin*, 21 December 1903, p. 5; 'Nécrologie', *Gil Blas*, 21 December 1903, p. 2.

4. Gaston Boudan, 'Madame Valtesse de la Bigne', *Au Pays Virois*, (October–December 1933), 164–9 (p. 165).

5. Yolaine de la Bigne, *Valtesse de la Bigne ou Le pouvoir de la volupté* (Paris: Perrin, 1999), p. 232.

6. Adrien Marx, 'La Plaine Monceau', *Le Figaro*, 21 June 1880, p. 1.

7. *Le Figaro*, 24 December 1910, p. 5; Claretie, p. 244.

8. Jean Chalon, *Liane de Pougy: Courtisane, princesse et sainte* (Paris: Flammarion, 1994), p. 151.

9. *Le Figaro*, 23 December 1910, p. 7; *Chronique des arts et de la curiosité*, 31 December 1910, pp. 320–1. All currency equivalents calculated according to: http://www.measuringworth.com/ukcompare/relativevalue.php

10. *Le Figaro*, 19 February 1911, p. 7; *Le Matin*, 4 March 1911, p. 6.

11. *England and Wales, National Probate Calendar (Index of Wills and Administrations), 1858–1966* for Louise Emilie Valtesse de la Bigne.

12. *Le Figaro*, 31 August 1910, p. 4.

13. Liane de Pougy, *My Blue Notebooks*, trans. by Diane Athill (New York: Tarcher Putnam, 2002), p. 181.

14. Pougy, *My Blue Notebooks*, p. 261.

15. Pougy, *My Blue Notebooks*, p. 104.

16. *Niagara Falls Gazette*, 1 October 1923, p. 11.

17. *Lehigh Brown and White*, 22 February 1924, p. 4.

18. *Lehigh Brown and White*, 22 February 1924, p. 4.

19. Celine Colassin, '663 – Andrée Lafayette', http://cinevedette4.unblog.fr/663-andree-lafayette/ (accessed 18 February 2015)

20. 'French Actress Quits Hubby and Goes Home', *Reading Eagle*, 26 November 1924, p. 1.

21. Philip Eade, *Young Prince Philip: His Turbulent Early Life* (London: Harper Press, 2012), pp. 165–6.

22. Eade, p. 166.

23. Eade, p. 167.

24. *Le Temps*, 24 December 1910, p. 3; *Le Figaro*, 24 December 1910, p. 5.

25. *Le Figaro*, 24 December 1910, p. 5.

26. *Le Matin*, 20 December 1910, p. 6.

Index